Teaching and Learning

Collaborative Exploration of the Reggio Emilia Approach

Teaching and Learning

Collaborative Exploration of the Reggio Emilia Approach

Victoria R. Fu
Andrew J. Stremmel
Lynn T. Hill

*All, Virginia Polytechnic Institute
and State University*

Merrill
Prentice Hall

Upper Saddle River, New Jersey
Columbus, Ohio

Library of Congress Cataloging-in-Publication Data

Fu, Victoria R.
    Teaching and learning: collaborative exploration of the Reggio Emilia approach/ Victoria R. Fu, Andrew J. Stremmel,
Lynn T. Hill.
    p. cm.
    Includes bibliographical references and index.
    ISBN 0-13-028783-0
    1. Education, Preschool—Philosophy. 2. Education, Preschool—Italy—Reggio Emilia (Province) 3. Public schools—
Italy—Reggio Emilia (Province) 4. Education, Preschool—United States. I. Stremmel, Andrew J. II. Hill, Lynn T. III. Title.
LB1140.3.F82 2002
372.21'01—dc21

2001030253

Vice President and Publisher: Jeffery W. Johnston
Executive Editor: Ann Castel Davis
Associate Editor: Christina M. Kalisch
Editorial Assistant: Keli Gemrich
Production Editor: Linda Hillis Bayma
Production Coordination: Carlisle Publishers Services
Design Coordinator: Diane C. Lorenzo
Cover Designer: Rod Harris
Cover Photo: Lynn T. Hill at the Virginia Tech Child Development Lab School. Anna Boa-Amponsem, the child shown in
    the photo, drew the art on the back cover.
Production Manager: Laura Messerly
Director of Marketing: Kevin Flanagan
Marketing Manager: Amy June
Marketing Coordinator: Barbara Koontz

This book was set in Galliard by Carlisle Communications, Ltd. It was printed and bound by R.R. Donnelley & Sons
Company. The cover was printed by Phoenix Color Corp.

Photo Credits: Wendlyn K. Bedrosian, p. 70; Carol Bersani, p. 75; Steve Bickley, p. 90; Jamie Brother, p. 38; Sara Ferguson,
p. 125; Victoria Fu, p. 100; Marty Gravett, pp. 211, 212; Lynn Hill, pp. 2, 27, 30, 32, 33, 66, 88, 89, 91, 94, 95, 96, 97,
99, 100, 105, 132, 136, 139, 140, 143, 180, 221; Scott Hill, p. 12; Kathy Kidd, pp. 173, 175; Pam Oken-Wright, pp. 200,
201, 204, 205, 206, 207, 214; Dee Smith, pp. 156, 157; D. W. Tegano, pp. 161, 176; Jon Utin, p. 106; Kelly Wells, pp. 25,
26, 34, 46.

Prentice-Hall International (UK) Limited, *London*
Prentice-Hall of Australia Pty. Limited, *Sydney*
Prentice-Hall Canada, Inc., *Toronto*
Prentice-Hall Hispanoamericana, S.A., *Mexico*
Prentice-Hall of India Private Limited, *New Delhi*
Prentice-Hall of Japan, Inc., *Tokyo*
Prentice-Hall Singapore Pte. Ltd.
Editora Prentice-Hall do Brasil, Ltda., *Rio de Janeiro*

Merrill
Prentice Hall

10 9 8 7 6 5 4 3 2 1
ISBN 0-13-028783-0

※

*F*or my mother, Chen-Te Chang Fu, and to the memory of my father, Shang-Ling Fu.
I hope this book reflects their belief that teaching is for change—Vickie

※

*T*his book is dedicated to the three people who have taught me most about
teaching and learning: Joel, Corinne, and Joan—Andy

※

*F*or Scott, Katie, and Meg, my most cherished partners
in this great adventure of life—Lynn

※

The Authors

Carol Bersani is director and pedagogical coordinator of the Paul H. Jones Child Development Center and a professor in Early Childhood Education at Kent State University. Her research is focused on teacher education and parent participation in schools.

Victoria R. Fu teaches undergraduate and graduate courses in child development and early childhood education with her colleagues Andy Stremmel and Lynn Hill. She is a professor at the Virginia Polytechnic Institute and State University (Virginia Tech) and serves as a pedagogical consultant at the Child Development Laboratory School. She values learning and teaching as a lifelong endeavor that happens in relationships. Her recent research and writing reflect her philosophy of teaching as inquiry from a social constructivist perspective. She has visited the schools in Reggio Emilia and finds that their philosophy and practice offer possibilities to make meaningful the role of teacher as researcher. As a member of The Lugano-Reggio Teaching Research Collaborative, she is actively engaged in recasting the Reggio Emilia approach to inform teaching in the United States. She has published extensively in professional journals and books, including *Affirming Diversity Through Democratic Conversations,* which she co-edited with Andy Stremmel.

Lella Gandini is an author, a correspondent for the Italian early childhood magazine *Bambini,* and adjunct professor in the School of Education at the University of Massachusetts, Amherst. She serves as Reggio Children Liaison in the United States for dissemination of the Reggio Emilia approach. She is co-editor of *The Hundred Languages of Children: The Reggio Emilia Approach—Advanced Reflections* with Carolyn Edwards and George Forman.

Jeanne Goldhaber, is an associate professor at the University of Vermont's Early Childhood PreK–3 Teacher Education Program. For nearly 10 years, she and the staff and students of the UVM Campus Children's Center have been engaged in the study of documentation as a process that promotes inquiry, reflection, and collaboration among all the protagonists of a learning community.

Marty Gravett has worked for 25 years in the field of early childhood education and child care, teaching, administering programs and grants, planning, consulting, and writing. Six years ago, inspired by the integrity and promise of the municipal preschools of Reggio Emilia, Italy, she returned to a preschool classroom. Currently a teacher-researcher at the Sabot School in Richmond, Virginia, she has twice visited the schools in Reggio Emilia. She holds a B.A. in Anthropology from the University of North Carolina at Greensboro, an M.S. in Child Development from Virginia Tech, and has studied and observed in early childhood settings in England and Denmark. A former Virginia Governor's Fellow and Richmond Urban Institute intern, she has served extensively on boards and commissions. Her two middle-school daughters and her husband are generous benefactors and proponents of her work.

Lynn T. Hill lives on a farm in Giles County, Virginia, with her husband, two daughters, and several dogs, cats, and horses. Her love of nature contributes to her work as the Studio Teacher for the Virginia Tech Child Development Lab School, where she is also the Director of Curriculum. She also serves as an instructor in the Department of Human Development, where she teaches undergraduate and graduate courses in Early Childhood Education. She has been inspired and provoked by the Reggio Emilia approach for over a decade and has been most profoundly affected by the concept of "an education based on relationships." In an attempt to understand and live this concept, she has collaborated on several projects, including The Blue Door Creative Re-Use Center; The Great Duck Pond Project, Blacksburg Middle School's attempt to open a Reggio-inspired program for sixth, seventh, and eighth graders; The Lugano-Reggio Teaching Research Collaborative; a study-abroad tour for Early Childhood Education majors; and several conferences on the approach.

Diane M. Horm-Wingerd is professor of Human Development and Family Studies at the University of Rhode Island. She specializes in child development and early childhood education, and serves as the director of the University of Rhode Island's two child development centers, the "lab schools" that fulfill teaching, research, and service/outreach missions for the campus and region. Her scholarly work has three foci: evaluation of programs that serve young children and their families, assessment of young children, and professional development of the early childhood workforce, especially the impact of participatory models. She was selected to be a Visiting Scholar by the U.S. Department of Education's Office of Educational Research and Improvement for 1998–99. As a Visiting Scholar, she worked at the National Institute on Early Childhood Development and Education on a variety of issues related to professional development.

Debra Jarjoura was a preschool teacher at the Paul H. Jones Child Development Center for 10 years. This lab school setting provided the opportunity to work with a mixed age grouping of children, as well as college students and parents. Debra is now a teacher at the Phillips Brooks Early Learning Center in Menlo Park, California.

Pam Oken-Wright is a teacher-researcher, consultant, author, and incorrigible thinker (ask anyone in The Reggio-Lugano Research Collaborative). She is particularly interested in children's construction of theory through conversation, representation, and play, and in all aspects of the adaptation of the principles of Reggio

Emilia to U.S. contexts. She lives in Richmond, Virginia, with her husband and young daughter.

Sharon Palsha, who contributed the chapter on inclusion in Reggio Emilia, is an investigator at the Frank Porter Graham Child Development Center at the University of North Carolina at Chapel Hill. Dr. Palsha has 23 years of experience in the field of special education. She taught for 8 years before returning to school to work on her doctorate. In her job of 14 years at the FPG center, Dr. Palsha oversees projects and conducts research related to young children with disabilities and their families. Her most recent project involved evaluating the preschool programs for children with disabilities operated by the North Carolina Department of Public Schools. Sharon has made four trips (in 1995, 1998, 1999, and 2000) to Reggio Emilia to study the world-renowned schools. Her Reggio Emilia journey of study, Sharon states, has had and continues to have an enormous impact on her life, both professionally and personally. Dr. Palsha is actively involved in sharing her passion for the Reggio approach at local, state, and national inservice presentations and workshops.

Alise Shafer is the founder and director of Evergreen Community School in Santa Monica, California, where she and her faculty make extensive use of documentation as a source of data for their classroom research on children's construction of knowledge. Her interest in the "ordinary" moments of classroom life has resulted in her most recent endeavor—a look at ordinary moments in five Pacific Rim countries. In collaboration with teachers, administrators, and researchers in Thailand, Korea, New Zealand, and Hong Kong, she is examining how teachers in five countries listen to children and support their thinking. Alise also teaches at UCLA Extension and at several local colleges and universities. She speaks at conferences throughout the United States and abroad. Alise, a graduate of Pacific Oaks College, lives in Los Angeles with her two teenage children who keep her life from being anything but ordinary!

Dee Smith teaches in the Early Childhood Program at the University of Vermont and is Head Teacher in the Campus Children's Center's Infant/Toddler Program. She has been interested in the foundational principles of the early childhood programs in Reggio Emilia and how these principles can support and enhance programs in this country. She is particularly interested in the role that collaborative documenting plays in staff development and the training of preservice teachers.

Andrew J. Stremmel is associate professor in Human Development and director of the Child Development Laboratory School at Virginia Polytechnic Institute and State University. He received his B.A. in psychology from the Pennsylvania State University in 1978 and his M.S. and Ph.D. degrees in child development and early childhood education from Purdue University in 1981 and 1989. He is a member of the Academy of Teaching Excellence at Virginia Tech and has taught courses on curriculum and program planning in early childhood education, principles of working with children and parents, perspectives on multiculturalism, and child development theories. His research interests are in the areas of early childhood education, particularly the formation and transformation of pre- and inservice early childhood teachers. He has written on issues of early childhood teacher education, including the application of Vygotsky's theory in early educational settings; diversity and the development of multicultural awareness in teachers; and images of teaching and the role of self. He has also written about intergenerational exchanges between preschool children and older adults. He has co-edited a book with Vickie Fu entitled *Affirming Diversity Through Democratic Conversations* and is currently working on a curriculum book, *Life in the Classroom: Teaching as Inquiry with Inspirations from Reggio Emilia,* with Lynn Hill and Vickie Fu.

Deborah W. Tegano is associate professor at the University of Tennessee in Knoxville. She has studied in Switzerland and Italy as a member of the Lugano-Reggio Teaching Research Collaborative and continues to be involved in translational research projects. She works closely with teachers and students in the Child Development Laboratory School and the public schools through the teacher education program in the Department of Child and Family Studies. Working with the pedagogical team, she has been instrumental in guiding curricular approaches for preschool and elementary children and in working to reconceptualize teacher education curriculum according to social constructivist frameworks. She has studied creativity with young children and is the author (with Jim Moran and Janet Sawyers) of *Creativity in Early Childhood Programs,* a National Education Association monograph covering 15 years of research with young children. She has also published in the area of play and problem solving with young children.

Preface

It is paradoxical that a preface is almost always written after the completion of a book. This one is no exception. We would like to share with you some of our thoughts regarding this book. The three of us worked as a team in putting this volume together. We are good friends and colleagues who really enjoy teaching and learning together and, more often than not, think collaboratively. These sentiments carried us through this project as we wrote and edited the book, sharing responsibilities.

In writing the chapters for this book, we—knowingly or unknowingly—were taking the next leg of our journey together to recast the Reggio Emilia approach to inform practice in the United States. This project created a venue for us to continue our conversations with purpose in a community of "us" who value learning and teaching, multiple perspectives, sharing stories, and conversations that provoke us to understand, to make meaning of our experiences, and to invent. For all of these enticements, we thank our friends who contributed to this book.

We would like to thank Lella Gandini for her friendship, collegiality, and generosity for her chapter, "The Story and Foundations of the Reggio Emilia Approach." In this chapter, the essential history and philosophy of the schools of Reggio Emilia are provided as a context in which the other chapters are based. We are privileged to hear her voice, one that has a lived knowledge of the Reggio experience.

In this way, her chapter provides a crucial bridge between Reggio Emilia and our experience to recast and reinvent its philosophy in the context of learning and teaching in the United States. Additionally, in the spirit of documentation, her chapter offers the opportunity for us and the reader to revisit and find new meanings and understandings about our work as teacher-researchers.

We would also like to thank the following reviewers: Jane H. Bugnand, Eastern New Mexico University–Roswell; Pat Hofbauer, Northwest State Community College (Ohio); Karen Menke Paciorek, Eastern Michigan University; Karen L. Peterson, Washington State University–Vancouver; and Colleen K. Randel, University of Texas–Tyler.

We invite you to join our exploration and our conversation. We hope you will share your stories, reflections, and insights with your friends and colleagues, wherever you are, so together we can build amiable communities for learning and teaching.

Vickie Fu
Andy Stremmel
Lynn Hill

Discover the Companion Website Accompanying This Book

The Prentice Hall Companion Website: A Virtual Learning Environment

Technology is a constantly growing and changing aspect of our field that is creating a need for content and resources. To address this emerging need, Prentice Hall has developed an online learning environment for students and professors alike—Companion Websites—to support our textbooks.

In creating a Companion Website, our goal is to build on and enhance what the textbook already offers. For this reason, the content for each user-friendly website is organized by topic and provides the professor and student with a variety of meaningful resources. Common features of a Companion Website include:

For the Professor—

Every Companion Website integrates **Syllabus Manager™**, an online syllabus creation and management utility.

- **Syllabus Manager™** provides you, the instructor, with an easy, step-by-step process to create and revise syllabi, with direct links into the Companion Website and other online content without having to learn HTML.

- Students may log on to your syllabus during any study session. All they need to know is the web address for the Companion Website and the password you've assigned to your syllabus.

- After you have created a syllabus using **Syllabus Manager™**, students may enter the syllabus for their course section from any point in the Companion Website.

- Clicking on a date, the student is shown the list of activities for the assignment. The activities for each assignment are linked directly to actual content, saving time for students.

- ❋ Adding assignments consists of clicking on the desired due date, then filling in the details of the assignment—name of the assignment, instructions, and whether or not it is a one-time or repeating assignment.

- ❋ In addition, links to other activities can be created easily. If the activity is online, a URL can be entered in the space provided, and it will be linked automatically in the final syllabus.

- ❋ Your completed syllabus is hosted on our servers, allowing convenient updates from any computer on the Internet. Changes you make to your syllabus are immediately available to your students at their next logon.

For the Student—

- ❋ **Topic Overviews**—outline key concepts in topic areas

- ❋ **Web Links**—general websites related to topic areas as well as associations and professional organizations

- ❋ **Read About It**—timely articles that enable you to become more aware of important issues in early childhood education

- ❋ **Learn by Doing**—put concepts into action, participate in activities, complete lesson plans, examine strategies, and more

- ❋ **For Teachers**—access information that you will need to know as an in-service teacher, including information on materials, activities, lessons, curriculum, and state standards

- ❋ **Visit a School**—visit a school's website to see concepts, theories, and strategies in action

- ❋ **Electronic Bluebook**—send homework or essays directly to your instructor's e-mail with this paperless form

- ❋ **Message Board**—serves as a virtual bulletin board to post—or respond to—questions or comments to/from a national audience

- ❋ **Chat**—real-time chat with anyone who is using the text anywhere in the country—ideal for discussion and study groups, class projects, etc.

To take advantage of these and other resources, please visit the *Teaching and Learning: Collaborative Exploration of the Reggio Emilia Approach* Companion Website at

www.prenhall.com/fu

Contents

Part I

The Place of Reggio Emilia
in the United States

What is our fascination with Reggio Emilia? Why do so many of us who have had the fortune to visit this special place come back to the United States with exciting aspirations of incorporating the principles of Reggio Emilia into our own programs? We know we cannot simply transplant the ideas and practices of another culture to our own communities with much success. But we can recast and reinvent these ideas, pausing to reflect on our values and beliefs about teaching and learning, about children and what we expect for them, in order to look more broadly at and think more deeply about our pedagogy. Each of the chapters in this section serves to help us in this regard. We are urged to reconsider what it means to teach and to develop a respect for different ways of seeing and knowing as we attempt to reinvent the Reggio Emilia approach and embrace a pedagogy of possibilities. Likewise, we are reminded that children, as valued members of the human community, are worthy of our deepest respect. Moreover, they should be seen as protagonists in their own learning and development. This has important implications both for how we teach and how we assess children. Is it possible for standards, accountability assessments, and Reggio-inspired curriculum to co-exist and support one another in a success-oriented society that gives great value to achievement, assessment, and accountability? As advocates for children, American educators must participate proactively in the standards and accountability conversation, and use accountability assessments as a basis to inform their teaching practice and improve children's learning opportunities, in much the same way that our Reggio counterparts use documentation to inform decisions about curriculum and facilitate children's learning.

Chapter
1

An Invitation to Join a Growing

Community for Learning and Change

Victoria R. Fu ◆ Andrew J. Stremmel ◆ Lynn T. Hill

The fundamental message of the teacher is this: You can change your life. Whoever you are, wherever you've been, whatever you've done, the teacher invites you to a second chance, another round, perhaps a different conclusion. The teacher posits possibility, openness, and alternative; the teacher points to what could be, but is not yet."

William Ayers (1998, p. xvii)

A COMMUNITY IN SEARCH OF POSSIBILITIES FOR TEACHING

In the clamor of questions and solutions raised about education in the United States, a voice beckons from a small town in northern Italy. In Reggio Emilia, one finds a community made up of "a remarkable group of teachers of various strips and specialties who have worked together for years, even decades, with parents, community members, and thousands of children, to set up a system that works." (Edwards, Gandini, & Forman, 1998, p. xvi) Countless educators in the United States have become inspired by the schools in Reggio Emilia and their approach to education as they try to untangle the problems of quality care and education, school reform, and services for children and families.

We want to place this book in the context of how it comes to be. We, the authors, are colleagues, teacher educators, and friends who enjoy and value our camaraderie in teaching and learning together, in the best sense of a community. We share a philosophy of teaching that is based on social constructivism, qualitative inquiry; a belief that a teacher is always in the making; and a desire to create communities for learning. For us, teaching is a lifelong project, and "projects are most meaningful when they involve others, when they touch on others' lives" (Interview with Maxine Greene by William Ayers, 1995, p. 323). As Hannah Arendt said, "For excellence, the presence of others is always required" (cited in Ernst, Miletta, & Rielly (1988). This calls for us to continuously invite and engage others to walk with us in constructing and living a pedagogy of relationship and possibility in what Greene calls a community in the making. This journey to change is not lived without its ups and downs. It is at times challenging, invigorating, and celebrating and at other times trying, doubtful, and testing the deepest core of our being. But a sense of community and the belief that we are doing the right thing has kept us going through thick and thin.

A few years ago we became interested in the work that is being done in Reggio Emilia. We quickly saw that its approach to teaching provides a possible framework that can better bring our teaching philosophy into practice. The principles of the Reggio Emilia approach reflect the essence of inquiry-based teaching that values:

- ❀ Children as protagonists, collaborators, and communicators in the learning process;
- ❀ Teachers as partners, nurturers, and guides in children's learning;
- ❀ Teachers as researchers;
- ❀ Parents as partners that take active roles in their children's learning;
- ❀ Environments (as a third teacher) that support learning through social interaction and exploration; and
- ❀ Documentation as a means for negotiated learning through communication (Cadwell, 1997, Gandini, 1998, preface).

In 1997 we went to Italy to attend the Reggio Children's Spring Institute. Being in Reggio together afforded us the opportunity to listen, observe, reflect, and share our different points of viewing and opened our minds to other possibilities for change and the further reconstruction of teaching and learning in our laboratory school and in our college classrooms. But foremost in our thinking was the importance of expanding our community to include others to reinvent and recast the Reggio Emilia approach to make it truly responsive to the social and cultural diversity of the United States. While we were there, with this intention in mind, we proposed to Reggio Children to bring a group of educators from the United States with us to study and learn together in Reggio Emilia.

When our proposal was approved in the summer of 1997, we began to contact colleagues who we knew were engaged in exploring the Reggio Emilia approach and invited them to join us on a study-research tour to Reggio Emilia. The breadth of possibilities of what we could experience and learn together in a community of learners captured all our imaginations. Together we could listen, observe, reflect, and make sense of our experiences in each other's company. In order to capture the diverse contexts of learning, our group, made up of preschool and public school teachers, child development program administrators, college students, and university professors, with different levels of knowledge of the Reggio Emilia approach, hoped to capture the diverse contexts of learning. We knew that these differences could provide a rich opportunity for exploration as we would bring different points of view and life experiences to the table which would challenge each of us to revisit and reflect on our practice in new ways.

We traveled first to Riva San Vitale, Switzerland, and spent one week at our university's Center for European Studies. During our stay in Riva we studied, learned, and listened to our colleagues' stories of adapting the Reggio Emilia approach. We developed a teaching–research agenda that would guide our work when we returned to the United States. More importantly, this week of living and learning together created a bond among us—a community in the making. We named our learning community the Lugano-Reggio Collaborative to represent the beginning of our journey in Riva San Vitale situated along Lake Lugano and the bridge to the next leg of our journey to Reggio Emilia to attend the 1998 Reggio Children's Winter Institute. This sense of community continued as we listened, observed, and dialogued in Italy; upon returning to the United States a listserv was created to further facilitate our conversation and sharing of ideas.

This anthology tells our stories—a group of teacher–researchers who came together because, first of all, we share a passion for teaching and learning. Secondly, we recognize that the Reggio Emilia approach affords a framework to effect qualitative inquiry as a central mode of teaching. Thirdly, we are keenly aware of a need to reinvent the Reggio Emilia approach in the cultural context of the United States to "make it our own." Last but not least, we believe that in order to do the above, effectively, we need the knowledge, experience, critique, and insights of a community of learners. So the final analysis is that this book is about a community of learners who embraces a pedagogy of relationships. We are open to learning with all its possibilities, not bound by what had been the experiences in Reggio Emilia, Italy, and the United States, but of what could be. This book tells the beginnings of our process of transformation in diverse settings, incorporating the principles of Reggio Emilia but reaching beyond—embracing the diverse voices of other philosophers, theorists, and practitioners in the United States and reconstructing our classrooms to create something new, full of hope and possibilities.

We want to share our stories because we believe that teaching is a way of life. The teacher seeks and challenges others to find meaning in the questions of life: *What is teaching? How should we teach? What does teaching mean?* (Garrison, 1997, p. 22). Also, we hold on to the belief that "teaching is for change" (Ayers, 1998, p. xvii), and change happens in relationships where social construction of learning and knowledge comes to life. "Pedagogy as a social relationship is very close in. It gets right in there—in your brain, your body, your heart, in your sense of self, of the world of others, and of possibilities in all those realms" (Ellsworth, 1997, p. 6).

The chapters in this book do not adequately represent the many ongoing teaching–research efforts among the members of our collaborative. However, the strands of the passion and thinking of other members are embedded in this volume for they are a part of us from the beginning of our journey. The stories in this book reflect what Greene calls a narrative of "a community always in the making" that examines and reexamines processes of human questioning (1995, p. 6).

THEMES AND ORGANIZATION OF THE BOOK

This book is about relationships in a community of learners who are engaged in action research. Philosophical and inquiring conversations are central to transforming the Reggio Emilia approach to be responsive to the social, cultural, and historical contexts of the United States. In this book, we bring to you four major themes:

1. There is a need to revisit and reconstruct our meanings of education and the image of the child;
2. Communities for learning can serve a function for teaching and learning across the boundaries of culture, disciplines, schools, ways of thinking, and to explore possibilities;
3. Inquiry-based teacher education can promote change in self and others in being open to possibilities "to what could be, but is not yet;" and
4. *Progettazione* (projected curriculum) and documentation can promote learning, research, and understanding of children's work among the children themselves, teachers, and families.

This book ends with a chapter of conversation among the authors reflecting on lessons learned and questions raised for further investigation.

In each chapter the author(s) shares actual stories that bring to life major concepts and questions for further reflection. The stories include those moments of transcendence, when we first got together in Riva San Vitale, that challenged us to think and lead to our subsequent exploration of the topics being presented in this book. This is done so the reader can get a sense of collaboration among the authors. In each chapter, questions are raised for further reflection and exploration—questions that continue to challenge us. We hope that these questions will challenge readers in their efforts to explore the possibilities afforded by the Reggio approach in their schools and classrooms.

The Place of Reggio Emilia in the United States

In the five chapters found in Part I, the authors propose issues that should be explored in adapting and recasting the Reggio Emilia approach in the context of the social–

cultural context of the United States. In this chapter, Victoria Fu, Andrew Stremmel, and Lynn Hill tell the story of a community in the making. Lella Gandini provides a context for understanding the Reggio Emilia approach by telling its history, underlying philosophy, and its current practice in Chapter 2, "The Story and Foundations of the Reggio Emilia Approach." Victoria Fu invites us in Chapter 3 to explore and make sense of "The Challenge to Reinvent the Reggio Emilia Approach: A Pedagogy of Hope and Possibilities" by revisiting the history, memories, and voices of the United States and the meaning of the art of teaching, as we make this approach *our own*. In Chapter 4, "The Cultural Construction of Childhood: United States and Reggio Perspectives," Andrew Stremmel provokes us to reflect on the images of the child, as a cultural invention and how these images contribute to current conceptualization of teaching and learning. Using a parable as an entry to Chapter 5, "The Reggio Emilia Approach and Accountability Assessment in the United States," Diane Horm-Wingerd suggests a different way of seeing the assessment and accountability policies and practices in the schools.

Amiable Communities for Learning

The three chapters in this part examine the possibilities for learning in diverse communities. Carol Bersani and Debra Jarjoura share with us in Chapter 6 a story of families and a school working together to construct a shared culture for learning in "Developing a Sense of 'We' in Parent/Teacher Relationships." In Chapter 7, "A Journey to Recast the Reggio Emilia Approach for a Middle School: A Pedagogy of Relationships and Hope," Lynn Hill shares the story of a learning community created by a group of middle school teachers negotiating change in their school to provide the best education to their students. It is a story of the many challenges they had to overcome, personally and professionally. In Chapter 8, "An Outstanding Education for ALL Children: Learning from the Reggio Emilia Approach to Inclusion," Sharon Palsha examines the approach to inclusion in Reggio Emilia and the many possibilities it offers to early childhood educators and parents who seek to provide high-quality inclusion and community-based early care and education programs.

Teacher Education: Inquiry Teaching and the Possibilities for Change

In Part III, the readers are introduced to the philosophy and practices of three university programs that incorporate the principles of Reggio Emilia into their constructivist, inquiry-based teacher education programs. In Chapter 9, "The Transformation of Self in Early Childhood Education: Connections to the Reggio Emilia Approach," Andrew Stremmel, Victoria Fu, and Lynn Hill share their vision of early childhood teacher education as a process of continual renewal and transformation. They take the position that teachers must learn to view themselves as change agents, researchers, activists, and reflective thinkers who are on a journey on continual renewal, reinventing, and reconstruction of self. Jeanne Goldhaber and Dee Smith tell their story in Chapter 10, relating of how the practice of documentation contributes to teacher inquiry and reconceptualization of the role of teacher as researcher in "The Development of Documentation Strategies to Support Teacher Reflection, Inquiry, and Collaboration." In Chapter 11, Deborah Tegano invites us to revisit the meaning of "Passion and the Art of Teaching" by challenging us to recapture the passion for teaching and encouraging us to find our own voices, and our students' voices, through the development of representational competence.

Progettazione and Documentation: Learning Moments Among Protagonists

The two chapters in this section illustrate the meaning of progettazione and the power of documentation as tools of learning in the classroom, among children, teachers, and parents. Alise Shafer in Chapter 12, "Ordinary Moments, Extraordinary Possibilities," paints for the reader in words and children's representations that watching and listening to children can uncover "the extraordinary within the ordinary" learning moments. Pam Oken-Wright and Marty Gravett alert us in Chapter 13, "Big Ideas and the Essence of Intent," to listen to children—as Carla Rinaldi (1998, p. 120) says "with an active mind and an active heart"—in search of their intent in pursuing projects and ways of knowing.

Reflections: Lessons Learned and Possibilities for the Next Steps

This text ends with a conversation among us, the authors, reflecting on our individual and the group's journey to reinvent the Reggio Emilia approach in the context of the United States. We will also share our vision of what might lie in wait for us as we move on to the next leg of our journey to learn, relearn, and reconstruct the Reggio approach. What will the reconstructed approach look like in the landscapes of classrooms and schools in our country?

AN INVITATION TO REINVENT

Every encounter is a moment of challenge, inspiration, and renewal. In reading our stories we hope you will continue your search for meanings and participate in the reinvention of the Reggio Emilia approach in your communities for learning—communities of children and families you touch and who in turn touch and move you daily. Together we can reinvent and reconstruct amiable schools, classrooms, and communities for change, valuing the three protagonists in teaching-learning relationships—the child, parent, and teacher—looking for and living with real projects that can transcend us. As Greene said:

In teaching . . . I feel successful if I can make it possible for students to come upon ways of being they have not thought of before. Part of that demands an activation of imagination; part, a refusal to screen the self off from the world. None of us is separate and autonomous; none of us can possibly be an "island" in John Donne's sense. We are, like or not, part of a "main" our imagination can bring into being." (Ayers, 1995, p. 323)

REFERENCES

Ayers, W. (1995). Interview with Maxine Greene. *Quality Studies in Education, 8* (4), 319–328.

Ayers, W. C., Hunt, J. A., & Quinn, T. (Eds.). (1998). *Teaching for social justice.* New York: Teachers College Press.

Ayers, W. C., & Miller, J. L. (Eds.). (1998). *A light in dark times: Maxine Greene and the unfinished conversation.* New York: Teachers College Press.

Bruner, J. (1996). *The culture of education.* Cambridge, MA: Harvard University Press.

Cadwell, L. B. (1997). *Bringing Reggio Emilia home: An innovative approach to early childhood education.* New York: Teachers College Press.

Edwards, C., Gandini, L., & Forman, G. (Eds.). (1998). *The hundred languages of children: The Reggio Emilia approach—advanced reflections.* Greenwich, CT: Ablex.

Ellsworth, E. (1997). *Teaching positions: Difference, pedagogy, and the power of address.* New York: Teachers College Press.

Ernst, K., Miletta, & Reilly, K. (1998). In the presence of others. In W. C. Ayers & J. L. Miller (Eds.), *A light in dark times: Maxine Greene and the unfinished conversation* (pp. 33–40). New York: Teachers College Press.

Gandini, L. (1998). Foundations of the Reggio Emilia Approach. In J. Hendrick (Ed.), *First steps in teaching the Reggio way* (pp. 2-25). Upper Saddle River, NJ: Merrill Prentice Hall.

Garrison, J. (1997). *Dewey and Eros: Wisdom and desire in the art of teaching.* New York: Teachers College Press.

Greene, M. (1995). *Releasing the imagination: Essays on education, the arts, and social change.* San Francisco, CA: Jossey-Bass Publishers.

Rinaldi, C. (1998). Projected curriculum constructed through documentation—Progettazionne: An interview with Lella Gandini. In C. Edwards, L. Gandini, and G. Forman (Eds.). (1998) *The hundred languages of children: The Reggio Emilia approach—advanced reflections* (pp. 113–125). Greenwich, CT: Ablex.

The Inaugural Meeting of the Lugano - Reggio Research Collaborative Participants in Riva San Vitale, Switzerland, January 1998.
Participants:
First Row: J. Goldhaber, University of Vermont; D. Smith, University of Vermont; A. Miller-Stott, University of Tennessee; C. Bersani, Kent State; D. Tegano, University of Tennessee; L. Talley, University of Tennessee; D. Jarjoura, Kent State; S. Steffens, Kent State; P. Whisnant, Forsyth Technical Community College; S. Palsha, University of North Carolina; D. Fernie, Ohio State; D. Doninelli, University of Georgia; C. Maderni, University of Georgia; J. Atiles, University of Georgia; P. Oken-Wright, St. Catherine's School; L. Hill, Virginia Tech; M. Gravett, Sabot School; R. Wilkerson, Virginia Tech; G. Distler, Blacksburg Middle School; K. Lyon, University of Nebraska; V. Fu, Virginia Tech; D. Wallace, University of Nebraska; J. Sawyers, Virginia Tech; K. Wells (with D. Novak), Virginia Tech.
Second Row: S. Ferguson, Sabot School; A. Golden, Sabot School; B. Gantz, Rainbow Riders Childcare Center; K. Snyder, Rainbow Riders; L. Landrum, Rainbow Riders; D. Lickey, Sabot School; K. DeBord, North Carolina State University; R. Kantor, Ohio State University; P. Cruickshank-Schott, Durham Early School; K. Palfi, Evergreen Community School; K. Singh, Virginia Tech; P. Harrelson, Richmond City Head Start; S. Murphy, Virginia Tech; T. Cacace-Beshears, Places and Programs for Children; A. Stremmel, Virginia Tech; S. Natili, Virginia Tech; C. Fox, Blacksburg Middle School; A. Shafer, Evergreen Community School.

Chapter
2

The Story and Foundations of the Reggio Emilia Approach

Lella Gandini

A FEW NOTES ABOUT BEGINNINGS AND DEVELOPMENT

It all started at a particular place and time, namely Reggio Emilia in 1945, just at the end of Italy's Fascist dictatorship and World War II. It was a moment when the desire to bring change and create a new, more-just world, free from oppression, was urging women and men to gather their strength and build with their own hands schools for their children. Some of these schools continued until 1967 (when they were handed over to the city government) thanks to the initiative and imagination of workers, farmers, and a famous group of the time, the Union of Italian Women (UDI Unione Donne Italiane).

In the region of Emilia Romagna, where Reggio Emilia is located, there is a long history and tradition of cooperative work done in all areas of economy and organization: agriculture, food processing, unions, entrepreneurship, solution of crises, and so forth. Therefore, for people to get together and start the schools, and

This chapter is adapted from "The Reggio Emilia Story: History and Organization" and "Foundations of the Reggio Emilia Approach" by Lella Gandini, previously published in *First Steps Toward Teaching the Reggio Way,* edited by Joanne Hendrick (Upper Saddle River, NJ: Merrill/Prentice Hall, 1997).

13

for teachers and parents to work together to run the schools now, is in line with established tradition, with a traditional and successful way of life, which, although occasionally disrupted under adverse conditions, is then revived as soon as feasible.

In the 1950s and early 1960s, a teachers' movement was active in Italy concerning the goal of innovation in education. With strong motivation and commitment, these teachers hoped to develop new ways of teaching in tune with the new democratic society, with the new realities of the modern world, and with greater relevance to the life of children. In this way they also hoped that the public schools would become nonselective and nondiscriminatory.

In this time of ferment, Loris Malaguzzi (deceased), founder and director of the Department of Early Childhood Education in Reggio Emilia, took time off from teaching to specialize in psychology at the Center for National Research in Rome. He was aware of the tremendous potential value of all these sources of energy and of combining these with his own energy and ideas. He soon became a leader, first along with others better known in Italy and then by becoming a point of reference for teachers of many regions wanting to bring innovation to schools for young children. It was Malaguzzi who was ready and able to support the schools started by the common people in Reggio in 1945 and who carried the battle to get the city government to take the running of the people's schools upon itself and open the first municipal school in 1963.

Some of their ideas found inspiration and encouragement in the writings of progressive educators from the United States, and other ideas were influenced by theory and practice coming from France, and later by child psychology and pedagogy coming from various countries. In fact, educators in Reggio Emilia have continued all along to keep updated on current and innovative research on child development and education.

The sixties in Italy were marked by the tremendous economic development known as "the boom." The transformation that took place brought to Italians a diversified economy with modern industries. Along with that there was a notable development in the areas of social services and workers' benefits. More and more women were entering the workforce and became engaged in the emerging women's movement. Furthermore, in the late sixties and early seventies, a strong student movement shook up the university system and the traditional values of a still highly stratified society. It was during those years of upheaval between 1968 and 1971 that a series of national laws were passed that became true landmark decisions. They included the establishment of free schools for children three to six years of age, infant–toddler centers for children three months to three years old, maternity leave, a new family law more favorable to women, and equal pay for equal work between men and women.

It was during this time that Malaguzzi was able to gather around him a group of devoted and competent educators who, along with parents and other citizens who felt strong ownership of the schools, supported his work toward creating and maintaining a very high quality in the programs. This group was determined to continuously update the preparation of teachers and explore new avenues of innovation in teaching young children. In some of the interviews that Malaguzzi granted late in his life, he presented a long list of scientists, philosophers, scholars, artists, and writers who had influenced his thought and therefore the work of educators in the schools that he did so much to shape. His complex system of education, which takes into account the human desire to "do nothing without joy" and which pays close attention to individual as well as group interests and potentials, is a form of socioconstructivism, i.e., knowledge and understanding are constructed through social interactions.

To respond to Malaguzzi's dissemination effort and in appreciation of the great interest developing in the United States about the work done in the schools of Reggio Emilia, in 1992, Eli Saltz of the Merrill-Palmer Institute and Wayne State University launched *Innovations in Early Education: The International Reggio Exchange,* a quarterly publication that carries articles by Reggio and United States educators who are reflecting on the translation to a different context of ideas from Reggio Emilia. In addition to this dissemination effort in 1994, there was an organization established called *Reggio Children* that serves to share knowledge in theory and practice through the distribution of books, articles, videos, and slides that document the Reggio approach. Since the 1980s, an exhibition from Reggio Emilia entitled "The Hundred Languages of Children" has toured the United States. Among the many messages that emerge from the exhibit and motivate audiences to learn more about Reggio Emilia's schools for young children, several are of special interest to art educators, as well as to the rest of us. The exhibit has documented the importance of "giving children opportunities to communicate what they are thinking at any stage of knowing" (Houk, 1997, p. 33).

BASIC PRINCIPLES OF THE REGGIO EMILIA APPROACH

An examination of some of the principles that have inspired the experiences in Reggio Emilia immediately reveals that these concepts are not new to American audiences. Indeed, many of the basic ideas that informed the work of educators in Reggio Emilia originated in the United States and are, in a sense, returning to their point of origin. From the beginning of their work in building their program, the educators in Reggio Emilia have been avid readers of Dewey, and over the years, in addition to studying Piaget, Vygotsky, and other European scientists, they have continued to keep abreast of the latest research in child development and education in the United States. However, their approach, based on continuous research and analyses of their practice, has caused them also to formulate new theoretical interpretations, new hypotheses, ideas, and strategies about learning and teaching.

In Italy, about 90% of the children three to six years old attend some kind of school, whether municipal, national, or private; in Reggio, 99% of preschool-age children are enrolled in a variety of such schools. Among these are 21 schools run by the municipality for children aged three to six years and 13 infant–toddler centers for children aged four months to three years. Children from all socioeconomic and educational backgrounds attend the programs. Children with disabilities are given first priority for enrollment in the centers and schools.

Educators in Reggio Emilia have no intention of suggesting that their program should be looked at as a model to be copied in other countries; rather, their work should be observed as an educational experience that consists of reflection, practice, and further careful reflection in a program that is continuously renewed and readjusted.

The following principles, or fundamental ideas, are presented one by one for the sake of clarity, but *they must be considered as a tightly connected, coherent philosophy, in which each point influences, and is influenced by, all the others.*

The Image of the Child

The educators in Reggio Emilia first and foremost speak about the image of the child. All children have preparedness, potential, curiosity, and interest in establishing relationships, in engaging in social interaction, constructing their learning, and negotiating with everything the environment brings to them. Teachers are deeply aware of the children's potential and construct all their work and the environment of the children's experience to respond appropriately.

Children's Relationships and Interactions Within a System

Education has to focus on each child, not considered in isolation but in relation with the family, other children, the teachers, the environment of the school, the community, and the wider society. Each school is viewed as a system in which all these relationships, which are interconnected and reciprocal, are activated and supported.

The Three Subjects of Education: Children, Parents, and Teachers

In order for children to learn, their well-being has to be guaranteed; such well-being is connected with the well-being of parents and teachers. Children's rights should be recognized, not only their needs. Children have a right to high-quality care and education that supports the development of their potential. It is by recognizing that children have rights to the best that a society can offer that parents' rights to be involved in the life of the school and the teachers' rights to grow professionally will also be recognized.

The Role of Parents

Parents are considered to be an essential component of the program, and many among them are part of the advisory committee running each school. The parents' participation is expected and supported and takes many forms: day-to-day interaction, work in the schools, discussions of the educational goals and psychological issues, special events, excursions, and celebrations. Parents are a competent and active part of their children's learning experience and, at the same time, help ensure the welfare of all children in the school.

The Role of Space: An Amiable School

The environment is the most visible aspect of the work done in the schools by all the protagonists. It conveys the message that this is a place where adults have thought about the quality and the instructive power of space. The layout of the physical space is welcoming and fosters encounters, communication, and relationships. The arrangement of structures, objects, and activities encourages choices, problem solving, and discoveries in the process of learning.

There is attention to detail everywhere—in the color of the walls, the shape of the furniture, the arrangement of simple objects on shelves and tables. Light, plants, and mirrors are used to help provide a pleasurable atmosphere while offering possibilities for reflection and exploration. However, the environment is not just beautiful—it is also highly personal. It is filled with the essence of the children. Everywhere there are paintings, drawings, paper sculptures, wire constructions, transparent collages coloring the light, and gently-moving overhead mobiles. The work and reflections of the children, their photographs, and the documentation of the experiences fill all remaining spaces. The results of so much work, thoughtfully selected by the teachers and the atelierista (teacher trained in the visual arts), literally surround the people in the school.

The Value of Relationships and Interaction of Children in Small Groups

In preparing the space, teachers offer the possibility for children to be with the teacher and many of the other children, or with just a few of them, or even alone when they need a little niche to stay by themselves. Teachers are always aware, however, that children learn a great deal in exchanges with their peers, especially when they can interact in small groups. Such small groups of two, three, four, or five children provide possibilities for paying attention, hearing, and listening to each other, developing curiosity and interest, and asking and responding to questions. It provides opportunities for negotiations and dynamic communication. Malaguzzi suggested that it is desirable that adults initiate the settings of such situations because a more homogeneous age group helps the communication among children in planning and decision making. This type of small group also favors the emergence of cognitive conflicts that can initiate a process in which children construct together new learning and development.

The Role of Time and the Importance of Continuity

Time is not set by a clock, and continuity is not interrupted by the calendar. Children's own sense of time and their personal rhythm are considered in planning and carrying out activities and projects. Teachers get to know the personal time of the children and each child's particular characteristics because children stay with the same teacher and the same peer group for three-year cycles. This process of looping further promotes the concept of *an education based on relationships.*

Documentation: Teachers and Children as Partners

To know how to plan or proceed with their work, teachers observe and listen to the children closely. Teachers use the understanding they gain in this way to act as a resource for them. They ask questions and discover the children's ideas, hypotheses, and theories. Then the adults discuss together what they have recorded through their own notes, or audio or visual recordings, and make flexible plans and preparations. Then they are ready to enter again into dialogues with the children and offer them occasions either for discovering or also revisiting experiences, since they consider learning not as a linear process but as a spiral progression. In fact, teachers consider themselves to be partners in this process of learning, which might proceed with pauses and setbacks but which is an experience constructed and enjoyed together with the children. The role of teachers, therefore, is considered to be one of continual research and learning, that takes place with the children and is embedded in team cooperation. Doing this kind of research, reflecting and listening to children together with other colleagues and with the support of the pedagogical coordinator (*the pedagogista*), contributes to a situation of continuous individual and group professional growth.

The Power of Documentation for Constructing Curriculum

It flows naturally that, to be truly respectful of children's and teachers' ideas and processes of learning, the curriculum cannot be set in advance. Teachers express general goals and make hypotheses about what direction the interests of children, activities, and projects might take; consequently, they make appropriate preparations. Then, after observing children in action, they compare, discuss, and interpret together their observations and make choices that they share with the children about what to offer and how to sustain the children in their exploration and learning. In fact, the curriculum is constructed in the process of each activity or project. It is negotiated and flexibly adjusted accordingly through this continuous dialogue among teachers and with children.

It is by the varied use of documentation, which is an integral part of the daily experience of teachers in Reggio Emilia, that this process is possible. Transcriptions of children's remarks and discussions, photographs of their activities, and representations of their thinking and learning while using many media are carefully studied. In many cases these different traces of documentation are then selected and arranged by the atelierista, along with the other teachers, to document the work (and the process of learning) done in the schools.

This documentation has several functions. Among these are to make parents aware of their children's experience and maintain their involvement; to allow teachers to understand children better, and to evaluate the teachers' own work, thus promoting their professional growth; to facilitate communication and exchange of ideas among educators; to make children aware that their effort is valued; and to create an archive that traces the history of the school and the pleasure of learning by many children and their teachers.

Cooperation and Collaboration as the Backbone of the System

Cooperation at all levels in the schools is the powerful mode of working that makes possible the achievement of the complex goals that Reggio educators have set for themselves. Teachers work in pairs in each classroom, not as head teacher and assistant, but at the same level. They see themselves as researchers gathering information about their work with children by means of continual documentation. The strong collegial relationships that are maintained with all other teachers and staff rely on this information to engage in collaborative discussion and interpretation of both teachers' and children's work. These exchanges provide ongoing training and theoretical enrichment. A team of pedagogical coordinators (pedagogisti) also supports the relationships among all teachers, parents, community members, and city administrators further supporting this cooperative system.

The team of pedagogisti meets once a week with the director of the whole system to discuss policy and problems related to the whole network of schools and infant-toddler centers. Each pedagogista is assigned to support three or four schools and centers, helping the teachers to sustain and implement the philosophy of the system. The support of each school includes work with the teachers to identify new themes and experiences for continuous professional development and in-service training. In each particular school, the pedagogista helps the teachers deal with educational issues concerning children and parents. However, the goal is to support teachers by promoting their autonomy rather than by solving problems for them. The complex task of the pedagogisti is to collaborate with the various parts of this complex system and maintain the necessary connections, while at the same time analyzing and interpreting the rights and needs of each child, family, and group of teachers.

The Interdependence of Cooperation and Organization

The high degree of cooperation requires much support, which is supplied by a careful and well-developed structure or organization. From the details of each teacher's schedule, to the planning of meetings with families, to the children's diet, *everything* is discussed and organized with precision and care. In fact, the high level of cooperation is made possible precisely because of such thoughtful organization. Likewise, the organization is achieved because of the conviction by all concerned that only by working together so closely will they be able to offer the best experience to the children. Educators in Reggio Emilia consider organization as one of their important values; therefore, at least 6 hours in the weekly schedule are set aside for meetings among teachers, preparations, meetings with parents, and in-service training.

The Many Languages of Children: Atelierista and Atelier

A teacher who is trained in the visual arts works closely with the other teachers and the children in every preprimary school (and visits the infant-toddler centers). This teacher is called an atelierista, and a special workshop or studio, called an atelier, is set aside and used by all the children and teachers as well as by the atelierista. The atelier contains a great variety of tools and resource materials along with records of past projects and experiences.

The exploration of materials, activities, and projects, however, does not take place only in the atelier. Through the years the roles of the atelier and the atelierista have expanded and become part of the whole school. Smaller spaces, called mini-ateliers, have been set up in each classroom; furthermore, teachers and atelieristi have been working more closely together to transfer to one another reciprocal knowledge and skills. What is done with materials and media is not regarded as art per se, because in the view of Reggio educators, the children's use of many media is not a separate part of the curriculum but an inseparable, integral part of the whole cognitive/symbolic expression involved in the process of learning.

Projects

Projects provide the backbone of the children's and teachers' learning experiences. They are based on the strong conviction that learning by doing is of great importance and that to discuss in group and to revisit ideas and experiences is the premier way of gaining better understanding and learning. Ideas for projects originate in the continuum of the experience of children and teachers as they construct knowledge together through the use of documentation as a tool of work that respects all protagonists. Projects can last from a few days to several months. They may start either from a chance event, an idea or a problem posed by one or more children, or an experience initiated directly by teachers. For example, a study of crowds originated when a child talked to the class about a summer vacation experience. Whereas teachers had expected the children to tell about their discoveries on the beach or in the countryside, a child commented that "crowd" was all that she remembered.

Another project on fountains developed when children decided to build an amusement park for birds. This project originated when teachers invited the children to revisit a topic that had been explored within the school in the previous year. After much discussion of their memories, the children enthusiastically supported the idea, that was expressed by one child, of constructing an amusement park for the birds on the school playground. Some children completed initial drawings of ideas that they thought would be useful in the park's development. Teachers transcribed the recorded conversations of the children and then discussed the transcription with the pedagogista. They then prepared more questions on the topic because it was clear that the goal of constructing an amusement park for birds was of great interest to the children and also offered many promising opportunities for combining learning experiences with pleasure. The project took shape as the hypotheses (possibilities) formed by the adults blended with those of the children.

CONCLUSION

In introducing brief remarks about the story of the schools for young children in Reggio Emilia and attempting to present some of their fundamental principles, I only touched some facets of this complex system. The source of this complexity is the fact that the system touches the lives of so many people who have been participants in the construction of its success. Furthermore, this dynamic educational approach, which is constantly questioning itself, changing, and inventing new ways of understanding and supporting young children's learning, teachers' development, and parents' participation, cannot easily be captured and presented by only one person and with only one language. The challenge is for all of us who want to offer the children in our own context and community the best possible opportunities to experience learning with pleasure, and to continuously find new ways to translate these ideas, reinvent them, and invent new ones.

REFERENCES

Houk, P. (1997). Lessons from an Exhibition: Reflections of our Art Educator. In J. Hendrick (Ed.), *First steps toward teaching the Reggio way* (pp. 26–40). Upper Saddle River, NJ: Merrill Prentice Hall.

Chapter

3

The Challenge to Reinvent the Reggio Emilia Approach: A Pedagogy of Hope and Possibilities

Victoria R. Fu

No way. The hundred is there.

The teacher*
is made of one hundred.
The teacher has
a hundred languages
a hundred hands
a hundred thoughts

*My apologies to Loris Malaguzzi for substituting the word *teacher* for *child* throughout to bring to the forefront the role of the teacher. You can also substitute the word *parent* for *child*. I did this intentional editing because, in my conversations with teachers and others, I have often felt that many have missed seeing the other protagonists who are reflected in the poem. I hope that in reading this poem as printed above, the other protagonists—the teacher and the parent—are made more visible. I trust that Malaguzzi had this intention in mind when he wrote the poem, for he strongly believed that children, teachers, and parents are collaborators in the teaching–learning enterprise.

*L. Malaguzzi No Way. The hundred *is* there. (Translated by Lella Gandini). In C. Edwards, L. Gandini, and G. Forman (Eds.), *The hundred languages of children: The Reggio Emilia approach— advanced reflections*. Greenwich, CT: Ablex. p. 3. Reproduced with permission of Greenwood Publishing Group, Inc., Westport, CT.

a hundred ways of thinking
of playing, of speaking.
A hundred always a hundred
ways of listening
of marveling of loving
hundred joys
for singing and understanding
a hundred worlds
to discover
a hundred worlds
to invent
a hundred worlds
to dream.
The teacher has
a hundred languages
(and a hundred hundred hundred more)
but they steal ninety-nine.
The school and the culture
separate the head from the body.
They tell the teacher:
to think without hands
to do without head
to listen and not to speak
to understand without joy
to love and to marvel
only at Easter and Christmas.
They tell the teacher:
to discover the world already there
and of the hundred they
steal ninety-nine.
They tell the teacher:
that work and play
reality and fantasy
science and imagination
sky and earth
reason and dream
are things
that do not belong together.

And thus they tell the teacher
that the hundred is not there.
The teacher says:
No way. The hundred is there.

Loris Malaguzzi

Look how carefully and intentionally she sorts natural materials she gathered to be used in different ways to create and represent.

The words of Loris Malaguzzi in the poem "No way. The hundred *is* there" awaken in us a need to attend to the many voices, languages, and abilities of children, parents, and teachers that are often lost in the teaching and learning process. His words encourage us to revisit, rediscover, reflect, relearn, and *reinvent* our lives as teachers. The words in the poem beckon us to embrace a pedagogy of hope and possibilities, of what Greene (1988) would call doing things, in this case teaching, as they ought to be and could be in an open world.

In this chapter, I wish to share with you some of my thoughts about teaching with inspirations gleaned from Reggio Emilia and learnings from being a teacher/ educator. I believe that it is critical for us in reinventing the Reggio Emilia approach to make it our own to: (1) reconsider the essence of teaching, and (2) take into account the diverse cultures and voices that are deeply ingrained in the social-political history of the United States. I invite you to rethink the question: *What is teaching?*

Creating a game may include planning by putting changing ideas on paper. "Sometimes an idea just sneaks up on you!"

THE CHALLENGE TO REINVENT—IS THE REGGIO EMILIA APPROACH A FAD?

As I travel around the United States, I hear many teachers wondering aloud whether the Reggio Emilia approach is a fad. I also hear stories of difficulties in attempting to incorporate the principles of the Reggio Emilia approach into their curriculum, often saying that this could not be done because of many real and/or perceived constraints that are imposed on them by national goals and school policies for education. The underlying sentiment of these stories is summed up succinctly by David Hawkins' questions:

> What has happened to many of the early childhood programs that were at one time actively adopted in the United States?
> Where are they now?
> Where will the Reggio Emilia approach be in a few years?

Painting on tiles needs concentration, and, at times, scaffolding by a good friend.

These questions, placed in the context of a society that is always looking for a quick fix, seeking "an educational renaissance" because "schools need a revolution in search of a miracle" (*Time*, cited in Eisner, 1994), warrant our exploration of the essence of teaching.

There are numerous reasons that could have contributed to the failure of many early childhood education programs. I will just mention a few that I believe are most prominent. The notion of a prefabricated, prescriptive program itself places limits on one's thinking and practice in ways that discourage orienting the curriculum to the diverse needs and dispositions of teachers and learners. Additionally, these programs are often based on theories with limited possibilities for creativity and an appreciation for the art of teaching. In these "model" programs, theories and ideas are used as blueprints to be followed, instead of using them as tools to construct curriculum and practice. After all, blueprints are not cast in stone but should be revised and reconstructed in the process of practice. Thus, in many instances, mandating the adoption of particular programs places teachers in a position to teach to the model, without taking into account what constitutes best practice. In short, many prepackaged, prescriptive programs have failed because the program developers have ignored the fact that in the field of education it is not possible to prescribe a formula that one is to follow. Effective approaches to teaching are based on "concepts and generalizations that can heighten one's sensitivity to issues, problems, and possibilities to which one might attend" (Eisner, 1994, pp. 122–134). The Reggio Emilia approach reflects this latter position, and its success can be observed in classrooms.

Above all, I think many programs have failed because they are based on a deficit perspective that undermines and devalues the strengths, voices, and potentials of teachers, children, and adults with different experiences and from different walks of life, especially those who are oppressed. We need to celebrate diversity and recognize the breadth of knowledge and ways of knowing that afford us to learn in "a hundred languages and a hundred hundred hundred more." As teachers who value the art of teaching, we need to be armed with a breadth of languages and tools in order to create multiple possibilities for teaching and learning.

For those who question whether the Reggio Emilia approach is a fad, I can say with confidence that it is not a fad when its principles are implemented with understanding and thoughtfulness. These principles are found in the practice of responsive teachers across time and space. The Reggio Emilia approach is neither a model nor a program. It is an approach to teaching and learning. It is a way of thinking, **a way of life** that promotes teaching as an art. The ideas of John Dewey, Lev Vygotsky, Jean Piaget, Howard Gardner, Jerome Bruner, and many other thinkers penetrate the principles and practices found in the schools of Reggio Emilia. The Reggio Emilia approach reflects the concepts of social constructivism and promotes listening to multiple voices, and observing and recognizing different ways of knowing, seeing, and making sense. It also encourages the co-construction of meaning and practice through inquiry, reflection, interpreting, and learning in the company of others. This orientation of a community working together to support education values children, parents, and teachers as protagonists in the teaching–learning enterprise. In the United States, we often pay lip service to the idea of collaboration. We need to learn from Reggio Emilia how to make this system of collaboration work in schools. For this system to work, we need to reinvent the Reggio Emilia approach in the social, political, and historical context of the United States.

I hear many teachers who are inspired by the Reggio Emilia approach express the impossibility of adapting it in their schools and classrooms, saying, "The Reggio approach is unreal. It cannot be done in the United States," and that "It cannot be implemented in my classroom . . . not in my school." It seems that the history of the culture of schooling in the United States, with its multitude of prescriptions and barriers, may have broken the spirit of many otherwise innovative teachers. On the other hand, many other teachers may have become so entrenched in doing things "as usual" that they are afraid to take the risk to change their ways of thinking and teaching. These ways of thinking and positing are alarming to me because teaching, after all, is for change that calls for the releasing of imagination. Change begins with teachers who are willing to change. Teachers with such a disposition recognize there are different ways of knowing and learning. They are willing to create opportunities for their students to experience learning in multiple ways. A curriculum inspired by Reggio Emilia challenges teachers to be creative, imaginative, and to learn and relearn with children, colleagues, parents, and others in their respective communities of learning.

The people in Reggio Emilia have to overcome and continue to be challenged by many social, political, and religious barriers in order to create schools that are responsive to the needs of children and families. Their ongoing struggle, same as ours, is reflected in the poem:

> The school and the culture
> separate the head from the body.
> They tell the child (*teacher*):
> to think without hands
> to do without head
> to listen and not to speak
> to understand without joy . . .
> They tell the child (*teacher*):
> that work and play
> reality and fantasy
> science and imagination
> sky and earth
> reason and dream
> are things
> that do not belong together.

Inspired and guided by the vision of Malaguzzi and his colleagues, teachers, parents, and children value the power of learners and collaborative learning. Through the years, in Reggio Emilia, they have continuously revisited the works of leading thinkers in conjunction with their own experiences in order to reconstruct their practice to meet the changing needs of the children they teach.

The history of the struggles in Reggio Emilia gives us the courage to reconstruct and reinvent the Reggio Emilia approach—to make it *our* own. That is, to re-create an approach that is dynamic and responsive to children in a diverse, democratic society. Reggio Emilia gives us the image, as Rebecca New says, that makes us "more keenly aware of our limitations as well as our possibilities" (1998, p. 280). In our effort to reinvent, we need to be "seeing things up close and large" and to embrace a pedagogy of possibilities (Greene, 1995, p. 16). We need to revisit the writings and works of thinkers, writers, artists, philosophers, and theorists in the United States, from diverse backgrounds and disciplines. On this journey, we will find meaning in the memories, voices, and history of the United States that can awaken in us a realization that transformations are conceivable and that learning is stimulated by a sense of future possibilities and by a sense of what might be. We need to reconsider the *meaning of teaching* and rediscover the *art of teaching*.

WHAT IS TEACHING?

There are three fundamental questions of life posed by philosopher queens and kings: What is life? How should we live? What does life mean? Carlina Rinaldi, of Reggio Emilia, who sees teaching as life, also challenges us to ponder the question, "What is life?" as we try to understand teaching in Reggio Emilia, *and* as we try to reinvent the Reggio Emilia approach to inform teaching in the United States. For us, who are

Teaching happens in relationships—when teachers tune into their students' needs and interests.

teachers, teaching *is* our life. So these questions can be reframed as follows: *What is teaching? How should we teach? What does teaching mean?* (Garrison, 1997). Good teaching reflects a philosophy that takes these questions into consideration. According to Dewey we need a philosophy that conceives of "education as a process of forming fundamental dispositions, intellectual and emotional, toward nature and fellow-men" (1916/1966, p. 338). The process of teaching is "an art guided by educational values, personal needs, and by a variety of beliefs or generalizations that the teacher holds to be true" (Eisner, 1994, p. 154). Teaching happens in relationships—a pedagogy of relationships that encourage teachers to be imaginative and tuned into their students' diverse needs and ways of knowing by using multiple tools (languages) to promote different ways of seeing, understanding, representing, and demonstrating one's knowledge. *What is your philosophy of teaching?*

ARTS, AESTHETICS, AND THE ART OF TEACHING

How do we know when teaching is an art? Eisner suggests that we should consider at least four senses when we try to understand teaching as an art. First, teaching is an art when it can be performed with such skill and grace that the experience is a form of artistic expression characterized by aesthetics. Second, teaching is an art when teachers, like painters, composers, actresses, and dancers, make their judgments and decisions based largely on qualities that unfold during the course of teaching. In the process, the teacher 'reads' the qualitative forms of intelligence that are emerging among the students and responds intentionally and appropriately to "organize classroom qualities, such as tempo, tone, climate, pace of discussion, and forward movement" (1994, p. 155). Third, teaching is an art when the teacher's action is not dominated by prescriptions or routines but is influenced by unpredicted qualities and contingencies. Fourth, "teaching is an art in that the ends it achieves are often created in process" (Eisner, 1994, pp. 154–156). We can use these four senses as points of reference, to critique our own teaching and gain insight of the art of teaching. The notion of *progettazione,* "projected curriculum constructed through documentation" (Rinaldi, 1998), can be used as a guide as we try to practice teaching as art.

In addition, Jim Garrison offers that we know when teachers are practicing an art by looking at the artifacts created by the students. These artifacts document the students' aesthetic, transforming representations of what they are learning and have learned. These "works of art" are found in the classrooms of teachers who are invested in a constructivist, expressive approach to teaching that fosters multiple ways of inquiry and discovery, of making sense. These teachers capture teachable moments (Garrison, 1997), when children discover problems that make them want to find answers, and these same teachers work with them to create projects for exploration. There is synchrony and rhythm between teachers and students, and among the students. These are moments of transcendence—when teaching is being done as an art. Teachers who embrace the notion of teaching as art take on the disposition of artists. They are passionate about their work and value different ways of seeing and knowing. They value their students' diverse voices and ways of knowing and recognize that ideas can be represented in different ways. Their classrooms are creative, involved, and connected to the passions and activities in the students' lives. The essence of teaching as art is captured in *progettazione* as curriculum is constructed in the process of documentation.

In short, the real art of teaching happens in relationships, a pedagogy of relationships, between and among the three protagonists—the child, the parent, and the teacher. It happens, for Dewey, when imagination is set free so we are able to explore "alternative possibilities for action within a selected context of ongoing activity" (Garrison, 1997, p. 96). To rediscover the art of teaching we need to bring to life our 100 languages, 100 tools for learning, for making sense, and communicating our ideas and knowledge. Where are the hundred languages? How can we use them in our teaching? How would arts and aesthetics enrich the lives of teachers and children? How do the arts release imagination and open up possibilities for teaching and learning?

We need to explore the arts and in the process we may learn about ourselves as teachers and the art of teaching. Each artifact—poetry, painting, sculpture, music, dance, drama, photograph, and so on—affords multiple ways of seeing, knowing, and interpreting. Personal and cultural biases and differences in points of view and knowing often emerge in these artifacts. These differences can provide opportunities for inquiry, critical reflection, conversation, and building intersubjectivity. Greene proposes that " 'art' be treated as an open concept" that can promote critical awareness and help us and our students keep the questions open and alive. Art affords us an

"Teaching is an art in that the ends it achieves are often created in process"—*(Eisner, 1994)*
Searching and collecting samples for a project on natural materials.

imaginary mode of awareness that can help us "break with the taken-for-granted, with the ordinary and the mundane . . . to achieve the reconstruction of experience" (Greene 1978, p. 173). That is, to realize that teaching is transformation of self.

In embracing art and aesthetics in our teaching, we may become more aware of the art of teaching in general and the aesthetics of *progettazione* in particular. Teaching, when done well, is in itself creative, imaginative, social, emotional, and intentional as well as cognitive—it is an aesthetic experience through which we invite and encourage our students to life. "There must be attending; there must be noticing; at once there must be a reflective turning back to the stream of consciousness—the stream that contains our perceptions, our reflections, yes, and our ideas. Clearly, this end-in-view cannot be predetermined anymore than the imaginative mode of awareness can be predefined" (Greene, 1978, p. 182). Do these words not resonate the principles of the Reggio Emilia approach?

ARTS, AESTHETICS, HISTORY, AND A PEDAGOGY OF HOPE AND POSSIBILITIES

Malaguzzi believed that children in any culture and at any place are born with a "common gift" of potentials and competencies. He also recognized a need to address the

Bringing the collections back to school.

issue of diversity in teaching and learning. ". . . The universality of children's potential opens up new questions with which so far we in Reggio Emilia have had little familiarity, but which the multicultural events of our time press on us with urgency" (Malaguzzi, 1998, p. 79). But, for us in the United States, multicultural events are deeply rooted throughout our history. However, we have not confronted these issues honestly and with purpose. We need to revisit our history and memory, no matter how painful, so we can understand where we came from, our fears and prejudices—and to embrace our fellow teachers, students, and parents from diverse backgrounds—in our effort to adapt the Reggio Emilia approach and make it our own. This is necessary to be true to the essence of teaching in a democracy.

The appreciation of arts is both an aesthetic and intellectual experience. Let us go beyond looking at records and reading historical accounts by engaging in what Greene would call doing "history from the ground up, of penetrating the so-called 'cultures of silence'" (Greene, 1988, p. 127). All forms of artistic endeavors represent artists' interpretation of the history, culture, and society of their time. Thus, in taking an artistic–aesthetic stance in the curriculum through revisiting the creations of diverse artists, we encounter the history, memory, voices, and hopes of the multitudes of immigrants and laborers who came to this country by choice, as well as slaves. Visiting these artifacts and reflecting on their historical significance, in reference to our current social and cultural experiences, would expand our understanding of our past, present, and hopes for the future.

Representing one's ideas through documentation.

Yes, Reggio Emilia has given us the courage to dream of possibilities. As we reconstruct the Reggio Emilia approach to make it our own, arts and aesthetics provide avenues for us to be free to see, shape, imagine, create, play with ideas, and transform. If we dare to travel down these roads in our teaching, we will be reenchanted with life and with teaching. In the process we will rediscover the meanings of the philosopher queens and kings: *What is life* (or *teaching*)? *How should we live* (or *teach*)? *What does life* (or *teaching*) *mean?*

The Reggio-inspired approach we are recreating will embrace a pedagogy of hope and possibilities of how schools could be. Schools, where children, teachers, and parents are protagonists teaching and learning together with "*a hundred languages and a hundred hundred hundred more*"—languages of possibilities and hope. If we embrace an expressive curriculum for one day, when children enter any classroom door they would experience what Toni Morrison hopes for our nation and the world—a classroom that "is already made for me, both snug and wide open, with a doorway never needing to be closed" (Morrison, 1998, p. 12).

REFERENCES

Dewey, J. (1934/1987). Art as experience. In J. A. Boydston, (Ed.), *The collected works of John Dewey: The latter works, 1925–1953*. Vol. 10. Carbondale, IL: Southern Illinois University Press.

Dewey, J. (1916/1966). *Democracy and education*. New York: The Free Press.

Edwards, C., Gandini, L., & Forman, G. (Eds.) (1998). *The hundred languages of children: The Reggio Emilia approach—advanced reflections*. (2nd Ed.) Greenwich, CT: Ablex.

Eisner, E. W. (1994). *The educational imagination: On the design and evaluation of school programs*. (3rd Ed.) Upper Saddle River, NJ: Merrill/Prentice Hall.

Ellsworth, E. (1997). *Teaching positions: Difference, pedagogy, and the power of address*. New York: Teachers College Press.

Garrison, J. (1997). *Dewey and Eros: Wisdom and desire in the art of teaching*. New York: Teachers College Press.

Greene, M. (1978). *Landscapes of learning*. New York: Teachers College Press.

Greene, M. (1988). *The dialectic of freedom*. New York: Teachers College Press.

Greene, M. (1995). *Releasing the imagination: Essays on education, the arts, and social change*. San Francisco, CA: Jossey-Bass Publisher.

Malaguzzi, L. (1998a). No way. The hundred *is* there. (Translated by Lella Gandini). In C. Edwards, L. Gandini, and G. Forman (Eds.). (1998) *The hundred languages of children: The Reggio Emilia approach—advanced reflections* (p. 3). Greenwich, CT: Ablex.

Malaguzzi, L. (1998b). History, ideas, and basic philosophy: An interview with Lella Gandini. In C. Edwards, L. Gandini, and G. Forman (Eds.). (1998) *The hundred languages of children: The Reggio Emilia approach—advanced reflections* (pp. 49–97). Greenwich, CT: Ablex.

Morrison, T. (1998). Home. In W. Lubiano, (Ed.), *The house that race built*. New York: Vintage Books.

New, R. (1998). Theory and praxis in Reggio Emilia: They know what they are doing, and why. In C. Edwards, L. Gandini, and G. Forman (Eds.). (1998) *The hundred languages of children: The Reggio Emilia approach—advanced reflections*. (2nd Ed.) Greenwich, CT: Ablex.

Rinaldi, C. (1998). Projected curriculum constructed through documentation—*Progettazione:* An interview with Lella Gandini. In C. Edwards, L. Gandini, and G. Forman (Eds.). (1998) *The hundred languages of children: The Reggio Emilia approach—advanced reflections* (pp. 113–125). Greenwich, CT: Albex.

Chapter

4

The Cultural Construction of Childhood: United States and Reggio Perspectives

Andrew J. Stremmel

The worst sin towards our fellow creatures is not to hate them,
but to be indifferent to them: that's the essence of inhumanity.

George Bernard Shaw

WHO IS THE CHILD? WHAT IS A CHILD? WHAT DOES IT MEAN TO BE A CHILD?

These are the fundamental philosophical questions posed to those who go to Reggio Emilia. Indeed, they are important questions for all of us who are interested in and work with young children. They quite possibly may be as ponderous and as baffling as the questions "What is life?" and "What is self?"

We all have our own answers to these questions. We have developed theories of the child that have been constructed based on our personal experiences. Whatever "image of the child" we have constructed is influenced by larger cultural, social, historical, political, and economic factors, in addition to our ideological constructions (see Kessen, 1979). Further, how we view the child is related to other important questions like:

> What does our society hope and expect for children?
> How should children behave?
> What do children think? What are they like at a given age or stage of development?
> What does it mean to educate children—how should we teach them and how do they learn?

These are searching questions and the answers are necessarily culturally defined and negotiated (Kessen, 1979; Matthews, 1994). If we embrace this premise, then we must also understand that we cannot see the child from one point of view. Different perspectives must be negotiated and socially reconstructed to get a more accurate portrait of the child.

This chapter focuses on images of childhood that stem from various points of view. First, I present images or interpretations of the child derived from the histor-

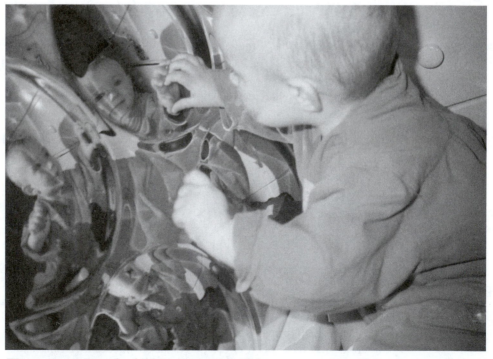

We cannot envision the child from one point of view.

ical, developmental, philosophical, and even theological views of theorists, educators, parents, teachers, philosophers, and others who have thought about children in our society. Then, I share the image of the child shared by parents and educators of the Reggio Emilia approach, ending with a call for us as a society to be more respectful and scrupulous observers of children and imaginative partners with them in inquiry.

HISTORICAL VIEWS

Consider if you will some images that persist from a brief look at our history. Understand that I do not claim to be a childhood historian, and by no means do these images, or glimpses to be more accurate, provide a complete picture of the history of childhood, but they do reflect the shifting nature of childhood.

For centuries childhood was not valued for its own sake but for its contributory value in service to mature and responsible adulthood. Children were viewed as "little adults" who, though they were obviously different than adults in many ways, were not thought to differ in the kinds of tasks they could be assigned or in the way they think and behave (Matthews, 1994, p. 8). Indeed, John Locke asked us to suppose the mind of the child to be like a blank slate void of all characters and without any ideas. Thus, by observing and participating in the world of adults, children learned how to become mature, responsible, and economically productive. It was not until the 17th century that the Western world began to recognize childhood as a legitimate period of human development (Aries, 1962). Yet, as I will argue in this chapter, the image of the child as an immature adult having unequal human value persists in the many ways we think about and behave toward young children in our society. A quick and rather haphazard review of the 20th century begins to shed light on this point.

At the beginning of the 20th century, changes brought about by an increasingly industrialized society, for example the establishment of compulsory schooling and child protection laws, also brought about a sentimentalized vision of childhood in which children were to be nurtured and protected (Corsaro, 1997, p. 194). Children now spent considerable time at home and in school, and parents and teachers were charged with the preparation of children for later life, particularly that of training workers for sustaining the nation's economy.

The 1920s and 1930s brought an emerging commitment to the systematic analytic examination of the lives of children, and along with this, prescriptions for how to raise and educate children. Mothers set out to raise self-reliant children. Laboratory schools and nursery schools were started to care for and educate young children. Measurements and milestones became the subject of intense scrutiny: an infant's height, weight, and age when she first sat up were charted with an exactitude worthy of the emerging science of nuclear physics.

The 1940s revealed a society intent on winning the war. Mothers went to work until the war was over, then were expected to stay home caring for their children, a job of utmost importance. With the publication of Dr. Spock's *Baby and Child Care* in 1945, the call came for lenience, flexibility, and the establishment of a strong mother-child bond. The 1950s brought the era of permissiveness as educators cautioned parents to be gentle and not too severe or strict in their discipline.

The 1960s were an era of idealism and activism with the passage of the Civil Rights Act of 1964, Head Start, and war protests. Children who misbehaved were now labeled "troubled children." Impoverished children were considered "culturally disadvantaged." Child psychologists perpetuated the romantic notion of child innocence toward the several forms of "If we could only make matters right with the child, the world could be a better place" (Kessen, 1979, p. 818). Almy (see Greenberg, 2000, p. 7) points out that in the 1960s, children's play became known as children's work, suggesting that work and the world of adults was more valued than play and childhood.

The last 25 years have seen the emergence of the "me" generation, an increasing need for quality child care as more and more mothers have entered the workforce, and greater focus on the social problems of childhood (e.g., poverty, divorce, teen pregnancy and non-marital births, violence, and victimization). Since the early 1980s, our schools have been increasingly scrutinized with a call for "back to basics" education and increasing accountability in a society that gives considerable value to measurement, achievement, and success, particularly in the global economy. Indeed, Goodlad notes this about childhood as we begin the 21st century, "Although childhood has achieved an identity as a market of consumers and an investment in future economic productivity, it has not been accorded existential human value equal to that of adulthood" (Goodlad, 2000, p. 87).

From the view of American children as "saviors of the nation," to more modern images of the "the hurried child," the "high-spirited child," and "the at-risk child," (and of course there are a host of other views), the transformation of childhood through the ages suggests that what it means to be a child is culturally, historically, theoretically, and philosophically complex. We now have numerous ethnographic and journalistic accounts that make us ever aware of the departures from our own ways of seeing children that exist, not only in other cultures, but within our own diverse society.

THEORETICAL PERSPECTIVES OF THE CHILD

Let us now take a closer look at our developmental theories, which have helped organize and guide our thinking and study of children. Over the years, we have adopted many different educational and developmental theoretical views of the child from Locke to Skinner, Rousseau to Piaget, from Dewey to Vygotsky. The child has been portrayed as a tender plant to be nurtured, an empty glass to be filled, a passive consumer of ideas, knowledge, and culture, and as an active contributor to his or her own development. We have been influenced by the ideas of Jean Piaget, whose careful observation of children and intriguing experiments with them provided us with new insights into the nature of the child. In recent years, the work of Vygotsky has challenged the Piagetian notion that the child constructs a knowledge of reality solely on the basis of private encounters with the world by proposing alternatively that the child's encounters are mediated through negotiation with others who have more skill or competence in given situations.

Our theories have continued to become even more sophisticated. For example, we now recognize that children learn primarily through establishing enduring and reciprocal relationships with other significant people in context. Urie Bronfenbrenner, in particular, has informed us that any study of the developing child must include an examination of how the child develops the parent (Bronfenbrenner, 1979. See Chapter 1). Likewise, a study of the parent-child relationship requires a study of the parent's relationship with his or her spouse, or a consideration that one parent may be lacking. The parents' relations with friends and neighbors and the conditions in their workplaces have an effect on the developing family, too. Moreover, any investigation of the network of family, friends, and colleagues would necessitate a consideration of the evolving social institutions and cultural practices that circumscribe them. Finally, any worthwhile study must be conducted over a long period of time because the dynamics of an evolving system take a while to manifest themselves.

Most recently, developmental psychologists have begun to challenge the notions that development is invariant, universal, and individualistic with a predictable pattern and process of change (see, for example, Lewis, 1997. See Chapter 1). We are coming to believe that development is less predictable, less certain, more random, and certainly more complex than previously believed, and as Howard Gardner points out, that there are multiple ways of learning, understanding, and knowing the world (Gardner, 1993. See Chapter 1).

If we embrace this premise, then we must also understand that our developmental theories present a somewhat limited image or interpretation of the child. We cannot see children from one point of view if we are to understand them more fully. Development is a social construction, and the image of the child as a continuous construction of social and cultural contexts is a difficult one to capture. Different points of view must be negotiated and socially reconstructed to get a more accurate portrait of the child.

As good and as useful as our theories are, they are problematic in presenting a complete image of the child. Though they may be increasingly less culturally problematic, they are most assuredly philosophically problematic. As Gareth Matthews aptly points out in his book, *The Philosophy of Childhood,* "children are not only objects of study, they are also, with us, members of what Kant called 'the kingdom of ends' " (Matthews, 1994, p. 27). Above all, we owe children respect. We need to be curious about children, and we need theories to stimulate research and challenge our understanding of them, but we must not let our theories dehumanize children and encourage condescending attitudes toward them. We must guard against letting theories caricature the child and limit the possibilities for educating, caring for, and simply being with them (Matthews, 1994, p. 29).

Skye 3	Gregory 3	Drake 3
Kelly 3	Eli 3	Meg 3

Multiple points of view must be negotiated to provide an accurate portrait of the child.

PHILOSOPHICAL VIEWS

I believe many of the wonderful stories written by Vivian Paley over the years demonstrate the limitations of theory in more fully understanding the child. The ideas represented in these stories (Paley, *Wally's Stories,* 1981) are not those of pre-rational, pre-scientific thinkers, but the wisdom of child philosophers. Children may not think the same way as you or I, but they do seem to understand something about their experiences, about life and learning, that we should honor and respect. According to Matthews, philosophical thinking in children is often left out of "images of the child" constructed from the theories of developmental psychologists (Matthews, 1994, p. 12). We are then forced to ask, "Do our developmental theories really tell us all there is to know about what our children are like?"

I will return to this issue shortly in discussing the view of the child held in Reggio Emilia. But before I do, I want to spend some time discussing views held by other adults in our society, including parents and teachers.

CURRENT PERSPECTIVES: IMAGES OF THE CHILD

Typically, as a society, we have considered childhood as something we pass through on our way to adulthood. We regard childhood as provisional, preparatory, and subordinate to adulthood as opposed to a unique and distinct time and place in the development of a person. We often disregard children's problems, squelch their creativity, deny their emotions, and generally ignore or diminish the significance of their daily experiences. For example, consider our heavy focus on child outcomes in our education system, while having little regard for children's experiences in the classroom. Consider our national obsession with standards and accountability (see Chapter 5), and our relentless efforts to remedy children's problems and deficiencies by teaching them discipline and isolated skills. Instead of treating children like passive receptacles into which knowledge or skills are poured, rather than testing them on facts that neither have much meaning nor interest for children, we should be spending time making sure that our schools and classrooms preserve and enrich children's innate desire to learn. Instead of "fixing" children by teaching them to memorize and be obedient, we should be helping them to develop dispositions of caring, fairness, and justice or how to engage in ethical reflection and live responsibly within a democratic society.

However, it is not only in our schools that children are treated as marginal members of society. Children are abandoned, abused, neglected, and criticized because they cry; they are born malnourished and addicted; their self-esteem is diminished daily by what we believe, what we say, and what we do. Consider these examples:

While waiting for a flight at Chicago's O'Hare Airport not too long ago, I overheard these two examples of our disregard for children from parents:

Father: "Hurry up, Ryan, you are poking along."
Mother: "No he's not, Rich, his legs are a third the size of yours."

Mother: (to a child who was curiously asking questions about everything on the plane) "Shut up! You ask too many questions."

How many times have I heard fellow teachers bemoan the lack of respect they receive from children by saying, "Children don't seem to have the same respect for authority as they did when we were young," when what they mean by "respect" is compliance with adult demands, however unreasonable. The truth is that children often "fail to show respect" (comply) because of how we act toward them: talking without listening; failing to consider their needs and perspectives; controlling their behavior through rewards and punishments; and failing to include their voices in classroom decision-making.

These very brief scenarios express our American attitudes toward children, which to me reveal an assumption that children aren't fully human. Parents and teachers alike seem to be expressing this when they are emotionally distant or absent from children, are unwilling to go at the child's pace, verbally deride or humiliate a child, or when they invade a child's world with adult expectations. Here, I offer two very personal stories.

One day I was traveling in the car, sitting in the back seat with my five-year-old son. It was common for either my wife or me to sit in the back with him when we went anywhere. He was drinking milk out of a plastic cup with a lid. Earlier in the morning he had been admonished twice for leaving the cup unattended in the back seat after spills occurred. As I was being dropped off at my office, I noticed that milk had trickled underneath where I had been sitting. Now both the seat and my coat were wet with milk. Once again, I chastised my son for his carelessness and displayed considerable anger toward him as I bid him and my wife goodbye.

Later my wife told me that my son cried the rest of the way home. Then she mentioned to me something he said that horrifies me to this day when I think of his words. He had asked my wife, "How can someone who is so important to me hate me so much?" Of course I don't hate my son, though these words, shocking as they are, demonstrate the feelings of a child who was deeply hurt by me. To me, this seemingly small and trivial incident painfully revealed the result of my anger and disdain in that particular moment, a common childhood occurrence, the spilling of a little milk. But of course I was inconvenienced.

Then there was the time when I took it upon myself to rearrange the things on my son's dresser —simply because I didn't like the way he had carelessly placed them there! Soon after having done this, he said to me, "Dad, I have things on there for a certain reason. Why are you moving them around?" Why, indeed? If I had been respectful, I would have taken the time and consideration to ask him if this was OK to do, or better yet, to pause and reflect on why I was even doing it. Again, while this may seem trivial and hardly worthy of print, I would argue differently, for it is the accrual of small gestures of respect that creates a climate where children are more likely to do the same.

As you can see, the simple understanding that children are worthy of our full respect, even when they seemingly are irritating, is oftentimes difficult to put into practice even by those of us who make a living teaching and advocating for children. I find it interesting how often my students, prospective teachers, use the terms "surprised" and "amazed" when they hear or see children doing things like sharing, problem-solving, negotiating, or acting out of kindness. This same level of amazement is not present when children display negative behaviors like hitting, grabbing, or name calling, which seem expected by students. Instead children are described as violent, obnoxious, rude, and annoying.

Herbert Anderson, bishop of the Evangelical Lutheran Church of America, relates this rather chilling reflection:

> Some years ago, a national magazine ran a story titled, "Do We Hate Our Children?" Most of the time I have been able to answer *no*. Then another story appears of a child being punched in the stomach or stuffed in a trash can or abandoned at McDonald's or pacified with toys and videos. Those stories prompt me to wonder again whether we may indeed hate our children or at least regard them with indifference (Anderson & Johnson, 1994, p. 3).

Do we hate our children? Do we regard them with contempt? In her book, *Suffer the Children,* Janet Pais writes that adults have contempt for children because they are small, weak, and needy (Pais, 1991, p. 9). This contempt underlies various forms of physical, sexual, and psychological abuse that adults frequently inflict upon children. The fact remains that anyone who is small, weak, or needy receives contempt in a society that glorifies size, strength, and self-sufficiency. And contempt for the powerless leads to oppression of the disadvantaged as well as to the abuse of children (Anderson & Johnson, 1994, p. 17).

Why do we hold the views we do? Why in a society with a high level of civilization do we diminish the child? Why in America are children, more than any other group, the primary victims of violence, abuse, and neglect? Corsaro suggests that it is because of their dependency on adults, in addition to their small physical stature, that children have little choice in where they live and with whom (Corsaro, 1997, p. 239). Another explanation lies in the understanding that our views are associated with images of motherhood, women, school, social services, and society in general. How can we change how we think about children and families in our society? Their present well-being and our common future depend upon this change.

AN ANSWER: REGGIO EMILIA

When I visited Reggio Emilia in January 1998 as a participant in our research consortium, I was especially interested in their "image of the child." Perhaps the most significant aspect of the Reggio philosophy is the teacher's deep respect for children who are viewed as being filled with curiosity and potential, who have rights—especially the right to learn and communicate using the many languages available to them. These languages are not only verbal, but also include other symbolic representations such as drawing, painting, clay work, collage, performance, movement, and music.

In Reggio, children are seen as strong, competent, and intellectual. They are viewed as inquiring, curious, and wondering. Indeed, the child's "why" is a research question not unlike the questions "What is life?" and "Why is life?" Children are seen as competent in the sense that they are open to the world, able to understand, know, and learn. Further, children are believed to be competent and ready to learn from the first moment of life. Children are competent in constructing an identity and their own theories. Children are also perceived as strongly motivated because they must "know" in order to live.

Children are protagonists in the development of their own identity and theories.

This philosophy of children as competent, born "ready" to learn, and to be protagonists in their own learning and development and not mere consumers of information and ideas, also implies that children are fully human from birth, and therefore, they are worthy of our deepest respect. I was deeply impressed by what I saw children doing in the Reggio Emilia schools. Children were not doing uninteresting and regimented learning tasks; they were not engaged in efforts to master isolated skills; they were not passive receivers of art, science, math, language, and culture. Here, it was quite evident that children were creators and producers of projects, encounters, and stories that reflected their attempts to make sense of and better understand their experiences. They were not preparing for school, nor were they mimicking what adults wanted them to learn; indeed, children were constructing and testing theories; they were seeking solutions to their questions; they were exploring the meaning of their lives of which school was just one part.

I believe Amelia Gambetti, liaison for the Reggio approach and executive consultant for Reggio Children, has stated best what Reggio Emilia is all about. "The Reggio experience is not a proposed model of early childhood education, but rather it is a stimulus and point of reference for those who want to reflect on the educational reality in their own countries and for anyone who recognizes the importance in investing in early childhood education" (RECHILD, April 1998, p. 4).

HOW CAN WE, AS A SOCIETY, LEARN FROM THE "IMAGE OF THE CHILD" CHAMPIONED IN REGGIO?

We can start by rejecting the view that childhood is less important than or subordinate to adulthood. By this I mean that we must reject the critical assumption inherent in stage/maturational models of child development that seems to suggest that childhood is merely a phase we pass through on the way to an increasingly satisfactory level of maturity (see Matthews, 1994, p. 16). The truth is that children are often more creative, more inquisitive, and more imaginative than adults who have become stale and uninventive with maturity and less likely to reconsider or reevaluate their assumptions (Matthews, 1994, p. 18).

We must celebrate children as part of the human community who are, therefore, worthy of respect. Urie Bronfenbrenner has suggested that we are experiencing a breakdown of the interconnections among the various segments of the child's life, for example, the family, school, neighborhood, and community, that make us human (Bronfenbrenner, 1972). In Reggio, community support and involvement contribute to the idea that children are fully human and worthy of respect. Children, parents, and teachers are all equally important in creating quality educational experiences. Social relationships are basic to the learning process and to the construction of meaning. Consequently, parenting and teaching must be viewed as human-centered activities. Our homes, our schools, and our communities must be places where children are known, understood, and valued. William Ayers challenges us to see children for who they are in all their fullness. He asks, "When we look out over our classrooms what do we see?" Do we see children with hopes and dreams, passions and interests? What are their concerns, their fears, their cares? Who is this person before me? What are her interests and areas of wonder? What effort and potential does she bring? In what ways does our teaching create a range of possibilities for children to make themselves known to us and become more whole and fully alive in the classroom? (Ayers, 1993, p. 28).

We must embrace the understanding that children are *competent and ready to learn from the first moment of life.* We must view children's curiosity and wonder as their way of making sense of and understanding their worlds. Children are indeed philosophers. Their "why?" is an attempt to answer questions about life such as "What is life?" and "Why is life?" Our role in this process, once we understand and know the meaning of children's questions, is to support them in reaching their solutions. We must try to create daily contexts in which children's theories, questions, and interests can be legitimized and heard. During a recent staff orientation of the Virginia Tech Child Development Laboratories, I reflected that the lab school was a sacred place because children were present and because learning was going to happen there. It was going to be (and indeed it is) a place, a community, in which we could find passion, joy, hope, dialogue, stories, wonder, and possibility.

We must learn to go at the child's pace. In this country, too often we see parents or adults walking ahead of children (as in my earlier example) dragging them along or yelling at them to hurry up. In other areas of life, especially in our schools, we expect children to all go at the same pace or at an accelerated pace; we push them, coerce them, and fail them when they can't keep up. In Reggio, children's own time and rhythms in the daily life of the school are respected. The school environment provides a sense of well being and contributes to teaching and learning. Anderson and Johnson (1994) suggest that going at the child's pace is a matter of simple justice and gentleness. It honors children and our common limitations.

We must respect children as partners in inquiry. We must listen to them and be more responsive to their ideas, feelings, questions, and the exciting new ways of perceiving the world that they can offer us. We must learn to see with children's eyes.

We must never forget and outgrow our own childhood. When teachers and children are seen as partners in learning, they teach us. They challenge us to reconsider and reconstruct our own childhoods, so that we can rethink and reconstruct the images of teaching we carry deep inside us. Robert Coles, the wonderfully wise and insightful psychologist, reminds us: "We should struggle toward childhood, and never forget it or outlive it" (Coles, April 1993, p. 58).

SUMMARY

Theories of child development, at their most limited, try to convince us that in knowing our children well, we don't in fact know them at all. They deceive us into believing, if we are not careful, that being with children is not enough to get to know them; in fact, in important ways they are strangers to us. However, at their best, theories remind us that childhood is unique and not just a phase we pass through on the way to maturity. They remind us that children *are* little people, but not little adults. If we take our theories seriously, they also help us, I think, to understand that children, like all people, need to be loved, feel safe, and be valued—all of us need and are dependent on others. On the other hand, we are also protagonists in our own development and destiny.

Who is the child? What is a child? The American child is a cultural invention. We cannot view children from any one point of view, and in particular a strictly developmental point of view, if we wish to understand them more fully. Both Sergio Spaggiari and Carlina Rinaldi remind us, "Knowledge of the child comes from being with them. We must listen respectfully to them, trusting our biological nature that has given us two ears and one mouth, to understand that the child is a protagonist in creating the reasons, the 'whys,' the sense of meaning of things, others, nature, reality, and life" (Spaggiari & Rinaldi, personal communication, January, 1998).

REFERENCES

Anderson, H., & Johnson, S. B. (1994). *Regarding children: A new respect for childhood and families.* Louisville, KY: Westminster John Knox Press.

Aries, P. (1962). *Centuries of childhood: A social history of family life* (R. Baldick, Trans.). New York: Knopf.

Ayers, W. (1993). *To teach: The journey of a teacher.* New York: Teachers College Press.

Bronfenbrenner, U. (1972). *Two worlds of childhood: U.S. and U.S.S.R.* New York: Russell Sage Foundation.

Bronfenbrenner, U. (1979). *The ecology of human development: Experiments by nature and design.* Cambridge, MA: Harvard University Press.

Coles, R. (April 1993). Struggling toward childhood: An interview with Robert Coles. *Second Opinion, 18*(4), 58–71.

Corsaro, W. (1997). *The sociology of childhood.* Thousand Oaks, CA: Pine Forge Press.

Gambetti, A. (1998, April). The winter institute: An international meeting on education. *RECHILD, 2,* 4. Reggio Emilia, Italy.

Gardner, H. (1993). *Multiple intelligences: The theory in practice.* New York: Basic Books.

Goodlad, J. (2000). Education and democracy: Advancing the agenda. *Phi Delta Kappan, 82*(1), 86–89. Bloomington, IN: Phi Delta Kappa International

Greenberg, P. (2000). What wisdom should we take with us as we enter the new century? An interview with Milly Almy. *Young Children, 55*(1), 6–10. Wash. D.C.: NAEYC.

Kessen, W. (1979). The American child and other cultural inventions. *American Psychologist, 34*(10), 815–820. Wash. D.C.: APA.

Lewis, M. (1997). *Altering fate: Why the past does not predict the future.* New York: Guilford Press.

Matthews, G. B. (1994). *The Philosophy of childhood.* Cambridge, MA: Harvard University Press.

Pais, J. (1991). *Suffer the children: A theology of liberation by a victim of child abuse.* Mahwah, NJ: Paulist Press.

Paley, V. G. (1981). *Wally's stories: Conversations in the kindergarten.* Cambridge, MA: Harvard University Press.

Spock, B. (1945/1968). *Baby and child care.* (3rd ed.). New York: Hawthorne Books.

Chapter
5

The Reggio Emilia Approach and Accountability Assessment in the United States

Diane M. Horm-Wingerd

THE COMPATIBILITY OF THE REGGIO EMILIA APPROACH WITH ACCOUNTABILITY ASSESSMENT IN THE UNITED STATES

When American educators are introduced to the Reggio Emilia approach, many agree that the approach is inspirational and sound, but quickly state that it could never be implemented in their programs. Although a variety of reasons are often given for this lack of confidence in the ability to successfully implement the Reggio Emilia approach, common reasons include state standards, state assessments, and pressures for accountability. Early childhood educators who work in primary school programs most frequently voice these concerns.

Although the assessment methods embraced in the Reggio Emilia approach are dramatically different than typical American accountability-driven tests, are the concepts incorporated in a Reggio-inspired curriculum incompatible with the standards-based approach implemented across the United States today? Does the demand for accountability necessarily prohibit the implementation of a Reggio-inspired approach? This chapter explores these and related questions. Special attention is devoted to implications for preservice and inservice professional development for early childhood educators and administrators.

A STORY AND ITS MORALS

As all early childhood educators know, difficult issues are often tackled in sensitive and successful ways in good children's books. The perceived chasm between good teaching and accountability assessment is no exception. A recent book by Dr. Seuss and friends presents interesting lessons related to teaching and accountability assessment.

In *Hooray for Diffendoofer Day,* a recently published book by Seuss, Prelutsky, and Smith (1998), the children of Diffendoofer School experience a bevy of creative, innovative teachers. Based on the description in the book, the teachers incorporated hands-on, experiential, meaningful, and fun activities into the daily school schedule. As noted by Miss Bonkers, one of the central characters in the book, the teachers at Diffendoofer School taught the children ". . . that the earth is round, that red and white make pink, and something else that matters more—we've taught you how to think" (p. 24). Interestingly, when faced with an externally imposed, high-stakes accountability test, the children in the story "know everything and more" and score 10,000,000%. This performance saves their school from demolition, prevents the children from being sent to dreary Flobbertown School, and even changes the personality of the principal from sad to jubilant.

Several themes and morals are conveyed in *Hooray for Diffendoofer Day.* These include:

❀ Accountability assessment is pervasive in the United States today.

Currently, calls for child-based results and school accountability are evident at both the state and national levels. Evidence suggests that the pressure for external accountability will increase, not decrease, in the near future (Jacobson, 2000; Shepard, Kagan, & Wurtz, 1998). Although the role and impact of accountability assessments have been discussed with increasing frequency in educational circles, the fact that the topic is featured in a Dr. Seuss book is evidence that the issue has transcended beyond professional discourse to be a pervasive component of contemporary popular culture.

❀ Accountability assessment is high-stakes and has an impact on children, teachers, and principals.

Accountability assessments are "external examinations, mandated by an authority outside the school, usually the state or school district, and administered to assess academic achievement and to hold students, teachers, and schools accountable for desired learning outcomes" (Shepard et al., 1998, p. 29). Accountability assessments are conducted to inform the public about the collective status of children—the performance of children in classrooms, schools, districts, communities, states, and nations is the focus (Kagan, Rosenkoetter, & Cohen, 1997 p. 7). Results from this type of assessment tend to be broadly disseminated and used for decision-making. Rewards and sanctions are sometimes attached to the results—for example, a student may be denied a diploma, a teacher may be awarded merit pay, or a school may be declared "in crisis" on the basis of accountability assessments. Thus, "stakes" or consequences are associated with the results. The stakes in *Hooray for Diffendoofer Day* were high indeed—if the children performed poorly on the test the school would be torn down and the children would be sent to dreary Flobbertown. However, as noted by Shepard et al., " . . . merely reporting school results in the newspaper is sufficient to give high stakes to assessment results with accompanying changes produced in instructional practices" (Shepard et al., 1998, p. 29), that is—"teaching to the test."

❀ Innovative, experiential, hands-on teaching and learning can produce good outcomes as measured by a typical standardized accountability test.

The children in *Hooray for Diffendoofer Day* performed well on the test. This aspect of the story is often surprising to American educators. Many American educators feel pressure to "teach to the test" as a technique to ensure good student performance on accountability tests. In "teaching to the test," teachers often narrow the curriculum and rely on inappropriate instructional practices (Kamii, 1990; NAEYC, 1988; NAEYC & NAECS/SDE, 1991). For example, to prepare students for the upcoming test, teachers may devote more time to the types of tasks that appear on standardized tests and drop important areas—such as self-discipline, desire to learn, and social competence—that are not easily measured on a paper-and-pencil test. In an effort to "get through the curriculum," teachers may rely on teacher-directed formal lessons at the expense of child-initiated exploration. As described above, the teachers at Diffendoofer School appeared to rely on hands-on, experiential, meaningful, and fun activities as a large part of the daily school schedule. How can this approach, similar to a Reggio-inspired approach, be associated with good test performance?

❀ The children responded positively, both in terms of their test performance and their love of learning, to the Reggio-like approach adopted in Diffendoofer School.

The children of Diffendoofer School proclaimed "We love you, Diffendoofer School, we definitely do . . . each day we love you more" (Seuss et al., 1998, p. 35). They expressed these feelings even after the accountability test! Many American educators associate the demand for accountability with stressed children. In fact, an acknowledged danger of "teaching to the test" and the "culture of accountability" is the negative socioemotional climate that is reported in American schools (Morgan-Worsham, 1990, p. 66). However, this did not appear to be the case at Diffendoofer School. How can this be so?

Hooray for Diffendoofer Day raises some important questions and challenges our assumptions about the necessary impact of accountability assessments. How can the children be so happy and demonstrate a love of learning in a school with a very high-stakes accountability test? How was it possible for the teachers of Diffendoofer School to implement a creative, hands-on approach when faced with an externally imposed accountability test? How did the children do so well on the test? As suggested above, these aspects of the story seem counter-intuitive to many American educators. What is the secret of Diffendoofer School? What can we learn from Diffendoofer School?

Another theme evident in *Hooray for Diffendoofer Day* may provide an answer to these questions. An important component of the story is that the content of the test mirrored, at least in part, what the teachers at Diffendoofer School taught. The teachers knew what was important for children to know and presented this essential material in innovative ways. How did this consistency occur?

THE ROLE OF STANDARDS

Accountability assessments should be comprehensive measures of important learning goals (Shepard et al., 1998). Consistency between the content of teaching and testing is imperative for accountability tests to be fair measures of teaching and learning. In contemporary American education, standards play an important role by serving as the common notion of *what* is important to teach and assess and to determine *how well* students need to know and perform. To conform to federal guidelines, states had until the beginning of the 1997–98 school year to develop and implement standards. State standards are typically comprised of both content standards and performance standards.

Content standards describe *what* children should know and be able to do. According to Hansche, "They are descriptions of the knowledge and skills expected of students at certain times throughout their education, often targeted at a specific grade level or at a cluster of grade levels" (Hansche, 1998, p. 12). Content standards outline "important ideas, concepts, issues, and other relevant information and skills to be taught and learned" (Hansche, 1998, p. 12). To illustrate, two content standards from Virginia's Standards of Learning (SOL) are listed below. These content standards are drawn from the English SOL for kindergarten children:

- ❀ The student will identify both uppercase and lowercase letters of the alphabet.
- ❀ The student will hear, say, and manipulate phonemes of spoken language.

The following are examples drawn from the Pre–K standards of Ohio's Competencies;

(Draft):

- ❀ Writing: The learner will produce some conventional words such as own name, mom, dad, and other familiar words from family/school contexts using scribble writing, invented spellings, and symbols.
- ❀ Reading: The learner will begin to demonstrate knowledge of some of the conventions of print, such as letter and word identification, identification of familiar words, etc.
- ❀ Scientific Inquiry: The learner will describe and group objects by similarities and differences.

As can be seen from these examples, although content standards may vary widely, they outline expectations for children's knowledge of specific content.

Performance standards describe *how well* children know and are able to perform—that is, performance standards name and describe the knowledge and skills at each performance level and specify "how good is good enough" (Hansche, 1998). Hansche notes that "to educators involved in the development of curriculum and instruction, performance standard typically means a description of what a student knows and can do to demonstrate proficiency on a content standard or cluster of content standards" (Hansche, 1998, p. 3).

Although standards are a central component of contemporary education reform in the United States, the merits of standards continue to be debated. Some view standards as the vehicle for aligning curriculum, instruction, and assessment and ensuring that *all* children achieve to high levels of performance. While standards have many proponents, others believe that the concept of standards is in conflict with the principles of "democratic education" (Noddings, 1997, pp. 188–189) and developmentally appropriate practices. For example, many believe that through standards the same level of performance will be expected of all students regardless of opportunities to learn (Noddings, 1997, p. 186); the onus for learning, and the blame for not learning, will be placed exclusively upon the child (Darling-Hammond & Falk, 1997, p. 191); or that failure and retention rates will be increased (Darling-Hammond & Falk, 1997, p. 191). As noted by Darling-Hammond and Falk, "Depending on how standards are shaped and used, either they could support more ambitious teaching and greater levels of success for all children, or they could serve to create higher rates of failure for those who are already least well-served by the education system" (Darling-Hammond & Falk, 1997, p. 191). Thus, it is important that standards and the associated assessments are crafted carefully to support learning for all children. It is also critically important to use accountability information "to inform teaching decisions, to trigger special supports for student learning, and to evaluate school practices" (Darling-Hammond & Falk, 1997, p. 191).

Relative to classroom practice, content standards are analogous to learning goals and guide the content or *what* of teaching. Performance standards outline *how well*. Teachers need to determine the *how*—the classroom approaches or methods to support children in learning the desired content to the desired level. So, although the broad content may be determined by the state or district standards, teachers determine the methods to approach the specified content in the classroom. As all good teachers know, there are a variety of ways to teach any particular skill or topic. Teachers can choose to adopt a teacher-directed approach and use drill and repetition. Teachers can also choose to adopt a laissez-faire approach and wait until children discover important constructs in the course of unstructured play. However, most early childhood educators agree that optimal approaches lie in-between these two points on the "continuum of teaching strategies" and that the best approach differs for various situations and individual children (Bredekamp & Copple, 1997). Congruent with the Reggio Emilia approach, contemporary notions of developmentally appropriate practice place a greater emphasis on teacher engagement and scaffolding.

Referring again to the sample state standards discussed previously, teachers could implement a plethora of approaches to support children's learning and development. For example, to support children's identification of both uppercase and lowercase letters of the alphabet, teachers could use flashcards and worksheets with repetition and drill. Alternately, teachers could "plan a variety of concrete learning experiences with materials and people relevant to the children's own life experiences and that promote their interest, engagement in learning, and conceptual development" (Bredekamp & Copple, 1997, p. 126). For example, in one kindergarten class the teacher built on the children's interest in business cards by providing sample business cards, blank index cards, markers, stickers, and other materials in the writing and computer areas of a classroom. Many children interacted with these materials over time, produced their own business cards, and learned a great deal about uppercase and lowercase letters. Thus, even with content standards that may be viewed as narrowly focused, teachers have the opportunity to implement a range of instructional approaches. In essence, content standards guide *what;* teachers design *how.* Standards should be viewed as a compass point or guide, not as an invitation or excuse for rigid, boring, teacher-directed lessons.

ACCOUNTABILITY ASSESSMENT IN CONTEMPORARY AMERICA

The available evidence suggests that the current calls for external accountability will increase, not decrease, in the near future (Shepard et al., 1998). Standards and accountability assessments are currently mandated for public schools. So, for early childhood educators working in kindergarten and primary settings, standards and accountability assessment are current realities that are likely to persist and increase. Standards and accountability assessment are also important for those who work with children younger than those served by public schools. There is an increasing emphasis on accountability in programs for young children (Jacobson, 2000; Kagan et al., 1997). For example, the 1998 reauthorization of Head Start includes the legislative mandate that all Head Start children know ten letters of the alphabet as a result of their Head Start experience. Many states are currently moving forward on the development of standards, expectations, or outcomes for preschool children. In a recent edition of *Education Week*, it was noted that policymakers in states with publicly funded preschools are frequently asking for data on how well these programs prepare children for kindergarten (Jacobson, April 2000, p. 1).

Given these realities, early childhood educators have an important choice:

1. Be active—early childhood educators can actively shape the future in this area through at least two avenues—by participating in the development of standards and accountability assessments and by designing and implementing programs that are tied to standards in child-appropriate ways.
2. Be passive—if early childhood educators are passive, it is likely that someone else will establish standards, design curriculum, and develop accountability assessments for young children. This someone else may or may not have expertise in child development and early childhood education and thus the resulting products may or may not be appropriate. Early childhood educators will then be in the position of living with the results or reacting to established policies.

Leaders in the early childhood field like Kagan, Rosenkoetter, and Cohen (1997) are recognizing the importance of shaping the development of standards and accountability assessments for young children and have initiated forums on "child-based results." At the keynote address of the February 2000 National Summit on School Readiness, Kagan told the audience that it is time for early childhood educators "to develop assessments that meet policymakers' needs and are developmentally and culturally sensitive" (Jacobson, 2000, p. 1). The Council of Chief State School Officers (CCSSO) has called for a variety of mechanisms and "next steps" to work towards uniting "developmentally appropriate assessment" and "accountability assessment" and to blend the expertise of early childhood and measurement specialists in accountability decisions (Horm-Wingerd, Winter, & Plofchan, 1999).

When discussing standards and accountability, especially in relation to programs for young children, the tone is often negative. However, it is important to remember that accountability is about assessing child progress *and* continuously improving it (Darling-Hammond & Falk, 1997). Thus, true accountability is tied to improvements in schools and classroom practices that enhance the likelihood that children will develop optimally. Similar to Goldhaber and Smith's (see Chapter 10) observation that the power of documentation in Reggio-inspired classrooms is in "trying to understand and respond to the meaning" of the collected information, the power of and challenge with accountability assessment lies in the use of results to improve learning opportunities. When used properly, school teams carefully review the results of accountability assessments as a basis for data-driven decisions in their efforts to strengthen programs. The goal is not to blame children, but to structure programs to facilitate optimal development of children. For example, accountability results may lead a team to decide that a professional development program is needed in techniques to support children's early literacy development or that summer programs are needed to sustain children's progress in reading, writing, and speaking. As noted by Rinaldi, documentation is part of progettazione, "the Italian term used by Reggio Emilia educators for all flexible planning—whether done by teachers, parents, or administrators—concerning any aspect of the life of the school and its connection with the community" (Rinaldi, 1998, p. 114). Teachers in Reggio-inspired classrooms use the process of documentation to inform classroom practice and sustain children's learning and to strengthen their own professional development through observation, reflection, and collaborative discourse (Rinaldi, 1998). Accountability assessment fulfills these same purposes at the school, district, or state levels. In this volume, Goldhaber and Smith (see Chapter 10) highlight the role of courage in the process of documentation by noting that teachers must demonstrate courage to analyze the results of their work and to use the information to change practice with the goal of enhancing learning and development. Similar to teachers' courage in the process of classroom documentation, teachers and administrators must demonstrate the courage to collaboratively review the results of accountability assessments and make data-driven decisions to effect school improvements.

The use of assessment information to inform classroom and school practices is a critical component of developmentally appropriate practices. Importantly, research demonstrates that developmentally appropriate practices enable young learners to meet high standards. As noted by Bredekamp and Copple (1997) in their NAEYC book entitled *Developmentally Appropriate Practice in Early Childhood Programs*, teachers need to actively create intellectually engaging, responsive environments to promote individual learning and development. This is accomplished through the use of a wide repertoire of teaching strategies and implementation of an integrated curriculum that has intellectual integrity and the opportunity to engage in experiential, hands-on learning (e.g., a Reggio-inspired approach). Thus, as demonstrated in *Hooray for Diffendoofer Day,* it is not necessary for standards and accountability assessments to run counter to appropriate classroom practice.

However, while it is possible for standards, accountability assessment, and developmentally appropriate Reggio-inspired classroom practices to productively co-exist and mutually support one another, the field is uneasy (Kagan et al., 1997). In addition to the perceived conflict between "standards" and "developmentally appropriate practices" that was discussed previously, Horm-Wingerd et al., (1999) outline additional reasons for the wariness of early childhood educators. These include:

1. A history of inappropriate use and over-reliance on norm-referenced tests. Early childhood educators are well aware of the countless examples of test misuse and the misinterpretation of standardized norm-referenced assessment results that were common in the 1980s and 1990s (Goodwin & Goodwin, 1993; Kamii, 1990). The problems associated with the misuse and abuses of standardized tests with young children were well publicized and the associated negative impacts on children, teachers, families, and schools were widely discussed. As noted by Schorr, the field's experiences in the 1980s "have left the early childhood community so traumatized at the possibility of unwittingly promoting further inappropriate testing, that many oppose any attempt to assess school readiness by testing or observing individual children, even if testing is done for the purpose of judging the community's provisions for preparing children for school entry and not the abilities or capabilities of individual children" (Schorr, 1997, p. 39). Although Schorr was commenting on readiness testing, the trauma she discusses has generalized to all forms of early childhood assessment, especially accountability assessments.

2. A lack of training and experience. Early childhood administrators (Thompson, 1990) and classroom personnel (Kagan et al., 1997) are often unfamiliar with assessment terms and approaches. Also, currently there is limited consensus in the field about the meaning of commonly used terms such as goals, benchmarks, indicators, outcomes, results, and assessment (Kagan et al., 1997). Due to their lack of specialized training, many administrators and teachers of young children feel uncomfortable with assessment, especially assessments that include high stakes for children, teachers, and schools.

It is likely that increased understanding and experience could partially address the worries of early childhood educators concerning standards and accountability assessments. Enhanced professional development is also necessary to support early childhood educators in meeting the challenge of demonstrating "increased competence, leadership, and advocacy on the broad topic of assessment in early childhood education" as we move into an era with increased attention on assessment and accountability (Groves & Horm-Wingerd, 2000). To avoid repeating the mistakes of the 1980s, early childhood educators need to enhance their understanding of and expertise in all forms of assessment in early childhood, especially accountability assessment. Professional development will be key to forging the productive and mutually supportive relationship among standards, accountability assessments, and classroom practices. Given this, what are the implications for preservice and inservice professional development for early childhood educators?

IMPLICATIONS FOR PRESERVICE AND INSERVICE PROFESSIONAL DEVELOPMENT

The American challenges of standards and accountability assessment do have implications for teacher development. These include:

❀ More emphasis is needed on the broad topic of assessment across all levels of teacher professional development.

Preservice preparation programs often do not include in-depth training on the various types of early childhood assessments and their appropriate functions and uses (Kagan et al., 1997). This is especially true with standards-based accountability assessments. Inservice programs are often "one-shot" seminars with little opportunity to implement new concepts with follow-up training. Thus, new and seasoned teachers are often unfamiliar with the process of systematically including various types of assessment into their daily program. A lesson Americans have learned from the Reggio Emilia approach is the importance of careful, ongoing documentation and analysis of children's work as the basis for classroom planning and teacher professional development (Goldhaber & Smith, see Chapter 10; Moran, 1998; Rinaldi, 1998; Tarini, 1997; Vecchi, 1993). Given the centrality of this type of ongoing assessment to high quality classroom practice, a greater emphasis is required on classroom assessment across all levels of teacher professional development. The emphasis on ongoing documentation will not only improve teachers' understanding of assessment but will enhance their classroom practice. As noted by Moran, when colleagues collaborate "to use data to inform teaching, previous ways of knowing and believing are often challenged, supported, and give rise to new perspectives, new knowledge, and even new beliefs" (Moran, 1998, p. 409). Moran goes on to note that the result is that teachers "return to the classroom with thoughtfully prepared provocations and anticipated responses to children's inquiry" (Moran, 1998, p. 410) that extend children's learning.

Relative to accountability assessment, many believe that the problems experienced with the over-reliance and abuse of standardized norm-referenced tests in the

1980s was based, in part, on the lack of training and experience of educators (Goodwin & Goodwin, 1993). Professional development on the topic of the proper role and functions of accountability assessment will hopefully diminish the possibility of misuse. Also, once teachers are comfortable and confident with their ongoing classroom assessment and documentation, it is likely that less anxiety will be associated with the sporadic assessments imposed by agents outside the classroom. Although these externally imposed accountability assessments often do have consequences attached for teachers and children, the information yielded by ongoing assessment should be the most influential force impacting classroom practice. As noted by Shepard and Graue, early childhood educators must be aware of the limitations of tests and not attribute greater scientific merit to them than is warranted (Shepard & Graue, 1993, p. 303).

✿ Greater understanding of standards and backmapping needs to be developed.

A positive relationship among ongoing classroom assessment, classroom practices, and accountability assessment can be fostered through standards. As discussed previously in this chapter, standards can play an influential role by formalizing expectations for children's development and learning and communicating these expectations to diverse audiences.

Currently, in American public education, standards have mostly been developed for use in K–12 educational settings. Although standards have primarily been developed for children in elementary classrooms, some states have developed or begun the development of standards for younger children. Even in states that have not developed preschool standards, the standards developed for older children have implications for younger children and those working in settings serving younger children. Backmapping involves understanding what the state standards written for grades three or four imply for teachers and children in grades two, one, kindergarten, and preschool settings. The overriding goal is not to "push-down" the curriculum but to work together in designing developmentally appropriate curriculum and assessments that enable children to progress through the developmental continuum that undergrid competence in reading, writing, math, social skills, and other important curricular areas. Even in the current climate of school reform, in which standards play a central role, the topics of standards and backmapping are rarely covered in preservice or inservice professional development programs for early childhood teachers and administrators. This lack of attention must be addressed for early childhood educators to work together to support children's progress.

✿ Shared responsibility for achieving standards across settings must be developed.

Both preservice and inservice professional development programs can play an important role in providing mechanisms for the development of shared responsibility for children's development and learning. Given this goal, it is important to structure professional development programs to include teachers who staff different levels and classes across preschool and primary settings. These opportunities are becoming more prevalent as funding sources and policymakers realize the critical importance of teaching "our" children instead of teaching the first-grade curriculum. These types of professional development opportunities are critical to ensure continuity for children as they progress through the patchwork of systems providing early care and education in the United States today (Kagan & Cohen, 1997).

❀ Participation of early childhood educators in the development of standards must be increased.

Committees representing diverse constituents often accomplish the development of standards. It is important that the voice of early childhood educators be part of the conversation and represented at the table when standards are developed. This implies that early childhood educators be active in volunteering or otherwise ensuring that their views and expertise are represented on such committees. In addition to ensuring the expertise and perspectives of early childhood educators are represented in the development of standards, participation on such committees is typically a wonderful professional development opportunity. These committees offer teachers the opportunity to discuss children, child development, factors influencing child learning, and other similar topics with colleagues—unfortunately, unlike the experience of teachers in the preschools of Reggio Emilia, the opportunity to engage in rich collaboration is rarely available in American education.

❀ Participation of early childhood educators in the design and implementation of accountability assessments must be increased.

As noted by CCSSO, "Early childhood educators and educational measurement specialists must work together to jointly derive satisfactory solutions to the need for developmentally appropriate assessments that can generate information for use in determining program effectiveness in supporting all young learners to achieve high standards" (Horm-Wingerd et al., 1999, p. iv). Collaborative work is needed to develop accountability assessments that mirror classroom practice—teachers can assist measurement experts in understanding the variety of ways young children can demonstrate knowledge and skills. Documentation as practiced in Reggio-inspired programs demonstrates that displaying "children's work in a wide variety of media provides compelling public evidence of the intellectual powers of young children" (Katz & Chard, 1996). Also, teachers should be more involved in the administration of accountability assessments to ensure that they are child-friendly and appropriate. As noted by Gallagher, teachers must have a stronger voice in the process of assessment of children in order to assure that any measures are appropriate (Gallagher, 2000, p. 506).

The state of Vermont has been a leader in including teachers in the state's second grade accountability assessment. During the 1997–98 school year, Vermont instituted an individually-administered reading assessment to determine the degree to which schools were making progress in meeting state standards in reading accuracy and comprehension. Teachers administer the assessment to second-grade students in individual sessions and determine the highest level of proficiency at which students read with accuracy and comprehension. Teachers are also actively involved in the scoring and psychometric study of the assessment. For example, all administrations of the assessments are audiotaped and a sample of tapes is selected and rescored by expert scorers who are teachers. The expert scorers also evaluate the sample audiotapes for consistency of administration. Feedback is given to teachers whose audiotapes are part of the sample and this information is helpful in their future administration of the assessment to individual children. Vermont requires six hours of initial training in administration and scoring with attendance at updates and calibration sessions required annually for all teachers who administer the assessment (see Horm-Wingerd et al., 1999, for additional information on Vermont's Developmental Reading Assessment). Anecdotal reports from teachers suggest that this experience has been a powerful professional development opportunity (S. C. Biggam, personal communication, April 25, 1998). This type of productive collaboration between assessment and early childhood personnel will not happen without mechanisms to support it. As noted by CCSSO, one platform for the cross-fertilization of these two specializations is preservice and inservice professional development programs (Horm-Wingerd et al., 1999).

✸ Opportunities for ongoing personal professional development in assessment that includes lessons about good staff development from Reggio Emilia must be provided.

As noted by Rinaldi, staff development "often attempts to pour ideas into teachers, to shape them, so that they could in turn shape the children" (Rinaldi, 1994, p. 97). Additionally she notes that staff development is too often sporadic and dominated by the words of "experts." She maintains that staff development must take on a new meaning to be effective. Following the practices of Reggio Emilia, staff development must be seen as a right and as a vital and daily aspect of teachers' work and their personal and professional identities. Rinaldi advocates that professional development must be "seen above all as change, as renewal, and as an indispensable vehicle by which to make stronger the quality of interaction" with children and among teachers. This type of professional development—ongoing professional dialogue and work among diverse colleagues—is much different than typical approaches used in the United States. Relative to the topic of assessment, approaches like that implemented in Vermont where teachers and assessment specialists work together to construct child-friendly methods of accountability assessment may be the most meaningful form of professional development. It is perhaps the American approach to professional development, more than the impact of standards and accountability assessment, that functions as a barrier to the successful implementation of a Reggio-inspired curriculum.

SUMMARY AND CONCLUSIONS: THE COMPATIBILITY OF THE REGGIO EMILIA APPROACH WITH ACCOUNTABILITY ASSESSMENT IN THE UNITED STATES

Goodwin and Goodwin note the "entrenchment of tests in American society" (Goodwin & Goodwin, 1993, p. 442) and outline several reasons to explain it. One of the most important is Resnick's observation that tests are seen as efficient tools for promoting equal opportunity and visible national standards by a large portion of American society (Resnick, 1981). The recent calls for accountability assessment suggest this view persists in contemporary America and has expanded to programs serving young children and their families. Italian early childhood educators at Reggio Emilia operate in a culture without this American belief in the value of or need for external assessments. This difference certainly has implications for programming for young children. Although implications are evident, the American belief in the power of tests does not preclude implementing a Reggio-inspired, developmentally appropriate approach. Also, as outlined, there are several avenues American early childhood educators can pursue to shape standards and assessments to be congruent with best practice in early childhood education.

REFERENCES

Bredekamp, S., & Copple, C. (Eds.). (1997). *Developmentally appropriate practice in early childhood programs* (Rev. ed.). Washington, D.C.: NAEYC.

Darling-Hammond, L., & Falk, B. (1997). Using standards and assessments to support student learning. *Phi Delta Kappan, 79*(3), 190–199.

Gallagher, C. (2000). A seat at the table: Teachers reclaiming assessment through rethinking accountability. *Phi Delta Kappan, 81*(7), 502–507.

Goodwin, W. L., & Goodwin, L. D. (1993). Young children and measurement: Standardized and nonstandardized instruments in early childhood education. In B. Spodek (Ed.), *Handbook of research on the education of young children* (pp. 477–492). New York: Macmillan.

Groves, M. M., & Horm-Wingerd, D. M. (2000). Understanding assessment: A critical need in early childhood teacher preparation. *Journal of Early Childhood Teacher Education, 21*(2), 199–205.

Hansche, L. N. (1998). *Handbook for the development of performance standards: Meeting the requirements of Title I.* Washington, D.C.: Council of Chief State School Officers.

Horm-Wingerd, D. M., Winter, P. C., & Plofchan, P. (1999). *Primary level assessment for IASA Title I: A call for discussion.* Washington, D.C.: Council of Chief State School Officers.

Jacobson, L. (2000, April 12). Focus on results trickling down to younger and younger children. *Education Week, 19*(31), 1, 20–21.

Kagan, S. L., & Cohen, N. E. (1997). *Not by chance: Creating an early care and education system for America's children.* New Haven, CT: The Bush Center in Child Development and Social Policy at Yale University.

Kagan, S. L., Rosenkoetter, S., & Cohen, N. (1997). *Considering child-based results for young children: Definitions, desirability, feasibility, and next steps.* New Haven, CT: The Bush Center in Child Development and Social Policy at Yale University.

Kamii, C. (Ed.). (1990). *Achievement testing in the early grades: the games grown-ups play*. Washington, D.C.: NAEYC.

Katz, L. G., & Chard, S. C. (1996). *ERIC Digest: The contribution of documentation to the quality of early childhood education*. Urbana, IL: ERIC Clearinghouse on Elementary and Early Childhood Education.

Moran, M. J. (1998). The project approach framework for teacher education: A case for collaborative learning and reflective practice. In C. Edwards, L. Gandini, & G. Forman (Eds.). (1998) *The hundred languages of children: The Reggio Emilia approach—advanced reflections* (pp. 405–417) Greenwich, CT: Ablex.

Morgan-Worsham, D. (1990). The dilemma for principals. In K. Kamii (Ed.), *No more achievement testing in the early grades* (pp. 61–69). Washington, D.C.: NAEYC.

National Association for the Education of Young Children (NAEYC). (1988). NAEYC position statement on standardized testing of young children 3 through 8 years of age. *Young Children, 46*(3), 21–38.

National Association for the Education of Young Children (NAEYC) & National Association of Early Childhood Specialists in State Departments of Education (NAECS/SDE). (1991). Guidelines for appropriate curriculum content and assessment in programs serving children ages 3 through 8. *Young Children, 46*(3), 21–38.

Noddings, N. (1997). Thinking about standards. *Phi Delta Kappan, 79*(3), 184–189.

Resnick, D. P. (1981). Testing in America: A support environment. *Phi Delta Kappan, 62*(9), 625–628.

Rinaldi, C. (1994). Staff development in Reggio Emilia. In L. G. Katz & B. Cesarone (Eds.), *Reflections on the Reggio Emilia Approach*. Urbana, IL: ERIC Clearinghouse on Elementary and Early Childhood Education. ED 375 986.

Rinaldi, C. (1998). Projected curriculum constructed through documentation—progettazione. In C. Edwards, L. Gandini, & G. Forman (Eds.). (1998) *The hundred languages of children: The Reggio Emilia approach—advanced reflections* (pp. 113–125). Greenwich, CT: Ablex.

Schorr, L. (1997). Judging interventions by their results. In S. L. Kagan, S. Rosenkoetter, & N. Cohen (Eds.), *Considering child-based results for young children: Definitions, desirability, feasibility, and next steps* (pp. 36–47). New Haven, CT: The Bush Center in Child Development and Social Policy at Yale University.

Seuss, T., Prelutsky, J., & Smith, L. (1998). *Hooray for Diffendoofer Day*. New York: Knopf.

Shepard, L., & Graue, M. E. (1993). The morass of school readiness screening: Research on test use and test validity. In B. Spodek (Ed.), *Handbook of research on the education of young children* (pp. 293–305). New York: Macmillan.

Shepard, L., Kagan, S. L., & Wurtz, E. (Eds.). (1998). *Principles and recommendations for early childhood assessments: The Goal 1 Early Childhood*

Assessments Resource Group report submitted to the National Education Goals Panel. Washington, D.C.: National Education Goals Panel.

Tarini, E. (1997). Reflections on a year in Reggio Emilia: Key concepts in rethinking and learning the Reggio way. In J. Hendrick (Ed.), *First steps toward teaching the Reggio way* (pp. 56–69). Upper Saddle River, NJ: Merrill Prentice-Hall.

Thompson, E. W. (1990). The dilemma for superintendents. In C. Kamii (Ed.), *Achievement testing in the early grades: Games grown-ups play* (pp. 39–47). Washington, D.C.: NAEYC.

Vecchi, V. (1993). The role of the atelierista. In C. Edwards, L. Gandini, & G. Forman (Eds.), *The hundred languages of children: The Reggio Emilia approach to early childhood education* (pp. 119–127). Norwood, NJ: Ablex.

Part **II**

Amiable Communities for Learning

In the schools in Reggio Emilia, an education based on relationship is valued. One of their goals is to build an amiable school where teachers, children, and parents all have a right to "feel a sense of belonging, to be part of a larger endeavor, to share meanings . . ." (Rinaldi, 1998, p. 114). In the United States there is an ongoing talk about school reform, and a sense of alienation and powerlessness penetrates the lives of students, teachers, and parents. It is time to take lessons from Reggio Emilia, to move beyond rhetoric and begin the difficult task of building amiable communities, where learning and teaching happen in relationships—an education based on relationship. Is this possible in the United States? In reading the three stories in this section, you will find that it is possible. You will travel with the protagonists, find meanings in their struggles, challenges, hopes, and perseverance, which may transform your classrooms and schools.

Chapter
6

Developing a Sense of "We" in Parent/Teacher Relationships

Carol Bersani ◆ Debra Jarjoura

As teachers of young children, we are committed to the belief that strong parent/teacher relationships are essential for children's success in school. As teacher educators, we have advocated for family-centered education where all parents are accorded deep respect and viewed as partners in the children's education. During the last decade, we have been greatly inspired by Loris Malaguzzi's statement that a goal of the educators in Reggio Emilia is to "build an amiable school, where children, teachers, and families feel at home" (Malaguzzi, 1993, p. 58). In such a school we believe that both individual identity and a sense of belonging to a community can be affirmed. The relationships established have a symbiotic quality where each person is viewed as essential to the other. This chapter is intended to describe one school's efforts to create such relationships leading to what we refer to as a sense of "we."

Our school, the Kent State University Child Development Center, has a history of respect for, and nurturance of, collaboration among families and teachers that began with the formation of the school some twenty-six years ago. From the beginning, the school faced challenges that were surmounted by everyone working together. The school for young children was opened in the 1970s in one room of a university-supported elementary school as a response to the growing need for childcare on campus. Donations of materials and equipment were provided by a local parent organization. By the 1980s, the school had expanded to include four classrooms but now faced a serious challenge. The elementary school was being closed and the building renovated for offices. Parents and teachers decided to organize a statewide lobby that eventually led to funding for a new building for the school, which opened in 1991.

Several years later, the teachers began to study the Reggio approach to early childhood education. As we read and discussed together, our minds were opened to possibilities for involving parents in ways that had not occurred to us previously. We came to a deeper understanding of family participation embedded within a system of complex and interdependent relationships. We began to see, quite slowly at first, how family participation was integral and necessary to our **daily** work with children. Constructing and sustaining these interdependent relationships required much time, reflection, and hard work. Our goal was to transform the culture of our school into a community of learners.

Within this overall goal, there were two research questions posed:

1. How do families and teachers together construct meaning about the purposes of early education and the work of the children?
2. How can the school communicate the values they hold for family participation?

These research questions served as a framework for the work of the teachers, parents, and administrators during the past five years. The stories in this chapter were drawn from multiple sources, most notably the records of the teacher and family/school

A child and her mother sharing a family photo album with the teacher.

meetings, transcripts of parent focus groups, and interviews with parents and teachers. As we reflected on this work, we noticed that an important first step for us was to articulate the values that we shared about schools and relationships within them. Then, we identified the ways we thought those values were and were not visible in the community.

MAKING OUR VALUES VISIBLE

The five values identified were individual identity, knowing each other, listening and sharing, inquiry and reflection, and collaboration. The process of making these values visible helped us to understand ourselves at a deeper level. It also gave us a clearer direction for our work with families.

Individual Identity

We subscribed to the belief that identity is a social construction, shaping and being shaped by the school (Dahlberg, Moss, & Pence, 1999; Fraser, 2000). We valued the individuality and the uniqueness of each person and family. Our school had committed to enrolling a diverse population of children and families. Acknowledging, accepting, and accommodating differences in family values was important to us. In making each family's visible identity, we hoped that "each one would feel enough of a sense of belonging and self-confidence to participate in the activities of the school" (Malaguzzi, 1993, p. 62).

Knowing Each Other: Building Relationships

We thought of our school as a system of interactions and relationships that was being constructed continuously as we worked and played together. We needed to understand better what it meant to really "know each other." We had informally observed that parents who enrolled their children in a program with one arrival and departure time developed closer relationships than those parents who enrolled their children in full-day programs with varying arrival and departure times. As our school was moving to full-day-only programs, we were challenged to think of ways that the school could more effectively support the development of friendships among families, children, and teachers.

The importance of these relationships was clearly articulated by parents. In the words of one parent, "I think the teachers must have this relationship with the parents in order to have a strong connection with the child." Another parent commented, "It gives children confidence to see their parents know about their work at school and know their friends." Parents also valued a welcoming atmosphere in the classroom. One parent commented how important it was to her that all the children in the classroom welcomed her and desired her presence there. These parents valued being a part of a community of learners.

Listening and Sharing

Our school was committed to open communication between home and school. In thinking about this value, we noted that often written and oral communication had been unidirectional and concerned with the agendas of teachers and the school. We thought Carlina Rinaldi's (1998) reference to the pedagogy of listening applied to our work with parents as well as children. To listen to parents was to actively seek and respect their points of view. How could we create a system of communication that focused on listening and a mutual exchange of ideas (Dahlberg, et al., 1999)?

Inquiry and Reflection

Our school had a history of being a research community that valued inquiry and reflection. As a result of our study of the Reggio approach, we came to recognize that, for the most part, the voices of the parents were absent from this work. How could we invite parents to participate with us in the study of children's ideas and work? Dahlberg, Moss, and Pence describe this way of working as:

> Parents and pedagogues (and others) entering into a reflective and analytic relationship involving deepening understanding and the possibility of making judgments about the pedagogical work (Dahlberg, et al; 1999, p. 77).

We thought that it would be a way to know each other better and to have more points of view regarding the children's work. Would our busy parents, almost all employed outside the home or going to school full-time, be willing to take on this role of inquiry and reflection? Could this change also contribute to a greater sense of community within the school? Would more parents participate in the school because of the intriguing nature of the children's thoughts, explorations, and constructions?

A Collaborative Organization

The values of individual identity, relationships, listening and sharing, and inquiry and reflection served as a foundation for our thinking about what was a truly collaborative way of working together. We valued collaboration, but did not fully recognize the power of collaboration in producing growth in an organization (Wasow, 2000). Did we confuse collaboration with cooperation or congeniality? The role of critique in collaboration was not well understood or comfortable for us. What would be needed for our school to meet the standards for family involvement developed by the National Parent Teacher Association, especially Standard V, "To include parents as full partners in the decisions that affect children and families" (1998, p. 5)?

We hoped that as parents came together, they would build relationships with other parents and the teachers that would create new possibilities for collaboration. Wheatley and Kellner-Rogers describe this generative phenomenon in their book, *A Simpler Way:*

Parents who come together to build a town playground do more than create a park. They discover how to work together. What began as a park project transforms into relationships and shared desires that then can create more and more for the community (Wheatley and Kellner-Rogers, 1996, p. 70).

MAKING ORGANIZATIONAL CHANGES TO SUPPORT THE WORK

One of the first steps was to examine our organizational structure for ways in which it supported or impeded our work with families. It was apparent that we needed to begin by rethinking the role of the parent advisory council in the life of the school. While there would be a good turnout at the initial meeting each year, by the end of the year only a handful of parents came to the meetings. We had examined such factors as the time and day of meetings, clarity of purpose for the group, and the relationship between the advisory council's work and that of the teachers. Shared ownership for the work of the group was not strong. We needed to change our **expectation** that not many parents would participate. Perhaps this shift in thinking would make a difference in how we approached our work with parents.

The teachers and members of the parent advisory council decided to start over to construct a school-wide representative body. Many mothers and fathers turned out for this initial meeting. Parents, teachers, and administrators together wrote a set of bylaws to give purpose to, and govern, the organization. After much discussion, they decided to name the group the Center/Family Connection (CFC). Representatives from each of the seven classrooms were identified, officers elected, and standing committees formed. The Center agreed to provide childcare for the meetings to ensure that all parents could attend.

The creation of this more-representative organization within our school gave us a viable structure for involving parents in decisions affecting both their children and themselves and working toward the sense of "we" that was desired. When issues, problems, or conflicts regarding purposes, policies, or procedures arose, as they surely did, there was a collaborative structure in place for studying and resolving them. Where once administrators were expected to solve all problems, now many were addressed within the CFC and its policy committee.

At the same time, the teachers made an important decision to offer monthly evening parent meetings in each classroom. The purpose of these meetings was to build friendships among families and teachers, provide an opportunity for parents to bring questions and concerns to the group for discussion, and study the work of the children. This concept of studying the work of the children, to be described more fully in the next section of this chapter, was a new way of working for both teachers and parents. It involved presenting some project, investigation, or other experience of the children to the parents for study. Parents were supported in their efforts to understand the philosophy of the school and their children's thinking and learning. Teachers gained new perspectives on the ideas of the children. Resources for supporting children's investigations were identified. Because the teachers would alternate studying work with social events, the parents were able to build friendships that extended beyond the classroom and the family's stay at our school. As with the CFC meetings, these classroom meetings were scheduled either directly after school or in the early evening. Childcare and food were provided so that families could more easily participate in this small community of learners.

CONSTRUCTING MEANING TOGETHER

From a social constructivist perspective, the discourse of making meaning involves deep and sustained dialogue regarding the philosophy and goals of the school and the work of the children. Dahlberg, et al., has described the purpose of this discourse as follows:

> The intention is to study and make meaning from actual practice, recognizing that in fact there may be many meanings or understandings, not attempts to reduce what is going on to fit preconceived categorical criteria (Dahlberg, et. al., 1999, p. 109).

This is very hard work! It is especially so in the context of accountability because it drives so much of American education, even at the preschool level. We learned early that constructing meaning together was a process that occurred in both informal daily encounters and in more focused dialogues.

There were many informal daily interactions among families and teachers that led to co-construction of meaning. These moments mattered greatly!   Parents were encouraged to spend time in the classroom at arrival and departure in order to build relationships with the children and to understand their work. Parents were also encouraged to spend at least one hour a month volunteering in the classroom. As parents had few daytime hours available for this participation, creative ideas were needed. Many parents used their lunch hour once a month. Teachers scheduled home visits as a way of getting to know families better. In all of these encounters, questions asked and observations and interpretations offered by parents were documented for later study by the teachers. Often, these thoughts were returned to the parents for discussion at parent meetings.

In addition to these informal encounters, teachers offered parents more focused opportunities to interpret the work of the children. Four encounters that were especially provocative in the process of making meaning were: (1) home/school journaling; (2) portfolio development; (3) project documentation and study; and (4) group parent/ teacher conferences. They provided the parents and teachers the opportunity to "be close to the child in a new way" (Fontanesi, Gialdini, & Soncini, 1998, p. 151). They also contributed to building a strong connection between the home and the school. Attendance at classroom meetings soared as parents, and sometimes grandparents and other extended family, attended.

Sharing meaning is constructed as parents participate in daily classroom experiences.

Home/School Journaling

At the beginning of the school year, each family was given a small spiral notebook with the child's photo and symbol on the cover. This journal circulated between home and school. For the toddlers, it was sent home nightly; for preschoolers weekly. The journal belonged to the family, and was to be given to them at the end of the year. The process of journaling was meant to convey to parents how important the child was to the teachers **and** the other children.

Teachers made entries related to the child's interests, discoveries, thoughts, etc., and responded to parents' questions. The teachers emphasized the joyful moments with children. In the first entry, teachers often asked parents to share their wishes for their child. It was expected that information sharing would be reciprocal. In reflecting on this process, one parent stated, "When teachers give parents ideas and parents give teachers ideas, both are richer." Another parent shared, "If my house was on fire, it would be the journal that I would grab first!" The journal represented a chronicle of her child's life in school, a memory that she could not capture in any other way.

While not a substitute for group dialogue about the work of the children, it often offered parents a way to **begin** that dialogue with teachers in a manner more comfortable for them. This was especially true for parents of toddlers in their first school experience and for parents of children with special rights who often had concerns about the most appropriate environment to support growth. Because the teachers' entries focused on the child within the community, families began to focus on the community rather than just their own child.

Portfolio Development

The first encounter families had with our school after admission was generally with the family services coordinator. The purpose of this meeting was for the coordinator to share information about the school and for the parents to share information about the child. At this encounter, parents were also introduced to the school's use of the portfolio to chronicle and study learning and development.

Each family was invited to prepare an introduction to the child's portfolio, which served to acquaint all readers with their child. One family dubbed this the "home page." A photo of the family was placed at the entry to the portfolio. After school began, preschool children were invited to tell a story about their family that was transcribed and placed in the portfolio. We wanted all readers to know our classroom families.

In each portfolio, throughout the year, teachers placed documentation of various forms: transcripts of small group conversations, drawings, stories, and photos of relevant project work. Teacher observations, interpretations, and reflections on the children's work were included, as well as photographs of the child's family participating in school experiences. These portfolios were placed in the greeting area of the room, a comfortable place where parents often sat with children. Children could share their portfolios with families on a regular basis. They were also discussed at monthly classroom parent/teacher meetings and in parent/teacher conferences and often taken home for further study. Parents were asked to offer reflections on the work within the portfolio. As parents and teachers contributed to and studied the portfolios, they were developing greater understanding of the child, the other children, and the theoretical underpinnings of the work of the teachers.

Project Documentation and Study

Understanding projected curriculum

At monthly classroom meetings, parents are encouraged to offer agenda items for discussion. In one classroom of three and four year olds, the parents of children new to the school expressed a desire to know more about the purposes for small group project work. Parents of returning children shared the knowledge they had gained during the past year. For the next meeting, the teachers planned a provocation for the parents based on an interest previously explored by the children. This provocation was to provide a way for parents to begin to understand project work, and, in particular, to understand the concepts of drawing to learn and co-construction of theory (Forman & Fyfe, 1998). The teachers asked a question that related to an interest of the children,

"How do worms move?" In small groups, parents discussed their ideas. They observed a box full of worms and discussed their observations. Each was asked to draw his/her theory of how worms move and to share and discuss it with the members of their group. Then, each group presented one theory to the entire group of parents. Amid laughter and sharing of knowledge and theories, parents began to construct together the meaning of uncovering the theories of the children.

The teachers felt that they were making progress toward the goal of making how children learn visible. Next, they wanted parents to join the teachers in looking more closely at the documentation of project work. In one classroom, the children and teachers were engaged in a project called "Looking at Ourselves." The children had been quite interested in exploring all aspects of their mouths. The teacher brought the question, "Where do our voices come from?" to the children for dialogue. At the next parent meeting, the teachers shared the transcript of this conversation. Parents spoke the children's parts and then discussed the children's theories. Speaking the voices of the children in a conversation helped parents to listen to the ideas and theories of the children.

Connecting parents more closely to the children's work

This short story from Debra Jarjoura illustrates a way in which the teachers used an interest of the children in order to deepen parents' understanding of children's representational abilities.

> I believe that children must have a sense of belonging in the school to be able to explore themselves, enter into successful relationships with others, and respond with confidence to the many challenges school presents daily. I also think that children need to feel that the home and school are connected. Within that connection they come to know themselves and to understand that they and their family are respected and appreciated. I wanted to find a small, concrete way to draw families into our classroom community to support the children in their on-going construction of identity.
>
> In my class of three-, four-, and five-year-olds, the children had been exploring their physical selves and feelings throughout the year. I observed that dramatic play was an important language for representing their ideas and images of self. In my opinion, children's fantasy play was an important source for identity construction.
>
> I decided to offer the children a provocation, photographing each of them in a dramatic role of their choosing. I asked them, "Who do you want to be?" I wanted the children to think about how they acted in that role as well as how they wanted to look. Soon after, I shared the photos with the children at our morning meeting. Each child told the group about who they were pretending to be in the photo. I asked them if they would like to use the photos to make paper dolls for their play. The children all liked this idea!
>
> With the photo as a reference, the children were invited to draw their pretend selves. While they worked, I recorded their ideas and stories about their drawings. Each of the many characters was challenging to represent in a drawing. How could they become a bird, princess, bus, dinosaur, Barbie? To some children emphasizing beauty was important, to others, power and control.
>
> While all this work was proceeding, the parents were kept informed through a daily reflection. I posed a question to the children: "Would they like to invite their parents to

make the paper dolls?" They were very excited about this possibility. I thought that this could provide an opportunity to connect the parents with the children's work by looking at how the children represented their dramatic roles. Could the children's enthusiasm be a catalyst for parents to enter the children's thinking? This could be a way for the parents to learn more about the children in the classroom and the dramatic play roles that they so often chose.

We began the evening for this special event with pizza for everyone. Then, the parents moved to the studio while the children played in the gym. The parents knew that they would be making paper dolls for the children's dramatic play. When they were shown their child's photo, drawing, and verbal description of their character, they were surprised to learn that they would need to interpret their child's work in order to make the doll.

For many, the first step was to cut out the figure of the child from the photo. Then they searched for materials to support the representation. This was such a challenge! While the parents were engaged, I documented their work. When the dolls were completed, I laminated them. They were ready to share with the children at the next morning meeting and then to be used in play. The children were delighted with their parents' interpretations.

We asked the parents to reflect on the meaning of this experience. They were interested in what their child and all the other children pretended to be. They noticed that, even if two children chose the same character, the ideas for construction of each doll were unique. One parent commented, "We learned a lot about the other children's families and it was fun to see the other parents' reactions to what their own child chose to be. We enjoyed playing and using the materials like the children and interacting socially with the other parents."

When we studied the documentation, we saw that the parents were interested in the ideas of all the children. This experience reflected the values and goals that the teachers held for their work: coming to know about each other, making all children visible, developing a sense of "we" with parents, and studying the ideas of the children together.

Studying project work using a protocol

Towards the end of the past year, the teachers were exploring how to bring multiple pieces of project documentation to the parents for study. The teachers had utilized a way of studying documentation adapted from a protocol developed by Steve Seidel at Harvard Project Zero (Seidel, 1998). The steps in this process, adapted for use with our parents, were:

1. The teachers present documentation of a project that is in progress, building a context for the work to be studied, but not commenting on it.
2. The parents describe without judgment what they have observed in the work. The teachers record the parents' descriptions.
3. The parents pose questions about the work. The teachers record their questions.
4. The parents speculate about the meaning of the work. The teachers record.
5. The teachers respond to the parents' descriptions, questions, and speculations and offer their perspectives on the work.

6. The parents and teachers discuss possible directions for the work and ways to support the children's thinking.
7. The parents and teachers reflect together on the meaning of this process.

The teachers chose this way of studying documentation related to project work because they thought it would encourage parents to look closely, and in an egalitarian way, at the children's thinking abilities. Studying multiple forms of documentation would offer parents a "more particular kind of knowledge that empowers and provokes them to reflect, question, and rethink or reconstruct the image of the child and the rights of children to quality education" (Forman & Fyfe, 1998, p. 256). We hoped they would be as amazed as we were with the strengths and rich potential of all the children. It would also give them an opportunity to celebrate the children's accomplishments!

One of the teachers, Laurie Kidwell, contributed this story of her use of the protocol in studying documentation with parents.

> We noticed the children talked about things that scared them. During morning meeting we asked the children to close their eyes and think of what was really, really scary to them. The children had many thoughts: ghosts, dinosaurs, monsters, mummies. One child assured the others that monsters were all in our imaginations. Several said that nothing scared them!
>
> I invited the children later to draw something that was very scary to them. After studying the drawings and the children's thoughts, I wondered if this work might be something to share with parents at an upcoming classroom parent meeting. I was familiar with the protocol as a tool for teachers to use in studying work and I wondered about whether parents would find it useful, too.
>
> I spread the children's work out on tables in the classroom. After introducing both the context for this work and the protocol, parents were invited to study all the children's work. Then, they were asked to describe what they saw. Parents noticed that the lists of things that scared the children were not reflected in their drawings. The parents thought that some stories accompanying the drawings seemed based in reality; others seemed to be from the children's imaginations.
>
> The parents asked many questions: "Are the children really afraid of the things they drew? Are there differences between boys and girls in what they fear? To what extent are these expressed fears influenced by television or by other children? Why did the teachers only offer black drawing pencils? How were the conversations recorded?"
>
> During the speculation phase of this work, the parents offered interpretations of the work, thought about sources for the children's ideas, and wondered, again, about how children influenced each other in this work.
>
> As they discussed the work further, the parents wondered if the children perceived that parents had fears? They thought about asking their children, "Do you think mommy and daddy are afraid of anything?" In thinking about their own children's work, parents thought of ideas for how they could support the work at home.

Parents and teachers in this classroom agreed that this way of studying the work was a window into what they were eager to know about the children and a way of listening to the children. One parent commented that it gave her a broader view of what was going on in the classroom, not just for her child but all the children. She also viewed it as strengthening the bonds among the families and with the teachers. The teacher was amazed at the richness of the ideas generated by the parents.

The power of this way of studying documentation with parents was that it seemed to make thinking visible—that of the children, the teachers, and the parents. It was not so much about parent education as helping parents to see the "preciousness of children's ideas, their problem-solving struggles" (Gambetti, 1999). All of the parents were drawn into the work because it was so interesting and thought-provoking.

Inviting parents to document in the classroom

After these experiences, parents often expressed interest in volunteering to document project work and other experiences in the classroom. They saw firsthand the importance that children and teachers gave to these records. They understood the role of documentor in the teaching and learning process. One parent commented, "I think this (documentation) helped the teachers to get a different perspective on the children's progress. They always thanked me, and I always learned something myself."

Group Parent/Teacher Conferences

Because we had engaged the parents in studying the work of the children across the year, it seemed a logical next step to have a group parent/teacher conference at the end of the year. In a mixed-age classroom of three- and four-year-olds, the teachers formed two groups: parents of three-year-olds and parents of four-year-olds. It was thought that parents of three-year-olds, whose children were returning for a second year, would have questions and topics to discuss that were different from parents of those age four, whose children were going to kindergarten.

Each conference began with the parents reviewing and sharing from their child's portfolio. Project books, records of projects completed throughout the year, were available for study. As the parents shared observations from their study, the teachers recorded what they had to say and noted questions that might be returned to the parents for further discussion. One parent commented that the portfolio made her child's progress across the year so clear to her. The teachers reflected that "the parents have so many of the same questions and concerns. Those who feel a bit timid to ask a question often are reassured when their question is shared by another."

After sharing their individual observations, posing questions, and discussing topics of mutual concern, the parents then proposed, discussed, and set goals for the coming year. They also identified ways that they could support each other across the summer and during the next school year. For the parents of four-year-olds, goals were focused on transitioning children to kindergarten while maintaining the important friendships that children had established in the classroom during the past two years. The parents of three-year-olds proposed provocations to offer the children in the coming year based on what they had observed in the work of their children. The teachers noticed that the focus had changed from "How is my child doing in school?" to "What are the children thinking and doing in school?" To the teachers, that represented a major shift in parents' thinking.

Making Visible Our Values Regarding Parent Participation

In a sense, all these small stories shared the element of making visible how much we valued and gained from parent participation in the life of our school. This visibility seemed multi-layered. Highly visible to the eye were the photos of all families carefully displayed in children's cubbies and in the portfolios. The many ways that family contributions are acknowledged in newsletters, on parent boards, and in notes sent home communicated this value as well. Less visible to the eye, but perhaps closer to the heart, were the many encounters that led to closeness between families and the school. Parents commented that children model what they see and feel. One parent said, "In observing the close relationship between the teacher and their parents, children learn a valuable lesson about life. If the adults in their lives show cooperation and respect, so will the children."

Parents participated with teachers in observing, interpreting, and reflecting on the children's work not only because the work was so interesting and engaging, but also because the teachers assumed a position of expectation that parents would want to participate. One parent commented, "The teacher expects me to come and I want to see and understand the work of my child and his friends."

Two years after beginning this way of working with parents, we had the opportunity to invite some parents to serve on a panel at a local early childhood conference. The topic for the panel was, "Parents in the Life of the School." With much passion, the parents described their roles and relationships within our school. At the conclusion of their presentation, a member of the audience asked, "Won't so much participation encourage parents to be more critical of the school?" One of the parents on the panel replied, "If I am critical of the school, I am critical of myself!" She valued and had experienced a sense of "we" in her interactions in the school. She had developed shared ownership with the teachers for what happened in our school.

Our goal continues to be that all parents experience this same sense of belonging and purpose. We know that this way of working together must be constantly negotiated and nurtured. As Loris Malaguzzi said, "We think of school as a sort of construction in motion, continuously adjusting itself" (Malaguzzi, 1993, p. 56). Our construction continues!

REFERENCES

Dahlberg, G., Moss, P., & Pence, A. (1999). *Beyond quality in early childhood education and care: Postmodern perspectives.* Philadelphia, PA.: Falmer Press.

Fontanesi, G., Gialdini, M., & Soncini, M. (1998). The voice of parents. In C. Edwards, L. Gandini & G. Forman, (Eds.), *The hundred languages of children: The Reggio Emilia approach—advanced reflections* (pp. 149–157). Norwood, NJ: Ablex.

Forman, G. & Fyfe, B. (1998). Negotiated learning through design, documentation, and discourse. In C. Edwards, L. Gandini, & G. Forman (Eds.), *The hundred languages of children: The Reggio Emilia approach—advanced reflections* (pp. 239–260). Norwood, NJ: Ablex.

Fraser, S. (2000). *Authentic Childhood*. Scarborough, Ontario: Nelson Thomson Learning.

Gambetti, A. (1999). Remarks to Cherry Valley Invitational Conference. Granville, Ohio.

Malaguzzi, L. (1993). History, ideas and basic philosophy. In C. Edwards, L. Gandini, & G. Forman (Eds.), *The hundred languages of children: The Reggio Emilia approach—advanced reflections* (pp. 41–89). Norwood, NJ: Ablex.

National Standards for Parent/Family Involvement Programs (1998). Chicago, IL: National PTA.

Rinaldi, C. (January 1998). Speech to Winter Institute in Reggio Emilia. Italy.

Seidel, S. (1998). Learning from looking. In N. Lyons (Ed.), *With portfolio in hand: Validating the new teacher professionalism*. New York: Teachers College Press.

Wasow, E. (2000). Families and schools: New lenses, new landscapes. In N. Nager & E. K. Shapiro (Eds.), *Revisiting a progressive pedagogy: The developmental-interaction approach* (pp. 275–290). Albany, NY: State University of New York Press.

Wheatley, M. J. & Kellner-Rogers, M. (1996). *A simpler way*. San Francisco: Berrett-Koehler Publishers, Inc.

A Journey to Recast the Reggio Emilia Approach for a Middle School

A Pedagogy of Relationships and Hope

Lynn T. Hill

For three years, I worked alongside a group of devoted and forward-thinking teachers at Blacksburg Middle School in Blacksburg, VA, as we attempted to rethink the Middle School experience. Our shared goal was to find a way to recast the Reggio Emilia approach to inform the teaching and learning in their school. The group consisted of thirteen teachers, one administrative assistant, two university support persons (of which I was one), and one parent. While dedicated to our belief that children (and teachers) deserve an educational setting that is respectful, interesting, challenging, and joyful, we found that the hard part was circumnavigating all the road blocks and barriers in the way of innovation. Some of the more difficult aspects of bringing our project to fruition will be shared in this chapter and include: finding the time and energy to devote to our cause, achieving a community of philosophy and practice, negotiating with administrators, attending to complaints from outside faculty members, and justifying our innovation to families and influential community members.

 I was completely captured by this experience and by the passion and imagination of the teachers who committed themselves to the effort. My own Reggio Emilia-inspired philosophy and my interest in the possibility of "bottom-up" school reform combined to guarantee that I would be an eager and willing participant in the journey. A careful review of this three-year inquiry tells the story of the beginning of an innovation and the process that led to it becoming a shared goal for school reform. Along the way we found that careful attention must be given to the multi-layered context which will affect the growth and development of an innovation. Personal issues, the leadership in the school, and community politics each played a role in this complicated and complex process.

The Personal Context

For our group, we found that the personal context included family responsibilities, life changes, dispositions of the members, time, and the ability to collaborate. For this group of hardworking teachers, life is a constant juggle. To add to the juggle and challenges, the work and devotion necessary to reform education at the only Middle School in a highly influential and competitive town complicates one's life enormously. In addition, within a group of this size it is inevitable that there will be unexpected personal setbacks. During the course of our work together, one or more of the group weathered the death of a family member, an illness of a husband, a mother-in-law who moved in with the family, and a miscarriage. Other life changes were more joyful, such as weddings, pregnancies, and births; but also brought pause to the progress of the group's work. Trying to juggle the responsibilities of teacher, mother, wife, daughter-in-law, grandmother, and reformer is much like "trying to change the tires while driving the car" (Meier, 1995, p. 151). The dispositions of these special educators kept us driving despite the occasional flat tire. We were, by our own definition, thick-skinned, passionate, and risk-takers. But we were also human, and, although extremely talented, had not yet mastered the ability to increase the number of hours in a day. So, time (or the lack of) was a major deterrent in the work of our group. In addition to these stumbling blocks, we discovered that we were skillful at cooperation, but that our ability to truly collaborate was not as finely tuned. Viewing the innovation through this complex personal context was an important component in helping us to understand what it takes to initiate and implement change.

The Leadership in the School Context

The context of leadership in the school had a decided impact on our group of reformers. A traditional hierarchy exists in most school systems, and it is fairly uncommon for teachers to initiate an educational reform effort. Most restructuring occurs in a "top-down" mode. These teachers attempted to cross the traditional boundaries in the system and were suggesting a "bottom-up" innovation. A careful look at the response from the school's leaders was important, as the status quo in the school had been shaken. Sensing that we were treading on fragile ground, we were cautious and planned carefully for each interaction with the principals.

In particular, the principals expressed concerns regarding the plans coming from the reform group. The primary concern was how the rest of the faculty might react to this attempt to change the way of schooling and education at Blacksburg. This topic was debated at each meeting with the principals. This careful attention, by the principals, to the dynamics in the school was another important issue that must be attended to when change is being considered.

The Community Politics Context

Blacksburg had enjoyed a reputation in the county for being innovative and forward-thinking. In the late 1980s, Blacksburg was the first junior high in the region to make an effort to adopt a middle school philosophy and to realign some of its practices to mirror the new philosophy. They have been proud of their teaming approach, of their no-bell system, and of their responsive scheduling. In several classrooms, teachers have adopted constructivist approaches with great success. "History Alive" curriculum supplemented traditional instruction and hands-on, interactive experiences were found in many classrooms in the school. In 1998, when the State Standards of Learning (SOLs) were initiated in Virginia schools, Blacksburg was forced to follow the mandate. There were no immediate concerns about this new requirement, but soon the media began telling the story of punitive consequences should a school fail to pass the standardized tests. About the same time, Blacksburg was becoming enthused by a new math curriculum called Core Plus. This integrated system of math promoted a constructivist approach to teaching and learning, and it was highly acclaimed by the math teachers at Blacksburg. The Central Office supported the new math system as did the principals at Blacksburg. So it came as a surprise to teachers and administrators when the school came under siege from discontented community members due to the fact that this nontraditional math curriculum had been adopted at the school. A public war was waged in the newspapers and at school board meetings. Angry parents voiced concern that their child would not be "ready" for high school with this "watered-down" math curriculum. Parents, fearful for their child's future, demanded that the school reconsider and reinstate the traditional program. Teachers and principals bore the brunt of this onslaught and reputations were diminished in the community. This shifting context had a decided impact on the reform effort at Blacksburg and was also explored as we tried to make sense of our processes.

HOW IT ALL BEGAN

Travel as a Conduit to Change

After years of hearing and reading about the schools in Reggio Emilia, Italy, I have had the privilege and pleasure to travel there on four occasions. Participation in the formal Study Institutes and living in and among the culture for approximately two weeks during each trip gave me a glimpse into a system of care and education that seemed unsurpassed in other areas of the world. During each trip I would spend considerable time studying and reflecting on what I saw, heard, and felt in the schools and in the city. Each time I was intent upon finding ways to reinvent the approach for the children, teachers, and families back home. Some changes have been made in the Virginia Tech Child Development Lab School where I work, but they have often been cosmetic—like the revamping of the environment. Other changes have been more purposeful and thoughtful—like the attention to the planning and vision of curriculum and the crafting of both beautiful and meaningful systems of documenting the children's processes and the life in the school. But still a piece seemed to be missing. When I read Howard Gardner's (1998) foreward in the second edition of *The Hundred Languages of Children,* I began to have a sense of that missing piece. Gardner helped me to identify the missing component—true community collaboration. Cooperation, support, and trust among a group of people is a rare experience. In our fast-paced society and in our schools, we have little time or patience for sharing ideas, cementing relationships, and achieving intersubjectivity. This special, sometimes unspoken, understanding among people who work and/or live closely takes time, energy, commitment, and skill. I, for one, have had very few opportunities to practice this skill of being a contributing member of a learning community.

The people who work in and for the schools in Reggio Emilia have been able to achieve something extraordinary together. Their commitment to children and to one another has enabled them to find ways to overcome adversity and to reach a level of early education that our children in the United States deserve as well. What would it take to achieve the level of experience that Gardner speaks of? What are the dispositions of the individual members of such a collaborative? What support factors would be necessary?

Sergiovanni has defined communities as being made up of "relationships of people who work in the same place (community of place), feel a sense of belonging and obligation to one another (community of friendship) and are committed to a common faith or set of values (community of mind)" (Sergiovanni, 1992, p. 63). This chapter tells the story of a group of teachers who were struggling to become a viable community based on Sergiovanni's definition. Their *hope* was that upon achieving this important status that they would then be able to provide a more meaningful education for the children in their care.

> Hope is definitely not the same thing as optimism. It is not the conviction that something will turn out well, but the certainty that something makes sense, regardless of how it turns out. It is hope, above all, that gives us strength to live and to continually try new things, even in conditions that seem hopeless. (Havel, 1993).

The History of the Project

This story really began in May 1997, after I returned from my second trip to Reggio Emilia, Italy. As always, I had been taken by the concept of collaboration and community that was so evident in their schools. But this time it became clear to me that this feature seemed to be the fundamental premise on which these world-acclaimed schools were built. The idea was played out in all aspects of the school. The buildings were designed to afford opportunity for conversation and meeting by thoughtfully placing a large and open piazza in the entry of the school. Here, I saw parents gathering to chat in the mornings, teachers meeting to collaborate about a lesson, and children laughing and playing and working on projects together. The strong bond and relationship was also obvious when you observed the documentation of stories about school events that were artfully and respectfully hung for all to see, revisit, and reflect upon. This form of communication in the schools seemed to serve to inform, to educate, and to build community pride. In addition, the curriculum was designed with the use of the "progettazione" which loosely translates "to project." Through the school projects, children, teachers, family members, and community members all worked together to explore and investigate a concept and then to document the process of coming to understand. In this way the progettazione offers the opportunity for all members of the school to work together to visualize and extend an idea. Many other strategies were in place that seemed to work together to create a place where interrelationships were fundamental. And because of this central emphasis, everyone seemed to thrive. Teacher-reported satisfaction was enormously high, with the average turnover in teachers occurring every 17 years! Children thrived and looked forward to the interest-based learning that sprang from the projects, and parents felt that they were true partners in their child's education.

I found myself plotting and pondering regarding this collaborative and amiable environment; I felt a strong desire to recreate this feeling back home. A small plan of possibility began to hatch then. Upon returning to Virginia Tech I discovered that the university had just announced that one of its seven missions would be to create what they were calling "a community of learners." I wasn't sure what that was, but I liked the term and what it implied so I pitched my idea to a couple of colleagues in my department. We took the idea to the Provost and she liked it, too, and so the Great Duck Pond Project was born.

The Great Duck Pond Project

There's a magical duck pond just over the hill from our lab school on the Virginia Tech campus. It's a place where residents from our small town gather all year round. Children feed the ducks, athletes run by, students study or ice skate, families picnic, and others of us sit and watch the happenings. It is at this special community focal point that the seed for the Reggio Emilia approach began to grow in our town.

The Great Duck Pond Project became a community project where teachers from preschool, elementary school, the Blacksburg Middle School, the Blacksburg High School, and several university professors came together to think about curriculum. We studied the Reggio Emilia approach together and began to imagine how we might use the duckpond as the impetus for a large community progettazione. Everyone committed to the project for one year and launched into various aspects of studying the pond and contributing to the communities' body of knowledge. Soon, each of the teachers in our collaborative, along with the children in their classes, were working on fascinating and authentic projects that had been inspired by the duck pond and the individual interests of the children.

The Great Duck Pond Project, summer 1997.

The following are examples of some of the projects. The lab school children chronicled the experience of a female mallard that laid her eggs on their playground. A mixed-age group of elementary school children got excited about the historical significance of the pond and wrote, directed, and starred in a play based on their research. At the Blacksburg Middle School, a group of sixth graders became the self-proclaimed stewards of the pond and dove into environmental projects that were aimed at cleaning up the pond and surrounding areas. The seventh graders decided to write a book of stories about the pond and set up a hot line and a website where people could share their humorous, romantic, and adventurous stories. The Blacksburg High School was also involved with a chemistry class doing advanced water-testing research and a photography class creating a gorgeous video. On campus, an Environmental Art class used the duckpond as their palette and produced a fascinating display that the town was talking about for months.

About mid-way through our year together, there was another opportunity to visit Reggio Emilia with the Lugano-Reggio Collaborative. Because the middle-school teachers, in particular, had been experiencing great success with their new brand of curriculum, two of them asked to join our delegation. And so in January 1998, we traveled together to Italy for two weeks. This time, as I toured and studied the approach, I looked at it with different eyes. Because of my new liaison with the middle-school teachers, Gretchen Distler and Carol Fox, I began to think about the application for this age group. We spent 14 days together talking and plotting and pondering.

Middle School participation

High School participation

University Student participation

It was an incredible experience for me and by the time we were ready to come home, the teachers were certain that they could make this approach happen at the Blacksburg Middle School.

The teachers had also been inspired by the concept of community that they had seen in the schools in Reggio Emilia. They longed to establish "relationships of respect and care" (Hargreaves & Fullen, 1998, p. 31) with their students because they realized that this would be the basis for intellectual as well as social development. Smaller class sizes, group project work, and collaborating teachers were pieces of their vision for a restructured system. They were already calling their effort "The Revolution" and were inspired and enthusiastic and couldn't wait to share it with their colleagues.

Once back home, the duck pond group continued to meet, and at the close of the school year the group put together a museum exhibit and a video about the collaborative project. The town's local television station aired the video and the exhibit

Once back home, the work began in earnest, spring 1998.

was displayed at the local Natural History Museum for the summer. The Reggio Emilia approach was becoming more widely known and understood in our town. The middle-school teachers decided to officially launch their "revolution" on the day after school was released for the summer. Their hope was that they would begin to share their understanding with others over the course of the summer and then see what the response was. If there was enough support, they hoped to be able to develop a "school within a school" at Blacksburg. My goal was to follow and to offer support to this group of middle-school teachers as they moved through the process of planning for change and curricular revision.

An Invitation to Reform

"Are you interested in working toward a 'Reggio-inspired' system?" This bold question was emblazoned across the top of the flyer that was placed in every mailbox in Blacksburg Middle School on May 20, 1998. Teachers, administrators, custodial staff, and cafeteria workers were all invited to the first meeting of the revolution that was scheduled to be held on the day after school was released for the summer. The two teachers who had recently returned from Italy were ready to launch their hopeful reform effort by sharing information with their colleagues. They had already approached their principal with their idea of creating a separate Reggio-inspired "school within a school." The principal had supported their enthusiasm for the Reggio philosophy and had suggested that they should go ahead and share their thoughts with other personnel. "When 10 people are on board and knocking at my door, I'll call the superintendent of schools and we'll see what we can do about accommodating your ideas," he told the teachers. And so they were ready to pitch their ideas to a gathering of potentially interested colleagues. Because they hoped for a strong turnout of committed persons at that first meeting, they used an introductory flyer to describe a possible "Reggio-inspired system." The flyer read:

This means that you may~

❀ Enjoy working collaboratively with students and other adults in a shared space.

❀ Encourage students to think about what something is not.

❀ Encourage students to think about what something could be.

❀ Encourage students to think about reciprocal relationships.

❀ Help students reframe the mundane and the ordinary.

❀ Emphasize in-depth knowledge of complete systems.

❀ Model on the adult level the kinds of democratic participation, collaborative learning, and conflict resolution you are trying to teach students.

❀ Allow students to question and analyze each other's work.

❀ Help students turn differences of opinion into problem-solving opportunities.

❀ Trust the students to debate among themselves to closure.

❀ Dispense occasions that challenge students intellectually and emotionally.

❀ Assume the perspective of a researcher.

❀ Find in yesterday's notes the problems to pose today.

❀ Encourage students to work and rework representations of their learning.

❀ Treat all answers as derivatives of a logic to be understood.

❀ Allow students slow, unhurried time.

❀ Learn from students as they try to learn from you.

❀ Value long-term study projects developed through inquiry and emergent curriculum.

❀ Understand the role of the environment to the learning process.

❀ Welcome and seek community and parent involvement.

❀ Be extremely flexible and open.

There were 23 people in attendance at that first meeting, including teachers, a guidance counselor, an assistant principal, three university faculty, and several community members. Three young students of the middle-school teachers were also there and their presence reminded us all of why we were choosing to spend our summer vacations thinking about school reform. The first meeting was spent in trying to frame the philosophy for the less informed members of the group. There was considerable debate and some misunderstandings as we struggled to share our dream of what might be accomplished at the middle-school level. By the end of the meeting it was quite obvious that this would not be a quick process, but rather would be one that would require a sizeable commitment of time and devotion to the cause.

The group continued to meet on a regular basis. Agendas for the meetings usually included philosophical discussions and problem-solving sessions. There were numerous issues that would have to be discussed before we could all feel confident that we were ready to proceed. Some of the dilemmas considered at length were: How would children be selected for inclusion in this system? Where would this special system be housed? Which teachers would be included? How would the daily schedule work? How would this shift in schedule impact the greater school community? How would children be evaluated in this new system? What does "looping" look like in a middle school? How would this new system work in conjunction with the State SOL standards? How do we go about informing families? How would we evaluate the overall system? The questions seemed to be never-ending and the answers were not readily available. It was obvious to us that we were in for a long haul and that we had much to accomplish.

Meanwhile, a small committee of the teachers began to make a concerted effort to set up a conducive environment in one area of the large middle school. In a large, open room with high ceilings and concrete floors and lots of windows affectionately known as "The Big Room," the teachers began to imagine a wonderful piazza/studio space. Meeting on weekends, they began to paint and to organize. They procured cast-off shelving from a shop that was going out of business and started to stock them. Orchids were hung in the windows and some areas were designated for documentation spaces. This process of rolling up our sleeves together to accomplish something that was a bit more tangible than our previous emphasis on the philosophical component of our project was highly rewarding for the group. It seemed to keep us motivated and enthused in the wake of the lengthy process of coming to a shared philosophy of mind.

Next, our group decided to organize a mini-retreat where we would work together to determine all of our concerns, to make a plan of action to solve problems, and to form committees to address the issues. From this time together we ended up with eight committees that would then work together to thoroughly research each issue and subsequently bring suggestions for solutions to the larger group. Committees included: Assessment, Community Outreach, Family Involvement, Supporting Theories, Professional Development, Scheduling and Student Enrollment, Physical Plant Needs, and Curriculum. In addition to the work that would come from these committees, we knew that we needed to have a position paper that would state our shared understanding and philosophy for this effort. We knew that such a document must be carefully worded as it would no doubt be scrutinized by those who had the power to approve or disapprove our intention.

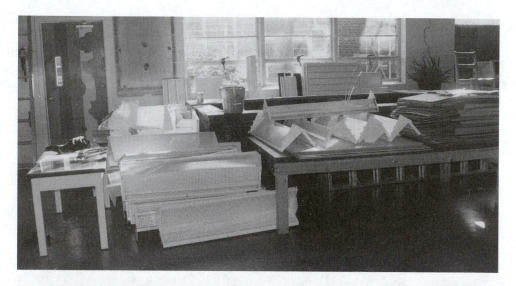

Building studio space

Lella Gandini Arrives on the Scene

Lella Gandini was in town for a series of lectures and symposiums, and she agreed to meet with our group of "revolutionaries." As she walked into the "Big Room," it was absolutely glowing. The 100 plus orchid plants that hung from pots in the large bank of windows were beginning to bloom, the fish pond filter gurgled gently in the back-

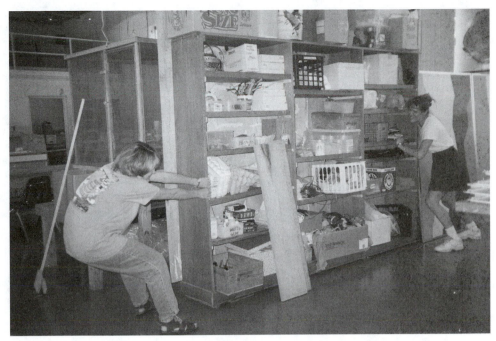

Building studio space

ground, and our large plywood table was covered with a tablecloth and child-made centerpieces. The enormous and blooming jade plant stood majestically on a large table in the room and was surrounded by pumpkins in a variety of shapes, sizes, and colors. Lella took one look at the space and said, "Oh my, this is a surprise. From the outside of the building I never would have guessed that I would find such a place inside." She proceeded to wander all around the room, stopping and touching and admiring many aspects. When she entered an adjacent classroom, she drew another breath. Suspended from the ceiling were hundreds of origami swans that had been crafted by the children over the years. These swans were subtly lit by the soft glow of lamps placed here and there in the room. Small groupings of tables included centerpieces and the typical bulletin boards had been transformed into gorgeous and respectful documentation spaces that boasted about the process of projects.

After Lella's leisurely tour around the space, we all sat down around the lovely table and began our conversation. Lella began by saying, "I am very impressed by the space and the energy that you are putting into this project. I am interested in hearing from you what aspects of Reggio you are finding appropriate for this age group. Children of this age sometimes have a very difficult time and sometimes are exhilarated by life, so there are these discontinuities that are very interesting but also very challenging."

The remainder of this special meeting was spent considering Lella's question. Somehow she had asked the exact question that we needed to be able to articulate in

Celebrating the process of learning

order to fashion our position statement. She urged us to "find a shared language or idea or it will be very difficult to move together." She was also adamant that we ensure our entire process was carefully documented as it might assist others whose struggle would come after ours. At the end of the meeting, Lella said, "You have provided fantastic hope for me." This was a very powerful statement and one that had a great impact on our small group of "revolutionaries." We were simultaneously touched by her sentiment and more determined than ever to continue our efforts on behalf of middle-school-aged children.

More Obstacles, More Solutions

In the following months, our group buckled down and began to meet in small committee groups to report our findings and suggestions to the larger group at our semimonthly meetings. Our base of operations had been moved, and we were now meeting in the evenings at a coffee shop where we had commandeered a small room with red walls and declared it "revolution central." Even though we were moving forward with the "obstacle and solution" part of our work, we were still bogged down in our efforts to write the position paper. We were uncertain as to how to begin to write such a "foreign" piece of prose. We had not had experience in this realm and we were much

An inspirational visit from Lella Gandini, fall 1998.

more comfortable with considering curriculum and scheduling issues. But still, the administration urged us to accomplish this very important task before they could begin to consider their full support of our project. As much as we wanted the "go ahead" for this effort, we could not seem to hurdle this particular barrier. Winter was upon us already and there had been several personal setbacks within the group. Finally, we had to admit that we would never be ready to open the doors of our new and improved middle school by the following fall. This admission was crushing but was tempered by our insistence that we did not want to risk falling on our faces by beginning with anything that was not our very best work. So we redoubled our efforts and committed to focusing on what needed to be accomplished.

Meanwhile, the State Standards of Learning were getting lots of press in our area of the state during this phase of our work. In addition, the new math program that had been adopted the previous year had come under attack from a very vocal group of parents and community members. These additional issues had a strong impact on the work of our group. We realized that we needed to learn from those who had gone before us, and so we decided that we needed to be able to articulate how our Reggio-inspired middle school would also meet state standards. So, one night at our coffee shop, we organized a session where we would take a long, hard look at the SOLs and a long, hard look at the brand of curriculum that we were suggesting and we would try to determine if these areas could be meshed. We came together that night thinking that this would be one of the tougher assignments that we had given ourselves. Much to our surprise (and delight) we found that when the standards were considered in an integrated way, as opposed to in an isolated fashion, there were multiple ways to ensure that required concepts were "uncovered." After this session, we felt confident that we could teach in this rich and integrated way and that we could also articulate our understanding.

Next, in an effort to assist in organizing our work and our thinking, I interviewed each member of the "revolution," each administrator, and several additional teachers who worked in the school but who had chosen not to participate in the effort. During the interviews we discussed each person's:

- ❀ Previous experience with innovation
- ❀ Description of the leadership style at the school
- ❀ Personal appeal for the Reggio Emilia approach
- ❀ Vision for the reform effort
- ❀ Impressions regarding roadblocks to the reform
- ❀ Ideas for the next steps in this effort

After organizing and categorizing the results of these interviews and using what we had learned from our friends in Reggio Emilia, we crafted a beautiful document of our shared knowledge and then gathered together at the coffee shop for a formal focus group. Together we reviewed the comments that had been shared during the interviews, noted some themes, and made some new plans for our next steps. Above all we noted that we certainly had attained a shared community of place and friendship, but as long as we still did not have a position paper, we could not claim a shared com-

An attempt to blend the SOLs with Reggio Philosophy, winter, 1999

munity of mind (Sergiovanni, 1992). So, "Write the Position Paper" was at the top of our list of things to do.

Since the summer months were now upon us, the teachers had more time to devote to our cause and we stepped up our efforts. Finally, in mid-July, we were looking at the latest draft of the position paper. We were thrilled with this accomplishment that had taken over a year to achieve, but we knew that our next step would be to convince the administration to approve our request to get started. We planned a meeting with the administrators for early August.

The administrators were receptive but cautious during this meeting. They were certainly gun shy from having just weathered some substantial backlash due to the math debates, and they wanted to be completely certain that they would not be walking into another ambush. They asked lots of "nuts and bolts" questions and encouraged us to present a more detailed plan at the next meeting. Our group then went back to the drawing board and put together a beautiful presentation about the Reggio Emilia approach and what it would look like in a middle-school environment. The presentation included PowerPoint, handouts, and documentation. All of our work had been put together in a handbook format that included detailed accounting of multi-aged grouping, small collaborative units, teachers as collaborators, the role of the environment, seminar-based instruction, documentation and representation of understanding and assessment, portfolio assessment, and family participation. This presentation was polished and thoughtful and the administrators sat up and took

An analysis of our work to date—discovering that we had a strong community of place and of friendship but that we lacked a community of mind (Sergiovanni, 1992).

notice. In the coming months we would also meet with county-wide faculty to share our vision and finally with the superintendent of schools. Having a background in school reform, our superintendent wanted to ensure that we had considered the many possible problem areas before launching our plan. It was at this point in our proceedings that our principal, Gary McCoy, declared how impressed he was with the dedication and intensity of the effort and noted that he had personally developed a "deeper sense of respect and obligation for our group and for the project." We had finally come to a place where we were expanding our community to include others whose expertise and wisdom would only strengthen our effort.

The Reggio-inspired middle school did begin in the fall of 2000. We began small, with a group of 150 sixth, seventh, and eighth grade students whose teachers shared common planning and visioning time. The integrated curriculum has been co-designed by teachers and students to meet state regulations as well as to inspire a joy for learning! Students are brainstorming topic options, working collaboratively, self-assessing their progress, and most importantly, finding the learning process to be exciting and inspirational. While the road has been long, we feel that we have only begun our journey.

> Collaboration: "A dynamic conjunction of forces and elements interacting toward a common purpose" (Malaguzzi, 1993).

MAKING SENSE OF THE JOURNEY

Dispositions and Attitudes of the Reformers

A question that begs to be answered here is, "How and why did the revolutionaries continue the effort although they faced multiple barriers thrown in their path?" Certainly, the attitudes and dispositions noted during the interviews and subsequent focus groups contain a partial answer to the question. These teachers "don't start what they can't finish," they are "passionate," "have a love for teaching and learning," "they work well under pressure," "they are not satisfied with the status quo," "they see possibility and have hope for the future," and they "are devoted to public education." In addition to these traits, they have achieved a sense of commitment and responsibility to one another and to the cause. They have struggled to attend every meeting, even though they've been tired and it would mean that they would get less sleep that night. They believed in each other and in their shared hope for a better system of schooling and education for the kids that they teach. They've had long conversations about social justice issues. They've agonized over the enrollment question (opt-in or opt-out). Their dedication to *all* children comes through in everything they say, do, write, and teach. In addition, they *like* each other. Although the meetings and the work of the movement took time from the other priorities in their lives, there was a magical aura in the room when this group was together. There was always a lot of laughter and good, natured teasing. They always began their time together with food, drink, and bantering conversation. They kept track of each other in a kind, sisterly way. They knew when birthdays and anniversaries were being celebrated. They planned baby showers and filled each other's freezers when times were tough. Several of them got together on a regular basis to do large chores at each other's homes. They were always talking about fixing a drainspout, seeding a lawn, or polyurethaning a deck. Finally, they shared a dream for this reform. When they eventually chose the symbol of the dreamcatcher as the logo for their movement, it was highly symbolic of their disposition of hope. One teacher wore a pin to one of the most recent meetings that said "Dreams are Hope." This thought seems to capture the essence of why they have stayed in the race, even though the hurdles have been plentiful and high.

Implications for Value in Other Settings

It is important to think of this story as an example and not as a model (Meier, 1995). There really can't be one way of progressing through a school restructuring process. As has been shown, the individual context in which the effort is attempted must be considered. However, summarized here are some of the lessons that we have learned from our own journey.

LESSONS LEARNED

Hurdling the Personal Barriers

The teachers who participated in the reform effort gave voice to several themes during the course of their 15 months together. One loud and clear anthem was obvious—they believed that a better system of public education was possible for their students and for themselves. This sentiment was reflected in the many, many hours of precious personal time that they were willing to give to this endeavor. A conflicting theme seemed to be that, "There are multiple forces that are out of our control that work in opposition to our best efforts." As we met together to talk, to plan, and to take action these forces would repeatedly be mentioned. There were not enough hours in the day or days in the week to devote to this work. Personal life changes and responsibilities often ate up the few excess hours that a busy teacher–mother–reformer might have to offer to the cause. Pregnancies, births, deaths, and accidents all took their toll on the group's ability to sustain focused attention over time. The myriad of extra work at school also demanded the time and energy of the group. Parent conferences, SOL testing, meetings regarding building or math issues demanded their attention. Time, or rather, the lack of time, proved to be the most frustrating roadblock during this process.

It is imperative that a community of place, friendship, and mind (Sergiovanni, 1992) be established within a group that attempts to restructure schools. As we found, this process cannot be rushed but needs to be savored. When a group of people share an intersubjectivity at each of these levels, then the commitment to one another and to their shared cause will be a powerful force to be reckoned with. In addition, the new allegiance and collaboration builds an attitude of courage within the group that will buoy them as they move toward opposition with a shared purpose, passion, and power. We suggest that a group might build this system of community through tangible work together, committee efforts around a shared problem, and extended time spent together during retreats, meetings, problem-solving sessions, etc.

Identifying funding support to "buy time" may prevent some of the exhaustion, guilt, and unhealthy compromises that might be made during such an effort. Stipends for outside research, paid planning time, or "duty" buyouts might assist the teacher–mother–reformer in her constant juggle of priorities as well as provide a sense of appreciation for the extra work that is being accomplished on behalf of the school.

Hurdling the Leadership Barriers

Each principal made it known that the peaceful co-existence within the school was a high priority for them. In this spirit we were asked to rethink many of our initial plans. The term "revolution" needed to be dropped because it might serve to ostracize others from the group of reformers. We were also cautioned to diminish the emphasis on how *different* this experience might be from all the good work that was already going on in the school. And we were advised that we could not expect teachers from outside the effort to be open to the suggestion of trading classroom space in order to give our small contingency proximity to one another. The administrators informed us that they spent a lot of time and energy ensuring that their large faculty felt safe and secure within their school system and that quick and sudden changes might "rock the boat."

While a certain level of dissonance is necessary for innovative change to occur, too much anxiety can also work against you. Heifetz suggests that the "level of distress must stay within a tolerable range" (Heifetz, 1994). Stacey concurs and reminds us that "to contain such anxiety, an individual requires a strong ego structure and a good enough 'holding environment,' which is to be found in the groups to which the individual belongs" (Stacey, 1996, p. 188). In the case of Blacksburg Middle School, the recent brushes with very public dissention may have left a level of distress beyond the tolerable range and an insecure feeling about the "holding environment."

Hargreaves and Fullan discuss the plight of the administrator as change is attempted. Their primary premise is that risk must be harmonized with security. In these ideal moments, teachers and administrators can feel a sense of being trusted and valued and of not being afraid to fail. In these moments they are "keen and ready to experiment, to take risks, and to try new approaches" (Hargreaves & Fullen, 1998, p. 110). However, if there was an aura of insecurity coupled with uncertainty, as in the case at Blacksburg, then a sense of fear and hopelessness may begin to spread among the faculty. In this case the wise administrator must develop strong collaborative cultures among the staff in order to rebuild the sense of hope and security. Rectifying this unfamiliar position may take time and may be the reason that they cautioned the revolutionaries to "slow down" and be willing to take small steps toward change. Certainly this position is understandable and part of the shifting system of politics and power that has influenced this attempt at reform.

As noted, this work cannot take place out of context. The teacher's efforts are very much influenced by the attitude of support coming from the administration in the school. Although, there were times when the reform group felt stymied by the suggestions from the administrators, they had to admit that they needed this broader way of viewing the plan in order to meet with success. We learned that nurturing a partnership between administration and teaching staff on behalf of kids can be a way to join forces and to also share the load. All members need to work together to remove the historical attitudes, beliefs, and stigmas associated with traditional American schooling where principals lead and teachers follow. As our reformers have mentioned, each group (teacher and principal) comes to this work with a unique perspective. Certainly it will take all points of view to be successful. As our wise principal, Gary McCoy, said at one meeting: "Can we stop being 'us' and 'them' and start being 'we'?"

Hurdling the Community / Political Barriers

During the course of this project, several community-wide issues brought Blacksburg Middle School into the public limelight. Heated public debates occurred regarding whether or not a new middle school should be built, whether or not a new system of math instruction should be adopted at the school, and how SOLs would be instituted in the school. All of this public dissent took its toll on the reputation of the school and on the process of this reform effort.

Careful attention must be paid to countering any outside influences. We suggest that a reform group should broadcast the good work of the reform effort. Use the fine art of documentation in schools, libraries, museums, at school board meetings, and throughout the community to exemplify the kinds of experiences that are occurring in your school. Sometimes, community dissent occurs because of a lack of knowledge. Parents do not like to be ill-informed where their children are concerned. Give them every opportunity to hear about the changes in multiple ways. Invite family and community members to be a part of the initial planning phase.

In addition, we recommend engendering support from like-minded others. Use every opportunity to broaden your base of support. Find university faculty that will champion your cause, talk with school board members, put out a notice in the county teachers' newsletter, and find colleagues. Don't be shy and don't be fearful. Be passionate and courageous. Invite experts into the community. Sometimes it is easier for others to listen to those from outside their immediate association. Find a way to host a forum, a conference, a series of dialogs that promote your position. Share the information.

A New System of Middle-Schooling

Finally, a very important result of this project was the development of a new system of middle-schooling based on the lessons learned from the Reggio Emilia approach. Using the fundamental principles from the approach, the reformers found a way to recast for a middle-school population. Our vision includes multi-age groupings, collaborative team teaching, a student-selected, integrated studies approach that we have termed "seminars," a new system of assessment by portfolio and other alternative styles of evaluation, a careful attention to the documentation and representation of knowledge using multiple languages, and a commitment to family engagement within the educational process.

Finding the Moments of Opportunity

The past three years of work with the teachers from the Blacksburg Middle School in their attempt to restructure their system have been an honor and an education for me. As I have attempted to understand what it takes to restructure education for a small group in a middle school, I have come to realize that there are many harmonizing and conflicting forces at work. What has become clear through this study is that the interplay of power, politics, and personalities embedded in the process, proximal interaction, person, and time has the most significant effect on the development of the innovation.

It is difficult to predict the moment when the forces will be in alignment. Many of the processes, experiences, and interactions took place on different planes and in different contexts. As we moved through our own effort at Blacksburg, we never knew when a setback would occur—a teacher might have an ill family member, a principal might have just received a new ultimatum from the central office, a community rumor

The group's representation of their emotions upon achieving a community of place, friendship, and mind!

Members of the "Revolution" at the groundbreaking ceremony for the new Blacksburg Middle School.

(From L to R: Lynn Hill, Virginia Tech consultant/author; Vickie Fu, Virginia Tech consultant; Reba Hoffman, 8th grade math teacher; Belinda Rossi, 6th grade language arts teacher; Carol Fox, 7th grade language arts/social studies teacher; Gary McCoy, principal; Gretchen Distler, 6th grade language arts teacher; Nancy Koebel, special education teacher; Jamie Simmons, administrative aide; Colleen Prosser, 7th grade math/science teacher; not pictured: Suzan Mauney, 8th grade science teacher, Nora Kenney, 8th grade language arts teacher.)

might be brewing about education. Each context worked for and against the development of the innovation and was in constant flux. How then, could an effort such as the one described in these pages ever find success? Successfully achieving the goal may be a matter of doing the research, engendering support, readying the troops, *watching for the moments of opportunity and being ready to seize them when they arrive.*

> When you look back, you see a clear path that brought you here. But you created that path yourself. Ahead, there is only uncharted wilderness . . . In the final analysis, it is the walking that beats the path. It is not the path that makes the walk (De Gues, 1997).

AUTHOR'S NOTES

I would like to add a few words of deep appreciation to the teachers and administrators who allowed me to have a front row seat during the course of their struggle to change the face of education and schooling for the children in their care. Your passion and commitment to a just and meaningful school experience was inspirational and I remain in awe of the work that you do. Thank you for the honor and privilege of being your colleague and friend.

This chapter is based on a previously unpublished dissertation by the author entitled, *TeacherWork: A Journey to Recast the Reggio Emilia Approach for a Middle School within the Context of Power, Politics and Personalities.* For more information, contact the author.

The Great Duck Pond Video is available for distribution. Contact the author for more information.

REFERENCES

De Gues, A. (1997). *The living company.* Cambridge, MA: Harvard Business School Press.

Edwards, C., Gandini, L. & Forman, G. (Eds.)(1998). *The hundred languages of children: The Reggio Emilia approach—advanced reflections.* Greenwich, CT: Ablex.

Gardner, H. (1998). Foreword: Complimentary perspectives on Reggio Emilia. In Edward, C., Gandini, L. & Forman G. (Eds.), *The hundred languages of children: The Reggio Emilia approach—advanced reflections* (pp. xv–sviii). Greenwich, CT: Ablex.

Hargreaves, A. & Fullen, M. (1998). *What's worth fighting for out there?* New York: Teachers College Press.

Havel, V. (1993). *Never hope against hope.* Esquire, 65–69.

Heifetz, R. (1994). *Leadership without easy answers.* Cambridge, MA: Harvard University Press.

Malaguzzi, L. (1993). For an education based on relationships. *Young Children, 49,* 9–12.

Meier, D. (1995). *The power of their ideas.* Boston: Beacon Press.

Sergiovanni, T. (1992). *Moral leadership: Getting to the heart of school improvement.* San Francisco: Jossey-Bass.

Stacey, R. (1996). *Complexity and creativity in organizations.* San Francisco: Berrett-Koehler.

Chapter
8

An Outstanding Education for ALL Children: Learning from Reggio Emilia's Approach to Inclusion

Sharon Palsha

For more than a decade, Reggio Emilia's outstanding municipal schools and educational approach for young children have attracted the attention and careful study of tens of thousands of early childhood educators from around the globe. Until recently, what appears to have gone almost unnoticed in all this attention is how Reggio is able to foster both the cognitive and social development of not only typically developing children, but also of children with all types of disabilities (Edmiaston & Fitzgerald, 2000; Elgas & Peltier, 1998; Gandini & Gambetti, 1997a; Gandini & Gambetti, 1997b; Kaminsky, 1997; Smith, 1998). A move to embrace the Reggio philosophy offers us the opportunity to enhance the lives of ALL children and ALL families. In Reggio Emilia, children with disabilities are referred to as children with "special rights," and they are given top priority in enrollment. Whatever the disability, every single child with special rights in the town of Reggio Emilia is offered a spot in the municipal schools, beginning at the age of three months.

This chapter takes a look at the thirty-year history of educators and parents working together to provide a carefully planned, high-quality inclusive experience for children with special rights. The chapter opens with a look at the historical beginning of the inclusive movement, both in Italy in general and Reggio in particular. Reggio's approach to inclusion is presented within the context of their key principles, as a point of reference and to emphasize the fact that these principles form the backbone of their educational system for ALL children. It is critical to remember, however, that although presented separately, these "principles or fundamental ideas . . . must be considered as a tightly connected, coherent philosophy in which each point influences and is influenced by all others" (Gandini, 1993, p. 5). At the core is Reggio's image of the child as powerful and competent. Rich environments, meaningful relationships, purposeful documentation, and small group project work are also vital to the educational experience for children with special rights. Individualized instruction for children with special rights takes place within a group context and is captured and promoted through Reggio's hundred languages. The chapter also includes how children with special rights are identified and assessed, and how they and their parents make their entry into the early childhood programs. The role of the consultant responsible for children with special rights, the methods used to provide needed therapy, and the staff development activities that assist teachers in including the children with special rights in the regular programming are discussed and compared to practices in the United States. Case studies are woven throughout the chapter to illustrate the careful and deliberate planning that goes into supporting and promoting the development of children with special rights. The chapter closes with implications for inclusive practices in the United States. Information for the chapter draws from three visits to Reggio Emilia to observe children with special rights in the municipal schools, dialogues with the schools' pedagogisti, teachers, and atelieristas, and two presentations by Ivana Soncini, the psychologist who oversees the educational services of children with special rights.

HISTORICAL BEGINNINGS

Since the early 1970s, international organizations have pointed to Italian education for children with disabilities as the most inclusive in the world (Berrigan, 1994–95). The inclusion movement started in Italy in the early 1960s when the country began closing its state institutions for people with mental illness. This deinstitutionalization movement created a parallel movement within education as Italians began to address the segregation of children with disabilities in the public schools. At this time there were two contrasting viewpoints in Italy to educating children with disabilities. The first position held that children with disabilities needed specialization, which translated into providing education in a separate setting. The second position held that children with disabilities needed a renewed school that was willing to change in order to accept and incorporate all children and their uniqueness. Italy took a stand to commit to the latter position, and in 1971 passed its first national law (118/1971), mandating that compulsory education of children with disabilities ages 6–14 take place in regular public school classes (Cecchini & McCleary, 1985). In 1977, a second national law (517/1977) was passed that outlined specific provisions to support and help assure *integrazione*. The word integrazione, or integration, is used in Italy when the child with disabilities achieves good results at both the cognitive and social level and is not simply inserted within a regular classroom (Vianello, 1996). Today in the United States, early childhood professionals use the term inclusion as the translation for the Italians' integrazione. Within this chapter it is important that the reader understand that this is how the term inclusion is used. The 1977 law limited the number of children in an integrated class to 20, with a maximum of two children with disabilities per class. The law also required that a support teacher be assigned to work with each class in which a child with disabilities was enrolled and established that local responsibility for the children be shared between the public schools and the local health units (Cecchini & McCleary, 1985). The 1977 law also made it obligatory that young children with disabilities, ages 3–5 years, be included in Italy's public preschools. In 1992, further legislation specified additional strategies to support inclusion. This law emphasized that the purpose of inclusion was to develop the child's potential for learning, communication, and social relations. The overall result of the inclusive efforts in Italy is that today 98.5% of all children with disabilities attend regular classes (Vianello, 1996).

In the early 1960s, while deinstitutionalization was occurring throughout Italy, another important event was taking place in Reggio Emilia. The parent-run infant–toddler centers and preschools were moving under the jurisdiction of the town. The educators of Reggio Emilia took this event and the deinstitutionalization movement as offering them an historic opportunity to act on their philosophy for all children. The question they asked themselves was, "What does difference mean to us?"

> Are we talking about a difference that is defined as standing out, a difference that removes, separates, divides, or sets boundaries? Or are we talking about a difference that presents opportunities for building relationships and exchange? (Soncini, 1999).

Reggio's educators made the choice to view differences as an opportunity to explore the nature of change and to build relationships. In 1967, Reggio became the first public preschool system in Italy to include children with disabilities (Kaminsky, 1997). This inclusion of children with special rights provided Reggio's educators with a vision of a reformed school that was willing to act on behalf of all children. Believing every child, no matter his endowment, to be powerful and competent with the innate right to the best education society could offer, Reggio made a commitment to focus on the potential and capabilities of every child.

ENVIRONMENT AS THE THIRD TEACHER

A high-quality environment, with attention to space, organization, materials, and aesthetics, is crucial to Reggio Emilia's early childhood programs. In fact, the environment is often referred to as "the third teacher." In Reggio's decision to include children with special rights, director Loris Malaguzzi stated:

> There is a difference between a child who can be reduced or a child who can be amplified depending on the favorable or unfavorable aspects of his/her environment. The broader and more varied the range of offers, features, activities, relationships the broader the possibility for children (Soncini, 1999).

Reggio's educators wanted to invite children with special rights into their schools to benefit from the richness of the environment they would experience and the meaningful relationships they would build there.

AN EDUCATION BASED ON RELATIONSHIPS

Education through relationships is another important principle in Reggio's approach to early childhood. Relationships with and among parents, grandparents, peers, educators, and the citizens of Reggio Emilia are viewed as critical for all children who attend Reggio's programs. Other significant relationships that are important in the life of children with special rights include those with educational and medical specialists. A team of curriculum specialists called *pedagogisti* is assigned to work at four or five municipal schools, assisting the staff with their educational programming. In addition to these general curriculum specialists, one pedagogista, Ivana Soncini, has the job of overseeing all the children with special rights enrolled in the Reggio schools. Soncini also has the responsibility of working with all the parents and teachers of these children and coordinating the services of the physicians, therapists, and psychologists from the Local Health Administration (L.H.A.).

Identifying Children with Special Rights

In Reggio Emilia, as is true throughout other Italian towns, the L.H.A. is responsible for identifying children with special rights. Their assessment of the child typically includes standardized testing and neurological and psychological evaluations (McCleary, 1985). Often the health team provides the family with a diagnosis. A distinguishing feature of the Local Health Administration is the continued involvement and relationship with the child, family, and schools (McCleary, 1985). This contrasts quite dramatically with related service care in the United States. For example, in the state of North Carolina, as well as in many other states across our country, a child with disabilities and his/her family receive related services through one lead agency from the time the child is born to age three years. When the child has his/her third birthday, the child and parents receive related services from a second lead agency. When the child enters kindergarten, another change in related services takes place. In Reggio Emilia, these constant transitions do not occur and usually the same specialists remain on the related service team over a long period of time to provide continuity of services to the child and family (McCleary, 1985).

Once the Local Health Administration's assessment is complete, they provide Reggio with the names of all the identified children. Soncini makes it her responsibility to contact each and every family to welcome them and their child into the municipal schools. What is important in the Reggio system is that the school reaches out first and introduces itself to the family.

Assessing the Needs of Special Rights Children

Entry into Reggio's programs for any child is a long process, but even more so for the child with special rights. Typically, six months before their child starts school, parents complete an entry application. Parents receive notice of their child's acceptance in March. In April, children and their families have an opportunity to visit the school that they will be attending, in order to meet the teachers, see the classroom, and interact with the children currently in the room. For the children with special rights there is an even more purposeful attempt to get to know these children before they come to school. It is extremely important for Reggio educators to know the children beforehand as a way of ensuring a warm entry into the school community. Coming to school is often the child with special rights' first introduction into society outside of his/her family context or medical experience.

The school's initial assessment of the child with special rights begins with a teacher visiting the child at home and interviewing the parents. In Reggio, parents of all children are totally involved in the entry process and are interviewed about their child's likes, dislikes, interests, eating, and sleeping habits. At the initial meeting with parents of children with special rights, Reggio's educators say that they often find the families in a kind of mourning for all the things that their child cannot do. According to Reggio educators, the tests that the Local Health Administration have conducted can be useful, but they certainly are not valid for all aspects of the child and primarily give the school staff and parents information about what the child *cannot* do. In contrast, Reggio's educators are looking for what the child *can* do. What is important in the Reggio approach is to have families begin to see their child in a way that they may never have thought about. Soncini states, "Reggio's educators are looking for what the child can do in the context of a rich environment and meaningful relationships. In school we are looking for the context of all the possible worlds that the child can encounter" (Soncini, 1999). In the personal interviews with families, another important objective is to inform the parents of children with special rights that the schools exist as a service to their child and family. These families must understand that the right to quality education is just as important for their child as for any other child in Reggio Emilia.

Family involvement is considered an essential element of Reggio's pedagogical approach. Parents are involved in day-to-day work in the schools, discussions of educational issues, special projects, and celebrations. A parent advisory council at each school helps facilitate an active home–school partnership. When children with special rights enter school, a major effort is made to include the family. Teachers help the parents find activities to "help with, so that they feel they are contributing to the well-being of their child and the other children" (Soncini, in Smith, 1998, p. 203). All parents of children with special rights are networked with the other parents at the school through the regular parent meetings. These parents are also networked with other parents of children with special rights across the town of Reggio Emilia to provide an extra support system.

The assessment of children with special rights continues once they arrive at school. Teachers carefully observe children to find and document the traces of what catches the children's attention. Observation and documentation are fundamental to Reggio's work with all children, but are seen as a particular benefit for children with special rights. In meeting with these children, the teachers' highest responsibility is getting to know the child first, outside his/her disability. The educators are particularly looking for information that can help build relationships. Reggio's philosophy holds that all children at a very early age have the capacity to make meaning out of their world and that this meaning needs to be shared.

Reggio makes every attempt to enroll only one child with special rights in any given classroom. More than two children with special rights are never placed in one room. If it does become necessary to include two children, it is arranged that these two children never have the same diagnosis. This practice discourages comparisons being made between the children.

Another policy in place in Reggio is that, if needed, an extra staff person is hired for the class enrolling children with special rights. The purpose of this support teacher is not to work solely with the child with disabilities, but rather to work with the whole class. When a child with mild delays (for example, a child with Down syndrome) is placed in a room, the two classroom teachers may decide they do not have the need for a support teacher (Gandini & Gambetti, 1997b). Other classroom teachers may request help during the initial period of adjustment to a child with mild delays, and then the support teacher is phased out as the child adapts to the routines of the school. The option to have a support teacher is always available.

In addition to receiving top priority in enrollment, another privilege children with special rights receive is that their parents have the right to select the municipal school their child will attend. The choice is based on whatever the parents feel to be most appropriate for their child and family (Soncini, 1999). These choices can include the presence of friends, the physical structure of the school, or the convenience of the school's location. Soncini shared a story of a family who chose La Villetta preschool, a three-story villa with narrow staircases for their child who was blind (Soncini, 1999). Soncini admitted that she and the staff had reservations about this request, and therefore they asked the parents why they had made this selection. The parents responded, "We feel if our child learns to master La Villetta's environment under the careful guidance of the staff and children in the school, he will feel confident to tackle all other environments he encounters for the rest of his life." Working together, the school and parents were able to ensure a successful life experience for this child. The school exemplified the importance of being able to work with families and to see the capabilities and competencies of every child.

SMALL GROUP PROJECTS

Project work is another key component of the Reggio approach. Small groups of five to eight children spend large parts of the morning working on projects. The individualized attention in the small groups is particularly important for the child with special rights. According to Ivana Soncini, it is another key to providing educationally appropriate programming. The small groups make it more likely that the child will enjoy the process and be motivated to go back and try things again. "Our goal is that all children want to come to school and that they develop a sense of autonomy" (Soncini, in Smith, 1998, p. 206).

Soncini explains, "We want the child with special rights to become part of the classroom routine, working on projects, cleaning up, helping make lunch, and playing and learning to get along with children and adults. Children learn best in small groups and we want children to be seen by their parents as competent. We want the parents to see their child participating in exciting and interesting projects" (Soncini, 1998). "Our hope is that we can avoid negative comparisons and pay attention to the particular gifts and contributions of each individual child" (Soncini, in Smith, 1998, p. 203).

EDUCATIONAL PLANNING—THE HUNDRED LANGUAGES OF CHILDREN

Delegates interested in children with special rights who attend Reggio's study tours always seem to have particular interest in Reggio's approach to children with autism. One delegate during the 1998 Winter Institute asked Ivana Soncini the following question: "Given how important relationships are to your system of education, I would think that children with autism, who have a difficult time with relationships, must be particularly challenging for you. And for that reason, I was wondering whether you include children with autism in your schools?" Soncini, with great sensitivity, answered that the educators in Reggio believe all children are born with the desire and capacity to form relationships. She stated,

> It is the responsibility of the educational staff to discover for the children with special rights, including children with autism, where the potential for their relationships begins. If, after close examination, we are unable to discover a trace of a relationship, then this is where the hundred languages come in. It is the educators' job to offer the child a hundred different opportunities to discover the trace of his/her desire for a relationship, and if we still do not find it, then we offer the child a hundred more (Soncini, 1998).

Soncini went on to say that in her experience Reggio's educators have been able to find such traces in all the children who attend their schools.

At the 1999 Winter Institute, Soncini illustrated how the educators' close observation and documentation of children with special rights works to find the trace of the child's relationship, and how this discovery allows them to build an educational plan that leads to broader and deeper relationships and learning. Elisa, a three-year-old with autism, entered one of the infant–toddler centers that serves children three months to three years of age. When she arrived, Elisa constantly ran around the center of the room like a merry-go-round. This behavior was very disorienting for the teachers; therefore, the first thing they desired was to figure out how to stop it. But, Soncini pointed out, how this occurred had to be handled very carefully. What Soncini stressed was the need to get to know this little girl. As is true for every child, Elisa had important traces to capture, so the teaching staff began their research. The teachers allowed Elisa to continue her running, and as she did they closely observed. The teachers began to notice and document that Elisa actually did have brief moments when she would pause. Through their careful and purposeful observations that were documented in their notes, through video footage, and through slides, the teaching staff discovered that Elisa was attracted to bright light. When she saw a bright light reflecting on the wall she would stop and pay attention. When she passed by an aquarium with the light on, she would pause. On a field trip to a gym in town she was attracted by the light pattern created by the sun on the gym floor.

The staff made a game with lights flashing on Elisa. They poured colored water into a lighted container of clear water. They projected bright slides on the wall of the classroom, and put Elisa in front of the light table. The purpose of these activities was to see if they could capture Elisa's attention, and they did. With this identified, how could they use this information to go further with Elisa? They selected Adriana as the classmate with whom they would begin to nurture a special relationship with Elisa. They set up the opaque projector and Adriana began to draw with bright colored pens on a piece of acetate. This, too, captured Elisa's attention. Elisa joined Adriana at the opaque projector and began making her own marks on the acetate. Elisa began to notice the connection between her drawing at the projector and the drawing projected on the wall. Elisa had started to put her own research into place by making these connections. For Soncini and her teachers, Elisa seemed to understand that she could leave a mark of herself. For a child with autism, the teachers saw this as a great sense of accomplishment since these children seem to have a fragile sense of identity.

Elisa's attraction to sunshine at the window continued. The staff designed and built a large double-sided plexiglass easel that they placed next to the window. Elisa began to paint there. On the other side of the plexiglass easel the teachers placed Elisa's friend, Adriana, who had worked with her earlier at the opaque projector. Soncini pointed out that children with autism often have a great deal of difficulty looking at themselves in a mirror. Through this activity Elisa could begin to make the connection of identity with her painting movements and action mirrored by her companion on the opposite side of the plexiglass. Elisa now had her first symbolic language that she could begin to use in future investigations. The teachers introduced smaller and smaller drawing surfaces on which Elisa and her friend could draw. A slide captured Elisa and Adriana working on a very small surface, their shoulders touching. The final slide documented Elisa's engagement at the end of the school year. Elisa stood at the light table, piercing holes with a small pen point on a black sheet of paper attached to a wooden frame. For Reggio, this is just one example of how the teachers start from the signal of the child and use this signal in the course of his/her learning experiences within relationships among materials, teachers, and peers.

DECLARATION OF INTENT

One or two months into the school year, after a lengthy period of observation and documentation of a child with special rights, the teachers, school pedagogisti, health team, and parents come together and write a Declaration of Intent. This document is comparable to the United States Individualized Education Program (IEP) in that it specifies the child's educational goals and objectives. But more importantly in Reggio, the Declaration of Intent is a written document involving the input of the municipal schools, the health authorities, and the family, that is designed to ensure that everyone is in agreement about how the child and family will be supported.

A primary difference in our IEP and Reggio's Declaration of Intent is evident on the first page of the document. The primary heading on this page is *Mondo Relazionale*—"The World of Relationships," with subheadings *Relazione bambino/famigila, relazione bambino/adulto, relazione bambino/bambini*—The relationship of the child with his family, with other adults, and with other children. A lengthy narrative of two to three typed pages describes the relationship of the child with his/her family, with the Health Unit, with teachers, and with friends. This in-depth description of who the child is in relationship to other significant people in his/her life and his/her school is in stark contrast to the IEPs that are written in the United States that simply list the child's goals, objectives, and competency criteria.

Another primary heading of the Declaration of Intent is *Relazione Oggetti/Spazi*—"Relationship of Time and Space." Information included in this section of the document covers the child's relationship with the space in his/her classroom and spaces throughout the school. On the final pages of the Declaration, the projection for the year is outlined and includes goals not only for the child but also for the family, classmates, teachers, and the health service team who will support the education of the child. For example, in the case of a child who is deaf, a goal will describe how sign language instruction will occur for the teachers and the entire class of the child's peers.

The Declaration of Intent is a flexible document that involves ongoing consultation, participation, and cooperation with the families, teachers, and related service health unit professionals. Parents and teachers collaborate throughout the year to provide written documentation of the child's progress.

DOCUMENTATION

Documentation, which is standard practice at the Reggio schools, is another critical component for children with special rights. Documentation serves as the history and collective memory of the school, but for the parents of children with special rights it allows them to see what their children are investigating and to see their children in meaningful relationships. This is particularly important for those children who are unable to communicate verbally. In addition to the large documentation panels on the wall, every child in the center has an ongoing portfolio of photographs, written observations, anecdotal records of significant events, and samples of the child's work. Educators take a great deal of time and make an effort to keep these records current and reflective of what is happening. These portfolios also capture the educational progress of the child. The documentation is a reflection of the collaboration among the family and educators to support the child's achievements. "The operative concept here is that the child is in relationships (especially with the other children) and is interacting and finding out who the child him/herself is and discovering who other children really are too" (Soncini, in Smith, 1998, p. 204). The documentation is always available to the family. Completed portfolios are taken by the family at the end of the child's three-year experience in the municipal schools.

TEACHER INSERVICE EDUCATION

Ivana Soncini also has the lead responsibility for ongoing staff development related to children with special rights. The staff development that teachers receive takes place on-site and is based on methods of careful observation and analysis. Videotaping is often used. For example, in the story of Elisa, we saw how careful observation and deliberate planning took a child from aimless running to being purposefully engaged in activities and meaningful relationships.

Every day Reggio's teachers are involved in observing, documenting, and interpreting the learning experience for the children and themselves and creating a learning environment based on their observations and interpretations. In Reggio, the educators' research skills are especially important in working with children with special rights (Soncini, 1998). Often for children with special rights, their questions may come silently, as they did for young Lucia in the 100 Languages of Children Exhibit. *Their questions* may come in the pointing of a finger, in the look of their eyes, or in the posture of their bodies. For this reason, Reggio educators stress that including children with special rights in their schools has made them better observers of all children. The rigorous documentation and reflection of teachers in Reggio Emilia stands in stark contrast to the practice of many American teachers who look to early childhood professors or researchers to provide knowledge, and then try to determine implications for their practice.

To make inclusion as successful as possible, all staff members at the school are included in any staff development sessions. In addition to the teachers, this includes cooks and other auxiliary staff, such as cleaning staff. Reggio educators believe that the communication between therapists and all members of the school community is essential so that everyone is available to support the potential of these children. It also means that wherever the child is, on the playground, in the bathroom, or helping in the kitchen, all staff members feel comfortable to interact with the child and to provide any needed support.

Reggio's on-site approach to staff development is dramatically different than what typically occurs in the United States, where groups of teachers from many different programs attend short workshops off-site. The teachers then return to their classroom and struggle to put into practice what they have learned. Often this challenge is intensified as they work in isolation from other teaching staff, and the responsibility of implementation falls solely to them individually. Reggio's on-site staff development demands staff collaboration, which is yet another critical component of their highly successful programs. Malaguzzi stated, "Teachers who work in isolation leave no traces. It is teachers who work together who have an impact" (Malaguzzi, 1992).

INTEGRATED THERAPY

The therapy children with special rights receive is also on-site. Educators have a strong commitment to finding the most appropriate methods and techniques for individual children. "What the Italian programs may lack in high technology and sophisticated equipment seems far outweighed by the caring and dedication that is expressed openly by teachers and health service team members" (McCleary, 1985). Once again the emphasis is on making sure relationships are established and that children are fully included. Therapists work with the child in the context of the family and the school. Very few, if any, therapy sessions are one-on-one with the child in an isolated therapy room; in fact, these only occur if requested by families.

Therapists also work with teachers to show them how to integrate therapy into daily classroom activities. For example, an observer in the Reggio schools would see a child who is in need of leg strengthening exercises at the table with classmates, feet on the floor, using the legs of the teacher to support his weight. To the casual observer this integrated therapy session by the teacher would go unnoticed. This natural integrated therapy looks quite different from the child who is strapped in a wooden stander for a certain time period each day.

Also, Reggio's educators see that developing peers can serve as co-therapists for their classmates with special rights (Soncini, 1999). This is true even with very young children. There is the example of an 18-month-old child with severe physical disabilities. Isabella entered the infant–toddler center with no use of her arms or legs. The teacher's approach was to hold her almost continuously and to protect her from the other children. However, observation and documentation of this approach showed that nothing was changing for this child. Soncini, in working with the staff, decided to construct a rubber "boat" that could hold and protect Isabella. The boat was placed in the center of the room and in a very short period of time the other children in the class began approaching her with their whole bodies. They touched her face and hands in the most sensitive and caring way. Eventually Isabella learned to sit by herself. Soncini and the teachers were convinced that it was because of the contact Isabella had with the other children in her class (Soncini, cited in Kaminsky, 1997). Reggio's educators have also found that the classmates often have a greater ability than the teachers to pick up the communicative signals, including gestures and other non-verbal methods, used by the child with special rights (Kaminsky, 1997).

CASE STUDIES: OBSERVING BEST PRACTICES IN INCLUSION IN PRACTICE

At this point in the chapter, especially if this is your first introduction to Reggio's approach to inclusion, you may be asking yourself the same thing I did when I first began studying Reggio's educational system: Does inclusion really work as well as it is described? Are Reggio's educators really able to provide inclusive services in this extraordinary fashion? I had to take a trip to Italy to see for myself Reggio's approach to inclusion in practice. At the time of my first visit, I had more than 20 years of experience in education and was keenly aware of the gap between the intent of our public laws for children with disabilities and the reality of how these laws are implemented in the United States. Over the course of three visits to Reggio Emilia, I observed children who are non-verbal and non-ambulatory, children with autism, children who are deaf, and children who are medically fragile. During my observations, all were fully included in the day's activities. All were seen as another one of the strong, competent, resourceful children attending the schools; all were acknowledged as children with full rights to a quality early childhood program that includes deep and satisfying learning experiences and personal relationships with teachers, families, and friends.

On my first visit to Reggio Emilia in April 1995, I observed a child with severe disabilities included in the four-year-old room at the Diana preschool (see Smith, 1998). Stella was a frail, non-ambulatory child with cerebral palsy who attended the Diana school for three years. On the day of my observation, Stella was included in the daily activities with other children so well that she went unnoticed by the majority of the other members of my delegation. In the four-year-olds' bathroom, she sat in a small wooden chair with a tray on the front that held a tub of water and water toys. Stella was the center of activity, surrounded by four classmates, all splashing, blowing bubbles, and giggling with delight. The support teacher was present interacting with the small group of five children.

Stella Is Fully Included in the Day's Activities

Soon the classroom doors opened, and all the mobile children ran outside for outdoor playtime. The support teacher moved Stella in front of one of the many mirrors inside the school. She took a brightly colored scarf and draped it around Stella's shoulders, and then began to brush Stella's hair. This interaction had a very positive tone, but I wondered if Stella was to be excluded from the outdoor playtime. A few minutes later, however, the teacher placed Stella into a stroller and moved with her toward the exit. As they went through the door, two of Stella's classmates met them. One of the little girls handed the teacher a bouquet of yellow flowers, and the other child laid a bouquet upon Stella's lap. Then these two children put their hands on the handle of the stroller and together moved with Stella and the teacher to the sandtable located on the back of the playground.

The teacher took Stella out of the stroller and leaned her against the stone table. She then positioned herself behind Stella. This stance provided the support Stella needed to stand and participate at the table. The other children were busily engaged in filling buckets, packing the sand, and then upturning the buckets to build a sandcastle. Everyone was so intent on their work that a few seconds passed before anyone noticed that Stella had lost head control and had sunk face down into her sandcastle. Slowly, she pulled her head upright. Although covered in sand, a bright smile lit up her face. Her classmates giggled, and one child ran to get a towel while the teacher gently brushed the sand away. Everyone enjoyed a laugh, and then the building commenced in earnest.

Andrea's Unique Language Results in Unique Educational Experience

In January 1998, I had the privilege of observing the inclusive educational experience and special language of Andrea. Andrea was a five-year-old child with special rights who spent three years at the Anderson preschool in Reggio. The morning of my observation, Andrea and four of his classmates were in the *atelier* (the studio for project work) with the support teacher. Recently this group of children had gone swimming at a community pool. A series of slides taken at their swimming outing was projected on the wall. Projecting slides depicting a special event or investigation is a technique that is often used to revisit an experience with the children. On this particular day, beneath the wall where the slides were being displayed, a large blue gym mat had been placed on the floor. Beside the mat was a bench. Andrea was truly the best at recreating the memorable plunge into the pool. He stood on the bench, held his nose, and shook from head to toe in anticipation of hitting the water. Once Andrea jumped onto the mat, he "swam" his way down to the end, and returned to the diving platform to wait his turn in line. Later, the teacher put out inflatable floats. The children each took a float and laid back to relax together in the pool they had created. Andrea was unable to verbally communicate, but was using gestures with the teacher and his classmates that appeared to be quite effective.

At the end of our morning observation, a special educator from Italy who was part of my delegation commented to Andrea's teacher that she did not recognize any of the signs Andrea was using as official sign language. Also, she stated her confusion about Andrea's diagnosis. Andrea did not appear to be deaf since he acted as if he understood many of his teacher's and friends' verbal comments. The teacher explained that Andrea was a child without a diagnosis. When he entered the Anderson school, Andrea's family was frustrated with the assessment of the Local Health Unit and had taken their young child to specialists in Rome to try and get some answers to their unanswered questions; however, the family returned from Rome with the same information. Andrea had normal hearing, but for a reason that was not identifiable, even by the doctors in Rome, he was unable to talk. Upon Andrea's entry into the Anderson preschool it was still important to his family that the teachers work with their son to try and develop his ability to speak. The teachers spent a year trying to produce recognizable sounds and to give meaning to any of Andrea's spontaneous guttural utterances. Finally, it was Andrea who introduced his own language to the adults in his life. Andrea began to make gestures that the staff could identify with people, objects, and events in his world. Wanting to be respectful of the language Andrea had created, the teaching staff took it upon themselves to learn his language and to teach it to Andrea's classmates! The teachers wanted to give credit to Andrea as a capable and competent child. Andrea's teacher did go on to point out that, since Andrea had not created signs for food, it was at mealtime that they were introducing official sign language to him, which he was learning with great success.

It was also mentioned that a goal on Andrea's Declaration of Intent was to have the teachers and classmates learn Andrea's sign language. Another goal on the document specified the group of friends with whom Andrea worked best and their goals for working alongside Andrea in projects.

Another story about Andrea involves his participation in a project that is a wonderful example of how teachers use these experiences to both individualize instruction and build relationships. 1996 was a city election year in Reggio, and the entire Reggio school system decided to have the children spend time exploring the city. This city-wide adoption of a project was quite out of the ordinary for the Reggio system, but was something the educators felt it was important to explore. However, how this city exploration would play out in each school or class would be unique. In the case of the Anderson school, Andrea and his classmates went into town and spent the day. The next day, during the morning assembly, the children began to share their favorite parts of the city. One child talked about how he loved the pigeons in the piazza, another child said his favorite part was seeing the fountain in the public garden, another child said how he loved the lions guarding the main piazza. The teachers quickly realized that all the children were telling their stories verbally, and that Andrea was not able to participate in this oral telling. They wondered how they might capture Andrea's story of his trip to the city. The next day the teachers allowed the children to take over the large piazza area in the school to recreate their town at school. Andrea stood at the corner of one of the block-built structures and began to pretend that he was playing a musical instrument. Everyone immediately recognized Andrea's action as depicting the saxophone player they had seen playing on one of the street corners during their town trip. Andrea could hum the tune! The teachers decided that one part of the class project would involve the children creating sounds for all their favorite parts of the city. The children flapped their arms and made whooshing sounds to signal the pigeons, they poured water into the sink to signify the fountains, and they roared for the lions. The children's sounds were played as slides taken during the class trip were shown. This wonderful slide show and soundtrack was entitled: Beyond Words: The City as Observed by Andrea and his Friends!

On my visit in 1999, I had the opportunity to return to Anderson preschool. Andrea had left to enter first grade. Soncini and the teachers worked to make the transition to public school as easy as possible for him. They arranged to have classmates who were Andrea's friends and who had learned his sign language placed in the first-grade class with him. The support teacher in his room from last year had moved from the five-year-old room to the three-year-old room.

Rosa Builds Relationships and Skills within an "Ordinary" Preschool Day

At the time of my visit, Rosa, another child with special rights, had entered Anderson school. Rosa, a non-verbal, cognitively-delayed child with health complications, required the use of a breathing tube which was connected at her nose. My observation of Rosa began when Manuela, the teacher, greeted Rosa and her mother at the door of the three-year-old room. As Manuela and the mother greeted each other, the mother handed Rosa to Manuela and began to wave good-bye. "Ciao, Mamma," Manuela said. After waiting for Rosa to wave good-bye, she and Rosa entered the room together. Manuela placed Rosa on the floor. Rosa quickly scooted on her bottom, propelling herself with her arms to the morning assembly, which was already underway. She took a seat at the risers among the other children. Manuela joined the group of children who, as part of their morning time together, were selecting either apples or oranges or both to eat for a morning snack. Manuela picked Rosa up and they went together to get a jar of prepared pureed fruit. They returned to the group and again took a seat on the risers with the other children, who were now eating. Manuela handed Rosa a spoon, then began to feed her with another spoon. Rosa ate eagerly. When there was a small amount of food left, Manuela held the jar and allowed Rosa to scoop and feed herself. Several children finished eating and headed for the bathroom. Manuela and Rosa joined them. Manuela supported Rosa under her arms so that she practiced walking as they made their way across the room. On their return from the bathroom, Manuela once again supported Rosa under her arms, but this time she had asked two classmates to join Rosa and her. The two children each held one of Rosa's hands and the four of them walked together back to the room.

The children in the class then moved into their small groups. Six children, including Rosa, went to the mini-atelier with Manuela to work with clay. Later Rosa left this group and scooted herself back to the main part of the room to join one of the other teachers and her small group of children, where she was welcomed. I was struck once again with the Reggio educators' attention to relationships. Rosa's morning activities had been purposely planned to ensure that meaningful relationships occurred. This began with the morning greeting of Rosa and her mother, continued through Rosa's entry into the group, and to the routine bathroom break that became a natural therapy session, including a hand-holding experience.

Filippo and His Classmates Reach Out to Each Other

On this morning visit to Anderson, I also had the opportunity to observe Filippo, a four-year-old child with autism. Filippo was in the main piazza area with a group of children playing on a large wooden structure. It had snowed the night before in Reggio, and therefore the children were enjoying gross motor play inside that morning. As I first began my observation, Filippo was running around the piazza area with little to no interaction with the other children in the group or with materials in the room. The teacher was sitting, taking notes about the children's play together. After some time, the teacher put her clipboard aside and joined in the children's play. She tied a large sheet to the permanent wooden play structure located in the piazza. The teacher invited Filippo to lie down on the sheet, which he did with great excitement. She began swinging him in the sheet as the other children gently pushed him. When his turn was up, a classmate, Cristina, extended Filippo her hand and helped him up. Cristina then lay down and took her turn at swinging. "Spinge, Filippo" ("Push, Filippo"), the teacher urged. With this encouragement, Filippo began to gently push Cristina. When her turn was finished, Filippo offered his hand to help his school friend up. The touching of another human being, which is often extremely difficult for a child with autism, was facilitated for Filippo through the deliberate planning of the teacher. This interaction was made possible through a language that Filippo apparently enjoyed tremendously.

The morning observation had come to an end and it was time for me to leave with my delegation. As I walked toward the bus stop with the group, I could hear the voice of Carlina Rinaldi, the director of Reggio's municipal schools, ringing in my ears. "Our focus is not on what the child cannot do, but on what he/she can do, or more importantly, on what he/she could do if in the right environments and in the right relationships" (Rinaldi, 1998).

IMPLEMENTATION IN THE UNITED STATES

Colleagues who accompanied me to Reggio Emilia in 1998 have started to share their beginning implementations in the United States. The Sabot School in Richmond, Virginia, has a long-time commitment to including children with disabilities in their program. For the past five years, the Sabot staff have been involved in the study of Reggio's approach and have looked to Reggio for inspiration and guidance to enhance the quality of their inclusive care. One night over dinner they shared their story of Wesley. Wesley is a non-verbal, three-year-old child with autism who entered the Sabot preschool last year. It took the teachers little observation time to discover Wesley's love of sand. Wesley would begin every school day by stopping at the sandbox on the school's playground. He would grab handfuls, hold both of his hands high in the air and watch the sand filter down. This behavior continued until a teacher would escort him inside. Once inside the walls of the classroom, his morning at the half-day preschool was spent largely in other sensory stimulation activities, such as flapping items in front of his eyes or against his chin, or dumping and refilling and dumping again containers of small objects. Once the playground was open to him, he would again head straight for the sandbox. How could the teachers turn Wesley's attention to sand into something that would expand his world and connect him to human relationships? The teachers introduced sand toys and hard animals, and placed other children in the sand area with him. Wesley dismissed everything and everyone. He pushed all the toys away, turned his back on the children, and returned to sifting alone in the sandbox. Challenged, but convinced of its importance, the staff knew they needed to continue to offer Wesley a hundred more possibilities. After careful discussion and thinking, they made a plan to pour a bucket of sand into the wagon on the playground. Would the sand entice Wesley to climb in? It did. A breakthrough had occurred. The director of the school then began pulling Wesley around the playground. Curious classmates asked what was happening. The director explained that Wesley was enjoying a wagon ride with sand. They all wanted a turn, both riding and pulling Wesley. The teachers had worked to help Wesley and his peers make the first step in a meaningful connection to each other, and in addition they broadened Wesley's playground activities. The teachers introduced more possibilities, such as obstacle courses through sand and rides down the slide into a pile of sand. Wesley's attention had been captured anew. His captivation with sifting sand continued; however, he was now able to make other choices when verbally or gesturally prompted. The teachers introduced signs to Wesley. One of the signs was "All done," which the teachers would ask of Wesley af-

The teachers and children at Sabot School have brought fall leaves inside the classroom for closer examination. Wesley is immediately engaged in touching the dry and crumbled leaves provided in the large storage box. He becomes so enthralled with the textures and sounds that he finds his own way to heighten the experience and climbs into the container with them. Observing and appreciating Wesley's intense research, his classmates later take a turn at doing the same.

ter he had sifted sand for a set period of time. When he would leave the sandbox he would always choose large motor play. Eventually he independently chose to spend less and less time at the sandbox. This year Wesley engages in play with classmates and teachers both outside and inside. He smiles and laughs with his friends on the play structure, swings, and seesaws. A new passion this year is initiating "horsey" rides on the back of his teacher. One day another child in the class had the idea of selling tickets for the rides. Again everyone in the room wanted a turn at what looked like a wonderfully fun experience. This led to more imaginative horse play by the entire class. Wesley's journey of blossoming into a social, well-loved, contributing member of the Sabot community continues to unfold as this chapter is written.

In Durham, North Carolina, at the Carolina Friends Early School, teacher Patti Cruickshank-Schott has been working to incorporate the Reggio approach in her classroom of five- and six-year-olds. Cruickshank-Schott writes a daily journal as one part of her documentation and reflection. This year she began an e-mail list to send her journal entry out each day to all the families in the class. Parents often responded and added their comments after reading about the children's day. They also began to use the list to let other families know about interesting child and family-related activities taking place in the community. Then unexpectedly, a family from the class wrote a letter stating their worry about their child being eliminated from the school because of the possibility that there was not room there for her and her learning differences. Since the staff did not receive a copy of this letter until it was posted to everyone, it seemed that it might result in a significant conflict and that the other parents may have received some misinformation. The school did, in fact, have a spot for this child. At that point, something very important happened: There was an outpouring of care and concern for the family and their child. The teacher's daily communication with parents had allowed a trusting relationship to develop beyond what she expected. In Italy, what impressed Cruickshank-Schott about Reggio's approach to inclusion was the focus on the relationship among the children, educators, and parents and the concept of group responsibilities for caring rather than our more American focus on individual goals and responsibilities. She was moved to witness the beginning steps of this occurring in her room and further inspired to trust and nurture the relationship-building process in her class for the benefit of all members of the school community.

IMPLICATIONS FOR PRACTICE IN THE UNITED STATES

Reggio's practices and the results they have achieved with young children with disabilities represent an enviable commitment to quality early inclusive services. Many factors are evident that contribute to the success of these programs and to the philosophical ideal that all children, regardless of the severity of their disability, deserve maximum educational opportunities and inclusion within society (McCleary, 1985).

How can we use Reggio's extraordinary approach to encourage and promote quality inclusive care and education for young children in this country? First, I would like to suggest that Reggio's pedagogical approach offers an opportunity to bring the general and special early childhood fields together to work on behalf of all children. For many years these two well-established programs have been largely supportive of their separate and unique personnel, skills, and clients, and this has often worked to impede inclusive efforts. Today, almost half the states in this country require general education students to take coursework on children with disabilities before receiving a teaching license (National Early Childhood Technical Assistance System, 1998). Other states have moved to a birth through kindergarten license that includes both regular and special early childhood training. Reggio's philosophy and practice represent best practices for both the field of general and special early childhood education (Bredekamp & Copple, 1997; Odum & McLean, 1996) and offer both general and special early childhood professionals many ideas for reflection (see Figure 8.1).

Secondly, and more importantly, I would like to suggest that a great possibility exists for those who are incorporating the Reggio approach to become the individu-

FIGURE 8.1   *Compelling Features of Reggio's Approach to Inclusion*

- ✤ Gives top priority in enrollment to children with disabilities
- ✤ Holds a strong image of ALL children as competent and full of potential, and having the desire and capacity to conduct research
- ✤ Provides high quality environments
- ✤ Views relationships and collaboration among children, parents, the community, specialists, and the school as critical
- ✤ Assesses children in a variety of settings; first and foremost is the view of the parents and the child in the home
- ✤ Promotes an active family-school partnership
- ✤ Promotes coordination and collaboration among the school, family, and support service agency (local health administration)
- ✤ Esteems teachers as researchers, who observe children closely to determine their languages for learning, and who, with great purpose and intentionality, have the children use these languages to build both cognitive and social development
- ✤ Individualizes instruction within a group context
- ✤ Develops goals not only for the child with special rights, but also for the family, teachers, specialists and peers who will support the education of the child
- ✤ Provides child–specific, on-site staff development that includes everyone on the school staff, including the cook and auxiliary helpers
- ✤ Provides natural integrated therapy with the teachers and children involved in delivering therapy
- ✤ Engages children in relationships and projects that are both exciting and meaningful

als who will provide the inclusive options that are needed to serve the children with disabilities and their families in this country. Experts in the field of early childhood special education (Bailey, McWillian, Buysee, & Wesley, 1998) recently suggested that primary barriers to inclusion in this country would be eliminated if the inclusive services in community settings were of high-quality, offered specialized instruction and services, and provided family-centered practices. Reggio's approach to inclusion encompasses all three of these values and more. To move further in our inclusive efforts, can we follow Reggio's example and open our doors to children with disabilities to have them benefit from the environments, activities, and relationships they would find there?

Once we commit to including children with disabilities in our programs, can we start with Reggio's image of the child and therefore focus on the competence and potential of every child? Could we approach inclusion as an opportunity to celebrate differences and put the emphasis on strengths, not deficits? This shift in emphasis would allow teachers to organize the curriculum to assist each child in reaching his or her potential. It would allow teachers to take more time to cultivate friendship and caring among children and adults.

Could we look to Reggio's approach as offering us the opportunity to begin to promote and value the observation, documentation, and interpretation skills of teachers as contributing to the knowledge base that guides our practice with children? Not only does Reggio esteem the child as researcher, but Reggio also demands that teachers conduct daily research. This research, in collaboration with parents and other educators, results in a highly individualized instruction.

Perhaps the most important question to ask comes from a basic principle in Reggio's approach to children: Can we resist the temptation to point out what we as teachers and educators cannot do, but instead ask ourselves what we can do, or more importantly what we *could do,* in our efforts to enhance the quality of our early care? This is the question that I believe will guide us as we strive to enhance the lives of all children and their families. One important change that does not cost an extra dime, or require the permission of a program director, is for us to begin to listen to and interact with children differently. This change in us as educators can begin today.

Children with special rights in the Reggio municipal schools are participating in an education that embraces all that is possible. The methods used in the Reggio schools are based on decades of studying and adapting the knowledge of educators, families, and children to provide an excellent program which benefits ALL children. As we move forward in the 21st century it would serve us all well to look at an educational approach to serve ALL children that has met with success for over half a century.

ACKNOWLEDGEMENTS

The author would like to extend a special thank you to Ivana Soncini for sharing Reggio Emilia's approach to inclusion with our study tour participants. Her stories contributed greatly to this chapter. It should be noted that the names of the children whose stories are chronicled here have been changed for this publication. I also want to thank Patricia Hearron, professor, Appalachian State University in Boone, NC; Molly Weston, editor of *ALL Together Now* at the Frank Porter Graham Child Development Center, Chapel Hill, NC; Pat Wesley, director of Partnerships for Inclusion at the Frank Porter Graham Child Development Center in Chapel Hill, NC; and Lella Gandini, liaison for the dissemination of the Reggio Emilia approach in the United States for their careful review and contributions to the chapter. I thank Sabot School teacher Denise Powers for sharing the Sabot School educators' experience with Wesley. I thank Patti Cruickshank-Schott, former kindergarten teacher at the Carolina Friends Early School in Durham, NC, and currently the director of the preschool programs at the World Bank Children's Center, for sharing her story. I also would like to thank Karen de la Motte, former Upper School Latin teacher at St. Thomas More School in Chapel Hill, NC, for her translation of Andrea's Declaration of Intent. Also, Wesley's parents have requested that it be noted that while attending Sabot, Wesley was also undergoing natural vitamin A therapy.

REFERENCES

Bailey, D., McWillian, R., Buysee, V., & Wesley, P. (1998). Inclusion in the context of competing values in early childhood education. *Early Childhood Research Quarterly, 13*(1), 27–47.

Berrigan, C. (1994–1995). *Schools in Italy: A national policy made actual.* Syracuse, NY: Syracuse University, Center on Human Policy.

Bredekamp, S., & Copple, C. (1997). *Developmentally appropriate practice in early childhood.* Revised edition. Washington, D.C.: National Association for the Education of Young Children.

Cecchini, M., & McCleary, I.D. (1985). Preschool handicapped in Italy: A research-based developmental model. *Journal of the Division for Early Childhood, 9*(3), 254–265.

Edmiaston, R., & Fitzgerald, M. (2000). How Reggio Emilia encourages inclusion. *Educational Leadership, 58,*(no. 1), 66–69.

Elgas, P., & Peltier, M. B. (1998). Jimmy's journey: Building a sense of community and self-worth through small-group work. *Young Children, 53*(2), 17–21.

Gandini, L. (1993). Fundamentals of the Reggio Emilia approach to early childhood education, *Young Children, 49*(1), 4–8.

Gandini, L., & Gambetti, A. (1997a). An inclusive system based on cooperation: The schools for young children in Reggio Emilia. *New Directions for School Leadership, 3.*

Gandini, L., & Gambetti, A. (1997b). The story of Luca: Including a Down syndrome child in the classroom. *Innovations, 5*(3), 7.

Kaminsky, J.A. (1997). An interview with Ivana Soncini, coordinator for inclusion of children with disabilities in the Reggio municipal infant–toddler centers and preschools. *Innovations, 5*(3), 1–6.

Malaguzzi, L. (1992, October). Presentation delivered to the 1992 Fall study tour delegation. Reggio Emilia, Italy.

McCleary, D. (1985). Intervention programs for young handicapped children in Europe: An overview. *Journal of the Division for Early Childhood, 9*(3), 195–205.

National Early Childhood Technical Assistance System (1998). *Programs for young children with disabilities under IDEA: Excerpts from the nineteenth annual report to Congress on the implementation of the individual with disabilities education act.* Chapel Hill, NC: Frank Porter Graham Child Development Center.

Odum, S., & McLean, M. (1996). *Early intervention/early childhood special education: Recommended practices.* Austin, TX: Pro-Ed.

Rinaldi, C. (1998). *Reggio's image of the child.* Presentation at the 1998 Reggio Emilia Winter Institute. Reggio Emilia, Italy.

Smith, C. (1998). Children with "special rights" in the preprimary schools and infant–toddler centers of Reggio Emilia. In C. Edwards, L. Gandini, &

G. Forman, (Eds.), *The hundred languages of children: The Reggio Emilia approach–advanced reflections,* (pp. 199–214). Greenwich, CT: Ablex.

Soncini, I. (1998). *Children with special rights.* Presentation at the 1998 Reggio Emilia Winter Institute. Reggio Emilia, Italy.

Soncini, I. (1999, February). *Children with special rights.* Presentation at the 1999 Reggio Emilia Winter Institute. Reggio Emilia, Italy.

Vianello, R. (1996). Learning difficulties in Italy: Didactic proposals for the class in which a pupil with learning difficulties is integrated. *European Association for Special Education,* 35–39.

Part III

Teacher Education: Inquiry Teaching and the Possibilities for Change

This section of our book awakens us to the processes and possibilities of personal transformation. "How," ask Jeanne Goldhaber and Dee Smith, "can we recast the traditional image of a teacher from one who knows all the answers to one who celebrates not knowing the answers and is excited by the prospect of the looking for them; from someone who sees teaching as a safe profession to one who sees teaching as an act of courage; from someone who views teaching as a solitary act to one who relishes teaching as a collaborative enterprise?" Among the responses to this provocative question is Andy Stremmel's advice to be aware of your inner self; to be alert to joys, struggles, passions, and questions. Jeanne and Dee contribute their research on documentation strategies as a supportive process to encourage reflection, inquiry, and collaboration. And Deb Tegano points to the passion and art of teaching as the combination of spirit and mind which encourage and support the transformation.

Chapter

9

The Transformation of Self in Early Childhood Teacher Education: Connections to the Reggio Emilia Approach

Andrew J. Stremmel ◆ **Victoria R. Fu** ◆ **Lynn T. Hill**

"The unaware life is not worth living."

Socrates

The quote by the great Socrates is a self-evident truth. Yet, how many of us are really aware of what's going on around us? How many of us are aware of our inner selves? Unless we are able to live attentively, being alert and aware to our joys, our struggles, our questions, and our relationship to others, we will miss out on opportunities to be present to ourselves and be open to change.

   Awareness is a fitting construct when describing the complex and challenging act of teaching. Without awareness, teachers become mechanical, complacent, and unresponsive to children. Without awareness, teachers become dependent on the shifting chain of events that characterize their work and lead to quick changes of mood and behavior. Teaching becomes nothing more than a series of actions and reactions that pull us away from our inner selves and the possibilities for awareness (Nouwen, 1975).

How does one develop awareness and understanding? How does one move from simply identifying with what one does and the outcomes of those actions to an awareness of the meaning and significance of thought, feeling, and action? How do teachers become alert to their inner voices as well as to the world around them so that awareness becomes part of their daily living with children? These are questions important to teaching, and indeed to life itself. In this chapter we focus on early childhood teacher education as the transformation of self, a continual process of becoming, in which teachers develop a greater understanding and self-awareness through reflection and the reconstruction of their experiences. We reason that it is through the reconstruction of experience that students of teaching discover that teaching is a complex journey that involves movement between the dialectic of certainty and uncertainty, knowing and not knowing, joy and sorrow, triumph and failure, faith and doubt. In short, teaching is a struggle with the question of "Who am I?" Further, we maintain that our primary role as teacher educators is to lead and challenge students

Education, like life, is self-transformation.

to develop the ability to puzzle over and question their work, and to move toward a deeper engagement with the burning and authentic issues of teaching that allow for self transformation and increased understanding, or, following Socrates, a "turning of the soul" (Haroutunian-Gordon, 1995).

Elsewhere, it has been asserted that beginning teachers must be not only students of teaching and the children they teach, but also students of their own development (Ayers, 1993; Bullough & Gitlin, 1995; Paley, 1990). Based on the notion of teacher as researcher, and adhering to a social constructivist, Reggio-inspired approach to teacher education, we regard teaching as a search for meaning and understanding and the negotiation of creative and meaningful relationships with those with whom teachers work. In addition, we view the self as the first source of search and research. In this chapter, we describe activities and experiences that encourage students to construct and reconstruct a knowledge of self and teaching through inquiry.

REPOSITIONING TEACHING: TEACHER AS RESEARCHER

Freeman (1998) contends that teaching, and the notion of a teacher's work, must be thought of as a process of doing research, defined as speculation, wondering, and questioning what we do. Consider the following self-reflective observation from a student in our Curriculum and Assessment course at Virginia Tech:

> There is the old cliché that "the eyes are the windows to one's soul," and though for many people this is the case, have you ever observed someone and truly wondered, "What is he thinking?" When I silently observe Madison wrapping several feet of green tape around his cardboard tube binoculars, or listen to him singing loudly (yet to himself), "Platypus walking in my play-dough, cause that's a really good song," while cutting out play-dough during dramatic play, I really wish I could delve into his mind and determine what he is thinking. Why does he create what he does? Madison's way of expressing himself seems to be through his constructions, yet when asked what he was making one day he replied, "I won't know until I am done." So what are his creative representations revealing to us about Madison? What does Hank, the tugboat, say to us as we view it as scraps of colored tape precariously holding together various pipe cleaners? My theory is that Madison would much rather be creating than taking part in social interactions, as he does not like to be disturbed and at times does not respond to others. Is he unable to interact socially or would he rather be inventing independently?

This reflection is the introduction to Freeman's framing statement of what she plans to study about a particular child in her classroom. In this assignment, we ask students, as teacher researchers, to "frame" what they want to find out about their "target" child. This framing statement articulates the themes or areas of the child's development that students will explore in the context of their current knowledge about children, theories of child development, and knowledge of self as a teacher researcher.

The concept of teacher as researcher permeates our undergraduate program in early childhood education at Virginia Tech, a five-year collaborative venture between the Departments of Human Development and Teaching and Learning within the College of Human Resources and Education. This program leads to teacher certification for grades pre-kindergarten through six. Students enter the program as freshmen in Early Childhood Education and begin an integrated and in-depth study of child development within family, school, and community contexts, the disciplines taught in elementary schools, and extensive and diverse opportunities for contact with young children in preschool and school-age settings. Over the first four years, coursework, field study, and internship experiences combine to enable students to critically examine various educational issues and approaches to teaching. Students earn a bachelor's degree in four years, and upon successful completion of the fifth year earn a master's degree and teacher certification.

The philosophy of our program is social constructivist and adheres to Dewey's notion that students construct knowledge through inquiry with the assistance of others (e.g., teachers, peers, and children) who help draw out their ideas and assumptions about the situations they encounter. According to this philosophy, prospective teachers learn to see themselves as researchers, activists, reflective thinkers, and agents of change. As teacher researchers, students develop the processes of inquiry and personal and professional renewal as a lifelong endeavor. Students are welcomed into a community of learners and co-mentored by early childhood education and elementary education faculty. Within this caring and safe community, they are instilled with the understanding that teachers, like their students, learn by carefully reflecting on their experiences. Through self-questioning and critical analysis of practice with young children, the opportunity exists to reinvent and reconstruct personal experience.

The idea that competence in teaching is not merely defined by action and activity, but by the ability to generate knowledge through theorizing, questioning, wondering, and discovering, is one of the basic principles of the Reggio Emilia approach. In Reggio Emilia, teachers are seen as active initiators of research in their own classrooms, as expert knowers of their children, and as creators of curriculum and knowledge as opposed to the common notions of teacher as technician, consumer, and transmitter of other people's knowledge (Cochran-Smith & Lytle, 1999). Similarly, in our Reggio-inspired child development laboratory school, students engage in the ongoing and reflexive process of connecting what they do with children to the way they are guided and supported in their own developmental journeys. In particular, teachers and students are engaged in the process of collaborative inquiry into the wonders, passions, and mysteries of young children and how this critical pedagogy encourages the transformation of self.

Our work at Virginia Tech reflects a recasting of the Reggio approach to inquiry in ways also consistent with recent shifts in how educational researchers have come to view the teacher as knower, thinker, and researcher. In moving from the perspective of teacher as consumer toward that of protagonist, it is necessary to think differently about the meaning of teacher research (Cochran-Smith & Lytle, 1999; Freeman, 1998).

To begin with, research must be redefined as something teachers do as part of their work. As alluded to earlier, teaching is more than action and reaction, it also in-

Students of teaching learn to see themselves as researchers, activists, reflective thinkers, and agents of change.

volves reflection and speculation. In addition to teaching skills, teachers must develop a questioning disposition toward the world leading to inquiry conducted within the classroom. Second, teachers must think of themselves as generating knowledge, not just using it. We cannot leave it to others to define the knowledge that is of most worth, nor can we let others define the knowledge that forms the basis of teaching (Ayers, 1993). Third, inquiry, both practical and social, is the foundation of teacher research. Here I mean that inquiry, as a routine and expected function of teachers' daily lives in the classroom, is about wondering what, how, and why they do what they do. Fourth, teachers as researchers must find new and varied ways to make public what has been learned through their inquiry. What we call documentation not only makes visible traces of child experience and learning, but it represents a public sharing and testing of ideas that are essential for creating a discipline of teaching (Freeman, 1998). Finally, teacher research must be considered hazardous work. There are no easy answers, only problems that must be addressed carefully, thoughtfully, and collaboratively with both

Research is something teachers do as part of their daily work.

hope and determination. In a society where nearly everything can be explained, quantified, and subjected to scientific analysis and control, teachers must persist in dogged pursuit of the complex and uncertain realities of the classroom with caring, compassion, and faith. Teachers who see themselves as researchers every day put their hope and faith on the line; they swim against the current when they know that what they may uncover is more uncertainty and that to care may be better than to know. This is risky business.

PROMOTING SELF-AWARENESS AND THE REINVENTION OF SELF

Given this new way of thinking, there are several important assumptions underlying our conceptual framework of teacher research as practical and social inquiry and as a way of knowing. Following a delineation of these assumptions, we discuss several of the things we do specifically in our program, particularly the lab school, to promote the self-awareness that leads to transformative possibilities.

From the first year, we want to instill in our students the notion that teaching as research is a way of knowing and being that extends across the professional life span.

We want them to know that teaching involves questioning assumptions and posing problems. We have two sayings that guide this thinking:

"Make the problem the project."
"Those with the problems are often the ones with the solutions."

Instead of seeing problems as something in need of fixing, of needing immediate answers, we view them as things to be studied and understood. Unless we learn to embrace our problems and questions and to pursue them through dialogue, reflection, and careful study, we cannot expect answers that are really our own. As Carlina Rinaldi, former director of the Reggio schools, would say, "To live is to question. To teach is to question." Unfortunately, this is difficult because we live in a culture where we are constantly encouraged to look for answers instead of listening to the questions.

An essential aspect of teacher research is reflection. In reflection we become present to ourselves. In practice, reflection leads to awareness and understanding. Change can happen only when we become aware of who we are, what we bring to teaching, and what our role is in relation to children and parents. Reflection helps us become aware of what is appropriate and possible in the classroom. It keeps us from being mechanical about our thoughts, emotions, actions, and reactions. When we are mechanical we get complacent; we start to feel good about ourselves and are subject to the ups and downs of teaching. When things are going great you feel as though you are a great teacher, but when things are going badly, you feel as though you are failing. To be aware of this is liberating and leads to what van Manen (1991) refers to as mindfulness and tact. Therefore, we believe knowledge of teaching is embedded in everyday practice, reflection, and questions about what we do. The classroom, then, is a site for inquiry—a place where knowledge is generated to improve teaching and create a more democratic and equitable learning community.

Exercises and Activities

In Reggio, one is confronted with the question, "Who is the child? (see Chapter 4 by Stremmel). Perhaps an even greater question, one that has been asked by the great philosophers of the world, is "Who am I?" This is a question that our students begin to pursue systematically as freshmen in the pre-professional seminar in early childhood education. This is a yearlong course designed specifically to help them begin to explore and think about who they are, what they care about and value, what has influenced their views and beliefs, and who they want to be as a student and a teacher. Three primary questions serve to guide inquiry in this first-year experience: *Who am I? Where did I come from? Where am I headed?* Among the activities that we offer to encourage this exploration are:

✤ An autobiographical sketch, which is a brief statement or paragraph that may include personal information, such as words students may use to describe themselves, something they love, something they fear, something they hope for, and something they feel passionate about, etc. (Ayers 1993). This activity is often a fun and easy way for students to begin thinking about themselves.

❀ The story of how they got their name—another fun and relatively easy activity that gives students an opportunity to research how they got their names and to tell the story behind it.

❀ A story of a time in their lives when the students learned something important about themselves. This is sometimes more difficult, but it helps students to reflect on significant events and people in their lives that have helped them to construct an understanding of self.

In addition, the seminar provides numerous opportunities for students to dialogue and reflect on significant experiences, or "hinge points," that have made an impact on who they are and who they are likely to become. These may be moments, events, encounters, or interactions that have influenced students to take a reflective turn in a new direction, to think differently about their reality, or to listen more attentively to their experience. After the first year of study, the focus of inquiry turns to self as a teacher and learner. Over the next three years of coursework and several diverse field placements, the following questions are tested and matured: *Who am I as a learner? How was I taught? Who am I as a teacher? Why do I want to teach? What is my role in relation to children and parents? What is appropriate and possible?*

The following activities, in particular, have been effective in exploring these questions. We will explicate a few of them here:

❀ Self Observations: Listening to Oneself
❀ Metaphors of Teaching: Who am I as a Teacher?
❀ Personal Narrative/Autobiography
❀ Representations (journal writing, reflections, physical models, poems, artistic portrayals, performances, etc.)
❀ Engaging in Practical Inquiry (pursuing "real questions," problem-based activities, projects, action research, etc.) and making discoveries public

In the first activity, students are asked to observe themselves as though someone else was doing the observation for an entire day. In this case, self-observation means to watch and listen to everything within and without oneself as though there is no personal connection whatsoever (de Mello, 1990). The aim is to study oneself without the desire to change what is, but to develop awareness and understanding. At the end of the day the student is requested to make sense of what was discovered and to share this with a peer, both in written and oral form. Below is an example:

> This morning I observed myself [in the classroom] much like I do the children each time I'm there. It was a difficult activity, trying to reflect on what I'm thinking, but still attempting to figure out what the children were doing and why. . . . While the parents were dropping off the children, I knew I was nervous. I know that being observed by parents makes me pretty uncomfortable. I don't think I'm doing anything terribly wrong, but I want the parents to approve completely. I took Christopher, Qi-Qi, Meg, and Martino outside to ride bikes on the playground. I really enjoyed myself with them. I know I work

better with smaller groups of people (children and adults). . . . I definitely know that I am more outgoing around children than adults I do not know. It's hard for me not to be more involved with the children I'm closer with, but sometimes that just happens. . . . I know that there are certain areas I need to work on, but feel that I learn so much each day that I am in the classroom.

In this brief reflection, the student is actually listening to herself, a skill that is essential to listening to others and developing awareness, which leads to mindfulness (Rud, 1995; van Manen, 1991). It is this kind of self-observation and reflection that can lead to transformation. In our experience, self-observation allows students to develop the ability to react less and act more, to question their decisions and search for meaning in their actions, and to see things from new and multiple perspectives.

A second very useful exercise is to have students identify metaphors of teaching (see Bullough & Gitlin, 1995, for a thorough analysis of teaching metaphors). This is so important to the negotiation of what it means to be a teacher that students are asked to complete this exercise periodically over the course of their formal teacher education, and to represent their images of teaching using multiple languages. One such activity asks students to imagine themselves as a teacher in the classroom, and then represent in some way (using any means of representation they choose) their definition of self-as-teacher. They are asked to explain their representation and share this in

Engagements in practical inquiry enable students to closely examine meaningful issues, rethink old positions, and look at teaching from a new and different perspective.

class. The transformative aspect of this assignment is that it provides opportunities for students to explore and analyze their mental images of teaching, including images of what is appropriate and possible in the classroom.

Writing personal narratives or educational autobiographies that reflect a social historical look at the experiences, events, and people who have helped students to construct their images of teaching and learning is also a very effective means for illuminating and challenging deep-seated beliefs and assumptions (Bullough & Gitlin, 1995). Being aware of the theories and beliefs that are informing one's practice is critical to taking ownership of and defending those views. This in and of itself is transforming.

Finally, engagements in practical inquiry (e.g., pursuing "real questions," problem-based activities, projects, and action research) enable students to closely examine meaningful issues, rethink old positions, and look at teaching from a new and different perspective. Projects that involve the pursuit of a "real" question, in which students pursue authentic and meaningful questions of interest to them, require original thinking and interpretation, multiple methods of inquiry, and promote the development of a deep and elaborate understanding of selected core ideas related to curriculum and assessment. This form of inquiry is part of the routine and expected function of teachers' daily lives in the classroom that can be documented in a portfolio and shared with others.

CONCLUDING REMARKS

Self-awareness and understanding are important in teaching, because we teach who we are. Our conceptions of ourselves as teachers are grounded biographically. Teachers need to know what theories, values, and beliefs are driving their teaching and be able to defend them and/or reconstruct them when conditions change. Furthermore, teaching is a relationship, a way of being and relating to others. Lella Gandini tells us that in teaching children, "we become aware of our way of observing and interacting with children." Understanding who we are and what we bring to our teaching enables us to understand that children also bring something to us. Listening to ourselves, we learn to listen to the child. When we listen to the child, the child becomes the teacher. This is an important transformation that allows us to learn and to experience children not as we are, but as they are. In closing, we raise a question that, we believe, all teachers must ask themselves: "How do teachers stay open to change in a success- and solution-oriented society that overvalues achievement, progress, and evaluation, in order to remain open to the transformative possibilities inherent in good teaching?" If teaching is a process of continual renewal and transformation, then, as William Ayers has noted, "teachers can never 'arrive,' in the sense that they have mastered the intricacies of their craft." Belief in the process of becoming means believing in the notion of reinventing yourself through the continual reconstruction of experience.

REFERENCES

Ayers, W. (1993). *To teach: The journey of a teacher*. New York: Teachers College Press.

Bullough, R. V., & Gitlin, A. (1995). *Becoming a student of teaching: Methodologies for exploring self and school context*. New York: Garland Publishing.

Cochran-Smith, M., & Lytle, S. L. (1999). The teacher research movement: A decade later. *Educational Researcher, 28* (7), 15–25.

de Mello, A. (1990). *Awareness: The perils and opportunities of reality*. New York: Doubleday.

Freeman, D. (1998). *Doing teacher research: From inquiry to understanding*. New York: Heinle & Heinle Publishers.

Haroutunian-Gordon, S. (1995). Soul. In J. W. Garrison & A. G. Rud (Eds.), *The educational conversation: Closing the gap* (pp. 97–107). Albany, NY: SUNY.

Nouwen, H. J. M. (1975). *Reaching out: The three movements of the spiritual life*. New York: Doubleday.

Paley, V. G. (1990). *The boy who would be a helicopter: The uses of storytelling in the classroom*. Cambridge, MA: Harvard.

Rud, A. G. (1995). Learning in comfort: Developing an ethos of hospitality in education. In J. W. Garrison & A. G. Rud (Eds.), *The educational conversation: Closing the gap* (pp. 119–128). Albany, NY: SUNY Press.

Van Manen, M. (1991). *The tact of teaching: The meaning of pedagogical thoughtfulness*. Albany, NY: SUNY Press.

Chapter
10

The Development of Documentation Strategies to Support Teacher Reflection, Inquiry, and Collaboration

Jeanne Goldhaber ◆ **Dee Smith**

We are sitting at tables arranged in a large square configuration in a spacious salon of an 18th century villa in San Vitale, Switzerland. Two floor-to-ceiling windows look out on the main road that leads to a tiny shopping area to the left. To the right, you can see a small but ornate church and bell tower which marks one of the town's boundaries. We are two of 40 American educators who have come together for a week to consider the ramifications of the theory and pedagogy of the Reggio Emilia approach to our own practice and professional settings. On this, the second day of the conference, one of the participants has the floor, and says offhandedly, "Well, we all know what documentation is, right?"

Vickie turns quickly to face her, and says, not unkindly, "Oh! Can you define documentation for us?" She then turns to the whole group, and adds, "Can anyone?"

Her question is met with uncomfortable silence, which is finally broken by a joyful squeal from the single and much doted upon six-month-old in the delegation. Everyone takes this cue as permission to start talking among themselves, leaving Vickie's question unanswered but lingering.

What *is* documentation? This is such a simple question, and yet, despite our seven years of study at the University of Vermont, we had never ventured to define this term, other than to refer to the words of Reggio Emilia educators such as Vea Vecchi or Carlina Rinaldi. It was time to construct our own definition, one that reflected our own experience, context, and history. So, that evening we struggled to write a draft of a working definition which incorporated what the practice of documentation had come to mean to us. It read as follows:

> Documentation *at the University of Vermont* is collecting, organizing, interpreting, and sharing traces of children's efforts to understand their social and physical worlds in order to: promote teacher inquiry and reflection; address and/or provoke children's theories, questions, interests, and concerns; build a community of learners among children and children, children and adults, adults and adults; nurture relationships among children and children, children and adults, adults and adults; and to advocate for children as competent and worthy of our attention, care, and respect.

In this chapter we tell the story of how we came to this working definition, as well as how this definition provoked further learning and investigation. Specifically, we describe our program and our efforts to learn about the Reggio Emilia approach, particularly in regard to the practice of documentation. We include a discussion of our early documentation efforts, which contributed to our growing awareness of the potential of the documentation process as a form of teacher inquiry and the corresponding need to develop a system to organize our efforts.

We discuss this system in detail in the hope that our experiences can support others who are eager to embark on this journey. By way of illustration, we report on a collaborative investigation in which the preschoolers explored their identities and roles as nurturers, mentors, and friends of the infants. We also describe a program-wide investigation of the children's developing ability to represent and communicate meaning. This project is particularly unique in that it included not only the teachers and a group of student teachers from our Campus Children's Center, but also another group of student teachers and their primary level classroom mentors from local public schools. Vignettes that describe student teachers' experiences are also included to breathe life into this discussion and give voice to their unique experiences.

We close this chapter with a personal statement that reflects our belief that the process of documentation is a powerful enterprise that has the potential to change how we view ourselves as early childhood teacher educators.

WHO WE ARE

The University of Vermont's (UVM) Early Childhood PreK–3 Teacher Education Program and the UVM Campus Children's Center are housed in the College of Education and Social Services. The PreK–3 program has approximately 80 to 100 undergraduate early childhood majors and the equivalent of 2.5 tenured faculty and professional staff. Administered by the PreK–3 program and with approximately 40 children (6 infants, 7 young toddlers, 9 older toddlers/young preschoolers, and 18 preschool-aged children), the Campus Children's Center performs a two-fold role: to provide full-time, year-round early education and care to the children of faculty, staff, and students of the university community, and to provide an educational laboratory setting for the UVM Early Childhood PreK–3 Teacher Education Program.

The PreK–3 program's academic courses and the curriculum of the Campus Children's Center reflect a shared social constructivist perspective. The infant–toddler and preschool program head teachers and PreK–3 faculty teach courses together and share responsibility for supervising practicum students in the Center. In addition, the Center's teachers serve as mentors to the practicum students and meet with the students in their academic classes to discuss issues and investigations relevant to their group of children. In these respects, as well as those that are less tangible but perhaps even more meaningful, we are a close and engaged community.

PROGRAM DEVELOPMENT TAKES TIME

Faculty, staff, and students of the UVM PreK–3 program and Campus Children's Center have been engaged in the joint investigation of the Reggio Emilia approach since 1991, when several of us participated in a delegation to Reggio Emilia. We returned overwhelmed by the challenge of interpreting our experience into our academic and children's programs. After making some relatively minor changes to our physical environment and experimenting with the use of projects and documentation, several of us decided to return to Reggio in 1993. This time we went with a different lens: we decided that we would focus on Reggio's practice of documentation. This decision reflected our own context and philosophical base and our belief that documentation's emphasis on observation and analysis would support our mission to prepare early childhood educators. Since that second visit, we have been investigating the role of documentation in teacher preparation and professional development and the extent to which the process of documentation can promote practice, which is characterized by teacher collaboration, reflection, and inquiry.

EARLY DOCUMENTATION EFFORTS

Our early documentation efforts primarily focused on capturing and interpreting images of children engaged in exploring their social and physical worlds. For example, we recorded and created panels of young toddlers' investigations of the texture and taste of uncooked oats and of an infant's joyful reunions with his image in a mirror. We invited older toddlers to reengage in a game of peek-a-boo by lifting a series of photographs which gradually showed more complete images of their faces. We documented children's motoric, social, and cognitive accomplishments, with the goal of promoting a rich and competent image of the child. Examples of these early efforts include panels that celebrated the infants' efforts to initiate and maintain interactions with their peers or those who discussed the preschoolers' concepts of infinity, good and evil, and life and death. Students were also documenting the children's experiences, although it should be noted that their documentation efforts were, at that time, often unrelated to those of the teaching staff.

A SHIFT IN FOCUS

In spite of our belief that documentation should be a "process" rather than a "product," we were spending far too much time creating the actual display of the collected information and far too little time trying to understand and respond to the meaning of that information. Fortunately, the toddlers' year-long investigation of the life, habits, and personalities of three hermit crabs transformed our definition of documentation from that of a "noun" to a "verb" through a number of simple yet transformative strategies: clip boards were hung in the classroom for all adults—teachers, students, parents—to record the toddlers' spontaneous questions or comments about the crabs; a panel was created that documented both the history as well as the in-progress crab investigations; a teacher kept a journal to record her reflections on the children's thinking about the crabs; parents attended meetings to discuss their children's investigations, and began to bring in transcripts and observations from home to be shared with the other children, families, and teachers. Documentation was becoming an active and interactive vehicle through which a community of children and adults was sharing the excitement of discovery and inquiry.

UNDER CONSTRUCTION: A "WORKING" DEFINITION OF DOCUMENTATION

Building on what we learned from the hermit crab investigation, we turned our attention to developing more process-driven strategies of documentation to promote more reflective and inquiry-based practice. We realized the important role organization plays in supporting reflection and analysis. Over time, our strategies evolved into a relatively straightforward and simple system that we still use. Teachers and student teachers put the day's observations, photographs, and annotated artifacts in the classroom's designated "documentation" basket. The fact that teachers and student teachers are invited to write their observations on whatever piece of paper is at hand (anecdotals are recorded on scraps of envelopes, torn-off corners of newsprint, etc.) appears to increase the likelihood of an observation being written. We have also found that identifying a basket as the "holding place" for the day's observations serves to protect them from being stashed and subsequently lost in teachers' pants or skirt pockets.

Teachers and student teachers discuss the materials collected in the basket during the children's rest time in order to understand at a deeper level the children's evolving questions, theories, and interests, and to plan experiences that will provoke further inquiry. Teacher discussions and meetings about the classroom are very informed with frequent reference to the "raw data" collected in the documentation basket.

The collected materials are then placed in looseleaf notebooks, which contain on-going documentation of a specific "thread" that is a current focus of active and child-driven inquiry in a classroom. In general, the notebooks contain dated anecdotal observations, transcripts, video logs, video prints, photographs, artifacts, and computer-scanned images.

FIGURE 10.1   *A transcript of a conversation about the classroom's hermit crabs (which was spoken in Chinese) between a mother and her two children while at home. She transcribed the conversation and shared it at a parent meeting.*

cc) How are Hermit crabs?　　　　　　　　寄居蟹呢？

la) walking . sleeping　　　　　　　　　走路 和 睡覺

cc) sleeping? or napping?　　　　　　　　睡覺？有沒有睡午覺？

la) no! no nap! don't nap!　　　　　　　沒有. 沒有睡午覺. 他們不睡午覺

cc) Are they not tired?　　　　　　　　　他們累不累？會不會累？

Ha) no　　　　　　　　　　　　　　　　沒有

cc) Why they are not tired?　　　　　　　他們為什麼不累？

ta) a little tired　　　　　　　　　　　他們有一點點累

cc) What do they do when they are tired?　他們累的時候怎麼辦？

Ho) they go back to their home to
　　　　sleep! (shell is their home, they sleep in
　　　　　the shell)　　　　　　　　　　他們回他的家 睡覺
　　　　　　　　　　　　　　　　　　（shell 是他們的家 他們在殼裡睡覺）

Ha.) they don't.　　　　　　　　　　　他們 沒有

ta) they do!　　(repeats: no no no yes yes yes)　他們 有 沒有有 沒有有 沒有有 . . . . .

Ha.) sleep! sleep! sleep. They sleep.　　睡覺. 睡覺. 他們睡覺
　　　in school. walking walking . they walk　在學校. 走路. 走路. 他們走路
　　　they hurt. claws hurt　　　　　　　他們會痛. claws 會痛.

cc) why hermit crab hurt?　　　　　　　為什麼寄居蟹會痛？

Ha) Big. small. Big and small.　　　　　大的. 小的. 大的和小的
　　　Big and small claws hurt.　　　　　大的小的 claws 會痛

cc) why their claws hurt?　　　　　　　為什麼腳會痛？

Ha) they walk.　　　　　　　　　　　他們走路

Ha) they walk too much.　　　　　　　他們走太多了

Ha .) Don't write too much!　　　　　　不要寫
　　　(He... took a pen started to draw)　弟弟拿起一支鉛筆 作畫

　　　This is a hermit crab. a lot of　　　這是 hermit crab. 好多腳 眼睛
da (lego) eyes. a big mouth, their　　　　一個 "好大" 的 嘴巴. 他們的腳 會痛
　　　claws hurt. make a small　　　　　一個小的 . 另外 一個小的.
　　　hermit crab. more small ones.

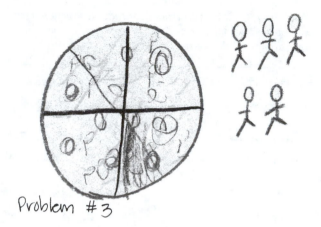

FIGURE 10.2 *The following observation accompanies this drawing, which is placed in a notebook that documents the children's evolving understanding of number and equity in the context of their year-long love affair with pizza. "I draw five children and one pizza cut in fourths. I approach Nadine and say, 'Uh oh, there are four slices of pizza for five children, how can you cut the pizza so that each child gets the same amount?' Nadine cuts the pizza once more along the diameter and counts the slices. Realizing there are now six, she colors one in and explains, 'You have to throw one out because then you have five for five kids and that's fair'."*

Each notebook is ordered chronologically with the most recent experience first. Actual artifacts, such as children's drawings or notes, are placed in plastic sleeves, as are observations and transcripts that have been recorded on scraps of paper. An investment in plastic sleeves to save the artifacts and observations proves worthwhile, particularly when it is time to review the development of a particular thread or to gather and present original artifacts in more formal and public formats. As a result, these more formal documentation panels and displays represent authentic and well-researched aspects of the children's experiences in the classroom.

The notebooks also serve other purposes. They are kept in the classroom so that they are available to families and visitors to the program. In addition, we require all student teachers who spend time in the classroom to read the notebooks before entering, so that they are informed and prepared to participate in the children's investigations.

THE INFANT/PRESCHOOL INVESTIGATION

A joint investigation between the infant and preschool rooms helped us to clarify our thinking further about the process of documentation and the corresponding need to be more thoughtful in how we organize and analyze the material collected in the notebooks. Over the course of a year, the infant and preschool teachers and student teachers observed, analyzed, and nurtured the infants' and preschoolers' interest in and theories about each other. This investigation provided a particularly high level of reflection and collaboration, and its richness required us to develop strategies to further organize and analyze the multitude of images, observations, and artifacts we collected. For example, one of the teachers decided to record her questions, along with her observations and hypotheses, as the investigation unfolded. Similarly, the need to trace the complex and transactional nature of the children's experiences emerged as the teachers cycled through a process that included observing, formulating questions, proposing theories or hypotheses, and planning experiences as provocations or extensions.

The infant/preschool investigation was formally documented as a panel and placed on the wall in the dramatic play area where much of the baby play occurred. By the end of the year, there were additional displays, several of which were made in duplicate so that there was one in both the infant and preschool rooms. These displays or panels presented and analyzed the meaning of the children's experiences as the preschoolers and infants learned how to be the agents and recipients of nurturing, mentoring, and friendship.

A SHARED FOCUS: THE DEVELOPMENT OF REPRESENTATIONAL COMPETENCE

The infant/preschool investigation convinced us of the power of a shared research question. Out of this conviction, we initiated a center-wide investigation of the development of representational competence. Specifically, we were interested in learning how young children become increasingly competent as meaning makers and communicators. A small Eisenhower Grant allowed us to include our primary level student teachers and their mentor teachers and to provide support in the form of on-site videotaping and consultation. Together, we gathered rich and provocative data that led us to unexpected research questions. For example, as we observed the ways in which the preschoolers and kindergartners represented their affection and caring for each other through their drawings, paintings, and writing, we looked for evidence of this social agenda in our infants. We were fascinated by our youngest children's efforts to engage each other in interactions through subtle messages of gesture, facial expression, and body movement. Similarly, the infant teachers' investigation of crying as a form of communication led to the preschool teachers' reexamination of the role of the adult when preschool-aged children cry.

Sharing the duties of our investigation took many forms. One of the student teachers collected the material related to the preschool's investigation of the communication thread and organized it into categories (such as the various functions of

FIGURE 10.3   *A flow chart that traces the unfolding of the infant/preschool investigation.*

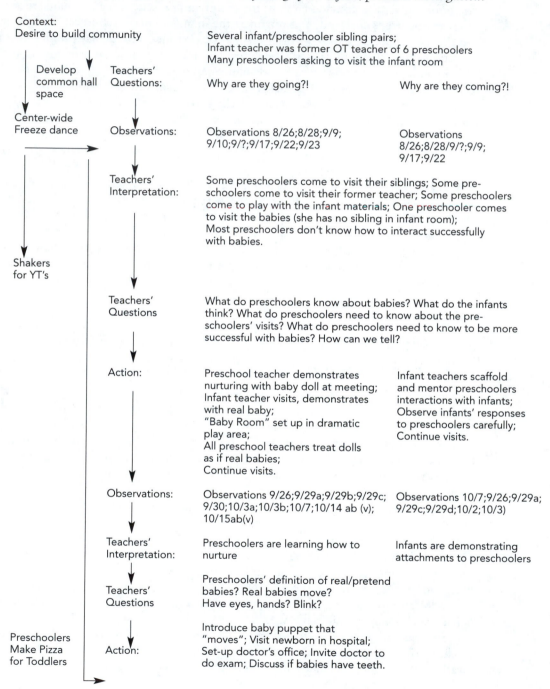

Context:
Desire to build community

Several infant/preschooler sibling pairs;
Infant teacher was former OT teacher of 6 preschoolers
Many preschoolers asking to visit the infant room

Develop common hall space

Teachers' Questions:

Why are they going?!   Why are they coming?!

Center-wide Freeze dance

Observations:

Observations 8/26;8/28;9/9;
9/10;9/?;9/17;9/22;9/23

Observations
8/26;8/28;9/?;9/9;
9/17;9/22

Teachers' Interpretation:

Some preschoolers come to visit their siblings; Some preschoolers come to visit their former teacher; Some preschoolers
come to play with the infant materials; One preschooler comes
to visit the babies (she has no sibling in infant room);
Most preschoolers don't know how to interact successfully
with babies.

Shakers for YT's

Teachers' Questions

What do preschoolers know about babies? What do the infants
think? What do preschoolers need to know about the preschoolers' visits? What do preschoolers need to know to be more
successful with babies? How can we tell?

Action:

Preschool teacher demonstrates
nurturing with baby doll at meeting;
Infant teacher visits, demonstrates
with real baby;
"Baby Room" set up in dramatic
play area;
All preschool teachers treat dolls
as if real babies;
Continue visits.

Infant teachers scaffold
and mentor preschoolers
interactions with infants;
Observe infants' responses
to preschoolers carefully;
Continue visits.

Observations:

Observations 9/26;9/29a;9/29b;9/29c;
9/30;10/3a;10/3b;10/7;10/14 ab (v);
10/15ab(v)

Observations 10/7;9/26;9/29a;
9/29c;9/29d;10/2;10/3

Teachers' Interpretation:

Preschoolers are learning how to
nurture

Infants are demonstrating
attachments to preschoolers

Teachers' Questions

Preschoolers' definition of real/pretend
babies? Real babies move?
Have eyes, hands? Blink?

Preschoolers
Make Pizza
for Toddlers

Action:

Introduce baby puppet that
"moves"; Visit newborn in hospital;
Set-up doctor's office; Invite doctor to
do exam; Discuss if babies have teeth.

communication). She wrote introductory essays analyzing each category and placed the notebook on the parent shelf as a public document to be shared with families, students, and center visitors. The other classrooms analyzed and shared their findings in various formats, including panels, slide presentations, and notebooks.

To this point, we have discussed our experiences primarily through the lens of the faculty and staff of our program. The following vignettes describe two students' experiences as they negotiated their developing understanding of the role of documentation in our program. We have included excerpts from their journals in the hope that you, the reader, will hear their voices as they share their feelings, frustration, questions, and theories.

ANNIE'S STORY

Annie began her practicum semester full of enthusiasm and eager to practice not only her skills with young toddlers, but her ability to document as well. She spent countless hours watching video tape, discussing children's play with teachers and fellow students, and documenting special moments in panel and book form for either parents or children, or both, to enjoy. As the semester progressed, she was challenged by our request to delve more deeply into one "thread" in the classroom. Everything was of interest to her! However, each time she viewed video tape, she found herself drawn to episodes involving children interacting with each other. In her journal, Annie began to hypothesize about the questions the children seemed to be asking. She wrote the following excerpt, in which she tried to put into words the thoughts and questions of the children she was studying:

> How do I express my intentions and desires with my developing communication skills? How do I enter into an activity that looks like fun? How do I get my friends to play with me? How do I sustain the interaction after I successfully initiate it? How do I manipulate my body to follow through with my plan?

With encouragement to narrow her focus, Annie became interested in how individual children approached each other to interact. She decided to view video tape of the children's interactions. It was in Annie's nature, however, to take on a little more than what was expected—in this case, she viewed a total of 24 hours of video tape taken in the young toddler room, beginning with tape from the prior semester! She found that although she had initially thought the children were highly individualized in their approaches to each other, there were actually many commonalties. She categorized the approaches as imitation, offering an object, touching, verbal invitation, laughing, and simply saying "Hi!" She found that one final category, eye contact, was present in almost all the approaches. By graphing her findings, Annie realized that at the beginning of the year, children spent more time initiating play through imitating, offering an object, and touching. By mid-year, the children spent much more time initiating interactions by verbal invitation and laughter.

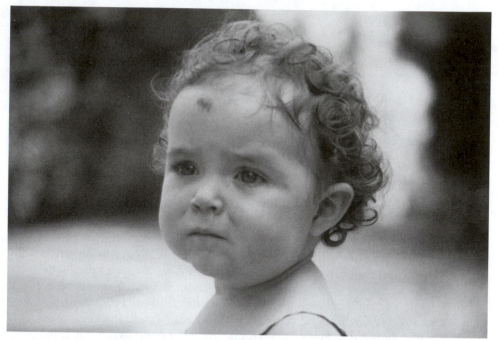

A pair of photographs capture the communicative power of an infant's facial expressions.

Annie was preparing to present her findings to the children's parents when she found information about a presentation by Honig and Thompson, "Toddler strategies for social engagement with peers" (1993), in which the authors discussed their findings related to how toddlers enter play with one another. Annie was delighted to find her research validated as she discovered her categories mirrored those of Honig and Thompson.

Reflecting on Annie's Experiences

Annie was an exuberant student teacher who had strong interactions with children, staff, and parents. She also enjoyed looking at short vignettes and documenting these to inform parents of their children's activities in the classroom. However, the idea of narrowing her scope of investigation to one area, and challenging herself to look at a deeper level, was a daunting task. She was excited *and* overwhelmed at the same time. With encouragement from staff, she found a method of inquiry which informed her questions. Though her investigation was of a totally different nature than the room's other investigations (involving questions related to the children's understanding of music, transparencies, and shadows), Annie looked to her peers and mentor teachers in the room to discuss her findings, to help her identify procedures for categorizing

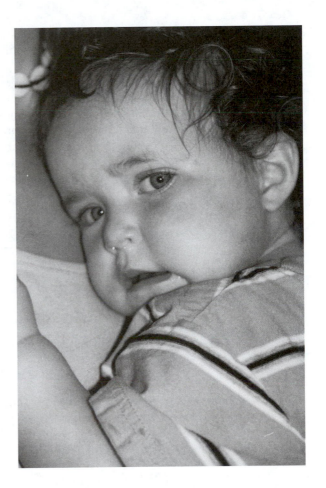

her data, and to collaborate in data collection. Annie's findings and collaboration benefited all the teachers as they became more sensitive to, and knowledgeable about, the toddlers' efforts to approach one another. Through this experience, Annie not only came to see herself as a more competent and confident teacher, she also extended her image of a teacher from simply practitioner to include the role of researcher.

JOAN'S STORY

Joan spent a semester as a student teacher in the infant room, which included children from 6 to 16 months of age. Joan had previous experience in the Center with older toddlers and preschoolers and also worked in a local child-care program with preschool-aged children. Her experience with infants was very limited, but she entered the classroom understanding that a significant responsibility would be forming relationships with the children and their families.

Based on her experience and previous course work, Joan understood the necessity of observing closely and was beginning to emulate the primary teachers' habit of formulating questions to guide their observations of children. After her second day in the classroom, she wrote in her journal, "I continue to observe the infants, but still feel like I am either looking too hard or not hard enough. I think I need to be asking more questions as I observe the infants." A few days later Joan began to sift through the infant room notebooks, organized by "threads," or interests of the children. The documentation she read reinforced her desire to question what she was observing. As she reflected on this, she wrote again in her journal:

> Observation has always been the key to learning about children, but there is also a lot of asking questions that needs to be done. I found that by following a thread, there were questions asked, and some were answered, but some remained. This, to me, is what documentation is all about.

Two weeks later, Joan was still observing, and still trying to narrow her focus of research for the semester. One afternoon Joan captured an amazing, lengthy social exchange between two infants on video tape. Joan reflected on the video clip in her journal:

> . . .Collin and Kyle were beginning to interact with each other on so many different levels. Their exchanges included physical touch, vocalization, and observation. It was a dance, possibly the beginning of a friendship. I can't wait to view the video tape of this interplay because there seems to be so much to see beyond what I saw originally. Why was this such a rich experience? How did this interaction begin, and how was it able to continue for such an extended period of time? What were the different levels of interactions with respect to the physical touch, vocalizations, and observation? Was this interaction instigated by one of the infants, or was it a combination of the two infants' interest in each other? This interaction has strengthened my interest in the social development of the infants, and the interactions they have. . . .

Joan continued to ask herself questions about the children's interactions, and the environment surrounding them. She spent hours documenting the experience to better understand the interactions. Her thoughts and conversations with others led her to look closely at the possibility of young children mirroring each other's actions, much like responsive care giving.

As Joan continued to study her observations and video clips, she decided to follow the infants' relationships as her "thread" for the semester. Her exact questions, however, were undeveloped. She began by documenting as many interactions as possible, and sharing them with staff and parents. She noticed that because of age differences, the children naturally tended to "pair off" in the classroom. Her questions continued to lead her to more observation, and her discussions with the classroom teachers and other students helped her to probe more deeply in her search for understanding.

As the semester progressed, Joan began to narrow her focus. She wrote to the staff and students in the infant room asking for their help.

. . . I would appreciate any video tape, Polaroids, or anecdotals on any interactions between those pairs of children. However, if there is an interaction that happens between two other children that just blows you away, I am still interested! I have narrowed my focus down to the following questions:

1. What draws these children together in an interaction? Is their interaction instigated by a mutual interest, an object, or companionship? Is there something else that brings these children together?
2. What are some of the cues the children are using to engage each other in such interactions? What is happening between the two children that is helping to prolong the interaction or make it so meaningful? (Smiles, touch, eye contact, observation, similar ways of exploring objects, mimicking. . . .)

As the semester came to a close, Joan organized a parent meeting to share her findings. She wrote in her journal:

We sat together and watched the clips one by one. The parents all watched their children engage in social exchanges, and frequently filled the room with laughter and affectionate thoughts.

Through dialogue, the meeting served not only to inform parents about their child's relationships at school, but to inform the staff about the children's rich relationships outside of the Center. It added to everyone's image of very young children as competent communicators. It was a joyful event which helped to bring closure to the semester for Joan in a very positive and emotional way. Joan wrote in her final journal entry:

I was so moved by the parents' conversations between each other and with how in tune they all seemed to be with their children! Ever since the moment I started the video and watched Collin and Kyle smile and squawk in turn, I was fighting tears.

Reflecting on Joan's Experiences

It seemed to us that Joan had learned not only about the children's relationships, but about her own connectedness to the families, her colleagues, and her profession. As we reflect on Joan's experience, we also see the significant role mentoring played in her experience. For example, Joan was in the company of teachers as they constantly discussed the relationships that were developing among the children involved in the concurrent infant/preschool investigation. In addition, room meetings between head teachers, teachers, and students often focused on the multiple investigations in the classroom, giving Joan the opportunity to apply the process of documenting to her own investigation. While the content of Joan's investigation was different, the cycle of inquiry was similar. Joan observed, reflected on her observations, revisited them multiple times, shared them with other teachers in the classroom, analyzed their meaning, and ultimately invited parents into the cycle of inquiry to add to her understanding of the children's competencies in forming relationships. Joan's experience clearly benefited from these multiple perspectives.

FINAL THOUGHTS

Looking back over both our own and our students' work, we return to a question which we have been exploring for several years: How do you recast the traditional image of a teacher from one who knows all the answers to one who celebrates not knowing the answers and is excited by the prospect of looking for them? from someone who sees teaching as a safe profession to one who sees teaching as an act of courage? from someone who views teaching as a solitary act to one who relishes teaching as a collaborative enterprise?

We recently talked about the image of the teacher at a meeting of all the student teachers in our center and asked them to reflect on why their image had changed since entering the program. Before the meeting began we had thought about all the things that may have influenced them. We were certain they would refer to the many assignments they had read which discussed the Reggio approach, constructivism, and documentation; to the many slide presentations they had seen over the past few years; perhaps even to a memorable lecture or two they had heard in one of their classes about the role of the teacher in the teaching and learning process.

We did hear some talk about these experiences, but by far the strongest influence was related to the power of being mentored within a collaborative learning community. For example, the students talked about the profound effect of having the classroom teachers ask them, "What do you think?" They talked about teachers in discussion with one another, intense about their work, sometimes in conflict over the meaning of a particular anecdotal observation or video clip. They were seeing a new image of the teacher who not only nurtures and cares for children, but also asks important questions and has the courage, stamina, knowledge, and skills to seek out their answers (knowing, of course, that their journey will ultimately lead to yet more questions).

Through our students' eyes, we see ourselves as the curious, intellectually, and emotionally engaged professionals we strive to be. We know, too, that we are at times quarrelsome, short-tempered, and frustrated by the realities of limited resources and multiple demands. Nevertheless, we appreciate how generous our students are in the lens they share and we recognize the powerful role we play in their development as early childhood professionals.

REFERENCES

Honig, A. S., & Thompson, A. (1993). *Toddler strategies for social engagement with peers*. Poster presented at the 8th Biennial National Training Institute of Zero to Three, Washington, D.C.

Chapter 11

Passion and the Art of Teaching

Deborah W. Tegano

Teaching as an Art, Art as Imagination, Imagination as Passion

To teach artfully means to combine spirit and mind. Loris Malaguzzi, the inspiration behind the schools of Reggio Emilia, explains something of the mystery of this mixture of spirit and mind when he talks of his personal experience of overcoming obstacles to birth the schools of Reggio Emilia. "It was a powerful experience emerging out of a thick web of emotions and from a complex matrix of knowledge and values promising new creativity of which I was only becoming aware" (Malaguzzi, 1998, p. 56). The schools of Reggio Emilia continue to offer inspiration to early childhood educators from around the world who find a sense of excitement and renewal, possibility and creativity, "discovery and serenity" (p. 63) in the very process of teaching.

Artful teaching combines the best elements of our inner intuitive sense with the best elements of our thinking sense. Teaching, then, requires both a source of inner energy and a sense of direction about where we are going. If we think of spirit as the energy that propels us to action, then spirit implies an intangible force responsible for forward movement, the "wind that fills the sails." Complementary to spirit, and yet unquestionably necessary for teaching, is the thinking sense that implies the logic and reasoning of mind that is responsible for finding direction, or "setting the course." In some sense, it is impossible to teach without this mixture of spirit and mind. On one hand, teaching that dissociates spirit from mind is either chaotic (energized random actions without pattern, form, or purpose) or prescriptive (objective-driven, but dry and lifeless). On the other hand, the elegant combination of spirit and mind yields teaching as an art and results in a passion about teaching. In the dictionary, passion is defined as emotion that compels action. Passionate teaching has an intensity that is characterized by goal-directed energy. This sense of passion is what we see, or perhaps *feel,* in teachers who work with children in Reggio-inspired classrooms.

In Chapter 1 of this book, Vickie Fu introduced the idea of the art of teaching and supported her ideas with contemporary thinkers like Maxine Greene (1988), Jim Garrison (1997), and Eliot Eisner (1994). In that chapter, Fu challenged teachers to follow Maxine Greene's advice and explore the arts as a means to exploring our own possibilities. Analogous to this is the suggestion that teachers strive to be both interesting and interested people (Welles, 1985). Fu asked us to think about the position of arts and aesthetics in our lives:

> Do you see the aesthetics of nature that surround us? Are you tuned in to the shapes, forms, lines, colors, sounds, rhythm, beats that integrate and play on each other in nature, in cities, in classrooms? Do you find connections between the creating and the creations of artists, sculptors, writers, musicians, dancers, and how you teach? Where are the hundred languages? How do you use them in your teaching? How do arts enrich the lives of teachers and children? How do arts open up the possibilities of teaching and learning? (p. 000)

The art of teaching evokes images of possibility, of the principles of form, beauty, and perception applied to teaching, and of intersubjective immersion in teaching. Let's think about each of these elements of the art of teaching.

Teaching is a creative act that is different in every moment. It means thinking extemporaneously, continually reasoning about what is happening and what may evolve next. Dewey said that, in teaching, our ability to reason is connected to our imagination. He continues that reason "must fall back upon imagination—upon the embodiment of ideas in [an] emotionally charged sense" (Dewey, 1934/87, p. 40). Dewey recognized the role of imagination in bringing life into the act of teaching. The art of teaching, then, involves imagination and possibility. In Dewey's Pedagogic Creed, he asserts his understanding of education and its relation to social progress as "the most perfect union of science and art conceivable in human existence" (Dewey, 1897/ 1998, p. 234). He states:

> I believe that when science and art thus join hands, the most commanding motives for human action will be reached, the most genuine springs of human conduct aroused, and the best service that human nature is capable of is guaranteed (p. 234).

As a philosopher, Dewey's words inspire us with passion—emotion that compels us to action. In Chapter 3, Vickie Fu notes, "Teachers who practice teaching as an art are passionate about their work, valuing creativity, uncertainty, different ways of seeing, knowing, and representing" (p. 000). These are images of possibility achieved through the art of teaching.

Imagination and possibility must have form, or they fall prey to randomness and chaos. This is an important aspect of teaching as an art. When teaching has a perceptible form, it may also have a sense of beauty or an aesthetic. One teacher, studying the Reggio approach, searched for a sense of how to find form in her teaching: "I am told to be a co-constructionist, a provocateur, an arouser of knowledge, a dancer with children following their lead." This teacher senses the possibilities of teaching in the poetic image of "dancing" in relationship with the children in her classroom. Her teaching has a perceptible form, an aesthetic, that is held together by her understanding of the principles of social constructivist approaches to education. Her understanding of herself as a "dancer with children" exemplifies her understanding of teaching as an art. The aesthetic of teaching is perceived differently in each movement, co-constructed in each movement, yet held together by core ideas and principles. The form and aesthetic of teaching are perceptible, though intangible. They are not found in detailed lesson planning or in developmental checklist data. Lesson plans and checklists are necessary for good teaching, though clearly, it is the intangible element of how we understand, interpret, and use this information that makes teaching an art. The form and aesthetic of teaching are sensed by teachers who have channeled imagination and possibility into myriad constructivist and social constructivist approaches to learning and have discovered that spirit and mind operate harmoniously.

Teaching artfully means being immersed in teaching in the same way that a painter is immersed in the process of painting, or, to use the previous metaphor, in the same way that a dancer is immersed in the dance. When painters, dancers, or teachers are passionate about their trade, the boundaries begin to blur into subjectivity. Am I painting or am I the painting? Am I dancing, or am I the dance? Am I teaching, or am I an intersubjective part of a powerful interchange between teacher and child? Is my teaching thus changed as a result of the interchange as a painting is changed with each brush stroke or a dance is changed with each movement? To be "a dancer with children" is to be immersed in the dance and to be open to the flow of movement and change as a partner in a special relationship.

Teachers who are passionate about teaching understand the process of teaching from an intersubjective perspective and look beyond measurable outcomes (a completed product) for the contextualized subjective *meaning* of a teaching and learning episode (the essence of the learning that took place). This disposition toward teaching involves the intangibles of intuitive understanding as well as analytical thinking; it takes both spirit and mind. Like any form of art, teaching that focuses on subjective meaning in context moves teaching into the realm of a delicate craft that requires exquisite skill and finesse. The craft of teaching implies intuition coupled with care and empathy. Vecchi discussed how her experiences of being an atelierista, a studio teacher who help(s) children find languages for symbolic expression of their thinking, have modified her views: "The 'reading' of reality is a subjective and cooperative production, and this is a creative act" (Vecchi, 1998, p. 143). So the art of teaching invites us to be immersed in the subjective and the intersubjective toward discovering "how creativity is part of the makeup of every individual" (p. 143).

In the best of worlds, teaching is both an art and an act of passion. Botstein uses Maxine Greene's work to observe: "What makes art—discipline, concentration, invention, action, the overreaching of one's own instincts" (Botstein, 1998, p. 70). These are the same words that we read and integrate into our understanding of teaching when we study the Reggio Emilia approach. Overreaching of one's own instincts means to go beyond one's own instinctual capacities. Passionate teaching pushes us to go beyond our perceived limits. In one teacher's words are seen her movement away from her perceived limits: "I have learned to seek knowledge like a child—to learn so I can teach and enjoy the process." Another teacher says, "I am in a new growth spurt in my life! Never would I have expected it at my age . . . My mind has regained more of its youthful elasticity and is stretching and growing to incorporate new thinking and ideas." With 54 years of combined teaching experience, these two teachers were reflecting on their experiences in a graduate class on the Reggio Emilia approach.[1] They illustrate the passionate voices of teachers who have discovered, or rediscovered, the experience of "overreaching" that is characteristic of Reggio-inspired educators. What makes *art* is also what makes passionate teaching—passion in teaching requires discipline, concentration, invention, action, and overreaching one's own instincts.

FINDING TEACHERS' VOICES

In this chapter, the voices of teachers demonstrate how the experience of studying the Reggio Emilia approach (REA) is renewing in and of itself. Discovering REA may be described as an "aha" experience—a continuous "aha" in a socially constructed and co-constructed world. For many educators there is an understanding that they have

[1]The summer course was a three-week intensive graduate level seminar on the Reggio Emilia approach.

come "home" to a philosophy that fits with an educational belief system that they have heretofore not been able to articulate. The works of the Italian educators from Reggio Emilia give form to a process of education that becomes a way of life for those who study these ideas.

One story of renewed passion is a personal one. Several years ago, my 25-year career as an early childhood teacher educator was becoming characterized by symptoms of stress and burnout. In an attempt to look deeply at my chosen profession and my work environment, I invited some of my colleagues to join me in an intraspective journey where each of us might articulate our professional and personal vision. Then I asked my colleagues to describe the optimal environment where this vision might be realized. I wrote:

> An environment that embraces innovation and change and stays open to the chaos inherent in the process of change.
> > Freedom to think.
> > Freedom to take risks.
> > Freedom to make mistakes.
> An environment where mutual respect is the highest priority.
> An environment that invites diverse perspectives and seeks discourse across disciplines.
> An environment that values the transfer of knowledge to applied settings and seeks challenges for problem solving in this arena.

Two years and three weeks later, I found myself attending the Winter Institute of the Schools of Reggio Emilia, Italy, with no predetermined idea that, indeed, my vision was being actualized. It was only by reflection, several years later, that I stumbled back upon my own words and realized that it was no wonder that Reggio-inspired ideas "fit" for me. Through my exercise of visioning, I had articulated for myself elements of what has been described by Malaguzzi and his colleagues so eloquently. My personal experience of "fit" is not unique. Other Reggio educators have expressed a similar sense of renewal, of belonging, of teaching in congruence with a system of beliefs and values, of a way of life. Malaguzzi's poem, "The Hundred Languages of Children," "encourages us to revisit, rediscover, reflect, relearn, and *reinvent* our lives as teachers" (p. 000).

The most telling evidence of this philosophy of life is inevitably revealed during the dialogue sessions at the week-long Institutes sponsored by Reggio children. As one follows the reflective process of Reggio educator Carlina Rinaldi's responses to inquiries from educators around the world, it becomes clear that her bottom-line answer of "What is life?" captures the essence of the Reggio Emilia approach to education. Reggio-inspired thinking *is* a way of life.

So, does passion replace burnout? What happens when we think deeply about our professional goals and about ways to bring these goals into our sites? Do we seek possibilities? Can we view educational philosophy as a vehicle to embody both spirit and mind? Can we teach from the heart? It may be a "stretch" to profess that REA is all of these things. Though it is clearly not a stretch to say that, for many educators, REA is a source of passion and one means for connecting with our intrinsic need to find meaning in our teaching.

This chapter considers the art of teaching as a means to engage our spirit as well as our mind, demonstrated in the essence of renewal and passion through teachers' stories. In looking at the quality of teachers' engagement, the nuances of context and teaching experience arise and become part of the interpretation of the phenomenon of professional development and teacher education.

The teachers' voices in this chapter come from several qualitative research studies focused on teachers' perceptions of the Reggio Emilia approach.[2] These studies were conducted across several years as teachers were introduced to and supported in working with Reggio-inspired ideas in a university laboratory child-care setting and in a number of public elementary school settings. The focus of the studies was on teacher education and on understanding the meaning of teachers' experiences in the context of their individual educational settings. The participants in the studies had diverse backgrounds and experiences. Some were preservice teachers, student teachers (in a teacher education program focused on child care), or teacher interns (in K–2 classrooms); while others were mentoring teachers in whose classrooms and under whose supervision the preservice teachers taught. Still others were child care and primary grade teachers who were involved in professional development projects focused on the Reggio Emilia approach. The university research team interviewed teachers and kept records at staff meetings and formal study group meetings.[3] The research team transcribed reflective dialogue, collected reflective journals, made detailed field notes about classroom practices and professional development activities, and dialogued intensively with teachers. The goal was to understand the phenomenon of teaching as it was perceived by the teachers—to understand the meaning that Reggio-inspired teaching held for the teachers. One overarching finding of these studies was the teachers' experience of passion and renewal associated with studying the ideas inspired by the Reggio Emilia approach.

One teacher dialogued about what she had come to understand about the phenomenon of Reggio-inspired teaching: "I am now beyond only seeing Reggio as a program that uses mirrors, shadows, and light play to teach children. I am trying to define and apply my own interpretation of collaboration, reflection, revisiting, and re-

---

[2]This chapter is based on the qualitative studies that explored the process of educational change influenced by the philosophy and approaches of the Schools of Reggio Emilia, Italy. The findings of these studies were presented at the National Association for the Education of Young Children conference (Toronto, 1998; New Orleans, 1999), as part of the Reggio-Lugano Research Collaborative preconference presentations at the Summer Conference on Recasting the Reggio Emilia Approach to Inform Teaching in the United States (Blacksburg, VA, 1999), and also at the American Educational Research Association Meeting (New Orleans, 2000). See references.

[3]The study groups were comprised of K–1 teachers and student interns across five elementary schools who were participants in a project funded by the State of Tennessee's Goals 2000, entitled *A Community of Learners: Partnerships in Early Education*. The Community of Learners project focused on helping teachers explore Reggio-inspried ideas, including the use of technology to create documentation of children's learning.

connaissance to use with my three-year-olds beginning in August. I will make a conscious effort to make sure that my children may utilize to the fullest their hundred languages." This quote touches the essence of continual and on-going learning when she says, "I am try*ing*." It also speaks to this teacher's recognition of the meaning of "The Hundred Languages" and her passionate commitment, to "conscious effort" toward achieving her goal.

Passion: New or Renewed?

Teachers' stories expressed a sense of passion about the experience of working with Reggio-inspired ideas. Interestingly, experienced and beginning teachers expressed this emotion differently. The expressions of passion were characterized by two themes: the theme of renewal for experienced teachers and the theme of discovery for beginning teachers.

Also, throughout our investigations into change, a sense of disequilibrium was described over and over again. A better description might be to say that teachers *chose* to engage in an internal struggle with their own sense of disequilibrium. Instead of ignoring a situation or a thought that engendered questions, these questions were recognized and welcomed and the struggle with a sense of disequilibrium was embraced.

Disequilibrium is a familiar idea in the literature on Reggio-inspired thinking (Edwards, 1998; T. Filippini, personal communication, June 1, 2000; New, 1998). We asked teachers to list three words that described their experience of Reggio-inspired ideas about teaching and learning (Groves, Tegano, & Eddlemon, 2000). This list demonstrates the nature of the struggle felt by teachers:

Enthusiastic	Confusing
Achieving	Struggling
Exciting	Overwhelming
Interesting	Challenging
Rewarding	Questioning
Enriching	Never-ending, without closure

Listen to the voice of one teacher after her fourth day in a summer graduate course about the Reggio Emilia approach:

> Before June 7, I felt that I was a child-centered early childhood teacher with a fairly good handle on child development and age-appropriate practices. On June 10, I am feeling unsettled, unsure, untidy, yet excited about REA. . . . This untidiness and disequilibrium is exciting and pushing me to make some of this theory, information, and application my own. Learning and changing are hard. . . .

This teacher had over 30 years experience in teaching young children. When we queried teachers, we found that the more-experienced teachers struggled to adapt their teaching as they analyzed and reflected on their practice (Tegano, 2000). One thread of our work with experienced teachers wound around their increased awareness of the process of teaching—their *own* process of teaching. Examining the process of teaching engendered an emotional response and one that produced the familiar sense of disequilibrium, even for sure-footed, veteran teachers.

At first glance, the previous word list was thought to represent apparently contradictory terms. However, in looking more deeply at the meaning of the words, it was obvious that these words are not mutually exclusive. Rather, it is the very juxtaposition of these terms that ignited the sense of struggle, and thus, the sense of disequilibrium. Piaget identifies disequilibrium as the intrinsic force behind development. The intellectual and emotional tension created by living between "enthusiasm" and "confusion," "achievement" and "struggle," "interest" and "challenge" is the experience of education in its finest moments. This is the place where both spirit and mind *feel* the tension—and *think about* and revisit the tension. Consider the words of another experienced teacher in her e-mailed reflection to her study group members: "We are all learning new possibilities. These new possibilities are presenting us each with some challenges. These challenges are resulting in growth." Disequilibrium moves teachers to higher levels (in this case, it is to deeper levels) of understanding and professional development. It is as though the process is like a spiral that twirls in both directions at once. It moves us to higher levels of professional development, while at the same time, it spirals us down into deeper and deeper levels of understanding.

Beginning teachers who are learning Reggio-inspired approaches did not seem to experience "struggle" in the same way as their experienced teacher counterparts. Disequilibrium was related to a sense of discovery for newer teachers. Perhaps this is because the process of completing a preservice teacher education program is about building a foundation for teaching—gathering, developing, and testing methods and experimenting with new ideas. New teachers report that *every* day brings confusion and presents a brand new challenge, whereas experienced teachers are probably not confused as much as they are perplexed or intrigued by daily classroom experiences. Experienced teachers may feel less confusion and more "choice making" in the activity of teaching (Fitzgerald & Tegano, 2000).

Is struggling, then, a more natural state for beginning teachers? Are new teachers accustomed to being unsure, off balance, challenged, and overwhelmed so that the discovery of new ideas is expected? The following is an excerpt from the reflections of a pair of student teachers working with preschool-age children. These student teachers were reflecting on their initiation and development of a very successful project about children learning how to draw their faces.

> In our reflection we recognized our role of facilitating scaffolding. [This was due] maybe in part to our lack of knowledge of art as well as trying to figure out the direction of the project. We did not realize that we were giving the girls the opportunity and confidence to take a risk, which possibly helped them to learn on the magnitude that they achieved. These are things we both learned and now know will always be prevalent in our classrooms. . . . [Our] perceptions of our role as teachers and the competencies of children have also blossomed. This became so much more than a student teaching project—it had so many results and influenced so many people. I could talk for days about it! M__ and I and the other teachers probably learned more than the children because, as we were teaching the children, they were teaching us! I think that this project and [my understanding of] the

Reggio approach are going to be very beneficial as I pursue my teaching degree. I cannot see teaching any other way!

There is a sense of passion through discovery in the voices of these student teachers. To recognize that children "learn on the magnitude that they achieve" may seem confusing, yet buried in these words is a powerful understanding, an "aha," a discovery. The rest of the reflection holds equally powerful evidence that these novice teachers experienced enthusiasm, achievement, and reward, while mucking about in uncharted territory ("our lack of knowledge of art," "trying to figure out the direction") that led to taking risks *with* the children. The process of working with Reggio-inspired ideas is summed up by the closing statement of this same reflection about Reggio-inspired teaching: "I want to and plan to surround myself with persons [who] not only [have] the knowledge but the belief!"

These new teachers experienced a sense of discovery and a passion about teaching that is inherent in the Reggio approach. With fewer preconceived notions about what comprises successful teaching, we find that beginning teachers are less likely to question new approaches and therefore more likely to take risks. Less experienced teachers don't possess the rich background and multitude of contexts that lead experienced teachers to a qualitatively different perspective for questioning the meaning of long-held beliefs. For experienced and so-called sure-footed teachers, deviation from the well-troddened pathway, being tripped up by a colleague's reflective provocation, or an "aha" that results in a loss of footing creates a noteworthy sense of disequilibrium and a feeling of being "unsettled," "unsure," and "untidy."

Experienced teachers utilize their rich context of teaching experiences. Unlike beginning teachers, many experienced teachers have pursued advanced study of various aspects of education. All experienced teachers have an extra 10, 20, or 30 years of living upon which to contextualize classroom events, to dialogue with children, teachers, and parents, and to compare theoretical perspectives about education. More experienced teachers may be able to put the teaching manual aside and feel free to step back and reexamine ideas and conceptualizations. The broad-based context of years of classroom teaching yields the ability to recognize the holes in one's own teaching, to look for what went wrong (or right), and to analyze from a greater depth of experience.

In addition, most accomplished teachers with years of experience have a positive self image of their teaching. They have experienced success in their teaching. They have experienced the children in their classroom as successful learners. When these teachers begin to explore Reggio-based conceptualizations of teaching, some of their struggle is with their recognition of themselves against this new image of teaching. Their long-held, positive image of "teacher" is brought into question by this new, also positive, image of "teacher." Again, one teacher's feelings of being "unsettled, unsure, untidy, yet excited about REA" illustrate this change in the image of teaching. Thus, the nature of the struggle is qualitatively different—richer and embedded more deeply in long-held or long-developing belief systems—for experienced teachers.

These differences between novice and veteran teachers withstanding, the infrastructure of Reggio-inspired professional development provides the foundation from which dynamic changes in teachers' dispositions toward teaching and learning are seen. Within this change, there is a sense of passion and renewal about a discovered, uncovered, rediscovered, newly constructed, or certainly co-constructed understanding of the process of teaching and learning.

COLLABORATION IN TEACHERS' VOICES

If passion in teaching is rooted in collaboration, then why do American school systems isolate teachers? Every teacher has experienced that surge of energy when he or she bursts out of the classroom, looking for someone, *anyone,* to share what just happened. Providing spaces for collaborative teaching or collaborative dialogue is an integral part of the Reggio Emilia approach.

In recasting Reggio-inspired ideas into the American system of education, we find that collaborative circumstances between teachers are often less than optimal. Fifty-nine percent of the participants who completed the 1990 Carnegie Foundation survey rated the quality of time for meeting with colleagues as "poor" or "not regularly available." Similarly, fewer than 10 percent of public school teachers reported that they were satisfied with their opportunities for collaborative collegial relationships (Darling-Hammond & Sclan, 1996). Teachers pass one another in the teachers' lounge or huddle together for overlapping minutes on the playground. Faculty meetings and staff meetings are usually consumed by talk of scheduling, testing, and other dispassionate topics. Generally speaking, our educational system makes no formal provisions for bringing teachers together for in-depth discussions about children's learning. Yet, when we do, we find elements of passion and renewal in the voices of teachers who experience the depth of true collaborative, reflective dialogue. Potential and creativity, flexibility and change are inherent in collaborative dialogue.

Throughout our study of teacher education and the Reggio Emilia approach, we were continually led back to the idea of teaching in pairs. When we investigated this idea (Tegano & Stott, 1999), passion reemerged as a salient theme. We created the co-teaching[4] support system that is so appealing in the schools of Reggio Emilia. The teaching pairs were *required* to engage in collaborative dialogue with each other, focusing on their reflection of experiences in the classroom. In addition, the teaching pairs were asked to engage their mentoring teachers in the collaborative sessions. The meaning of this experience seemed to be connected to their understanding of support and to their conceptualizations of their pedagogical development, both expressed with a sense of discovery and passion about their role as teacher.

For some new teachers, collaboration gave them support as they entered uncharted waters in their first experiences in an inner-city elementary school. They con-

---

[4]Preservice student teachers were paired for a full-day, one semester experience in a Child Development Laboratory school classroom for infants through preschool. Likewise, another group of preservice primary grade teachers were paired for a semester-long experience (nine hours per week) in a K–2 public school classroom as part of an undergraduate methods course.

nected collaboration to an understanding of community and to the metaphor of teaching as a journey. "As I look back . . . , I see the importance of colleagues. Having a partner in this class . . . there for support and a resource . . . I have shared ideas, thoughts, frustrations, and concerns with my partner . . . [It has] given me a different perspective . . . it makes me want to be a part of a community." One teacher said that her teaching partner "offered feedback, suggestions, and an understanding of what I was experiencing. She was a part of this journey and gave me strength the entire way" (Tegano & Stott, 1999). These students valued the support inherent in collaborative teaching. At a deeper level, there is a subtle feeling that these students recognized the intangibles of teaching that are necessary if teaching is to be renewing, motivating, and energizing. Darling-Hammond and Sclan (1996) remind us that committed teachers feel efficacious and motivated. In the best of worlds, education is a process that nurtures our spirits as well as our minds and, in some way or another, these young teachers *got* it or *felt* it. "Community," "journey," and "strength" are vivid and potent images of teaching. Framing education as a journey and a place where one may find (or seek) community is a manifestation of the subtle intangibles of passion in the art of teaching. These words give form, poetics, and perception to the art of teaching.

These preservice teachers were also aware of some shifts in their developing pedagogy, especially with regard to reflection as a part of collaboration. In talking about the role of reflection in her collaborative experience, one student said, ". . . putting aside time to think about the effectiveness of teaching is really important. . . . This is what will take me beyond the worksheets." Another student said that reflecting in a collaborative setting helped her take "steps toward a more complex thinking process. I . . . ask myself more questions about . . . what can be done to make it more valuable to the children . . . It allowed me to think forward about the next steps I could take" (Tegano & Stott, 1999, p. 6).

Intellectual Vitality through Collaboration

The principle of relationship in the Reggio Emilia approach extends to the collaborative nature of the teachers' work with one another, with children, and with the community (Spaggiari, 1998). Teachers in one study group called this *intellectual vitality* (Tegano & Stott, 1999). The dictionary definition of vitality is "the power to live . . . ; power of an institution . . . to go on; mental . . . vigor, energy" (Neufledt & Guralnik, 1997). The sense of vitality felt by Reggio-inspired teachers fits with the sense of passion present when teaching is seen as artful. Just as the art of teaching happens in the pedagogy of relationship, relationships are the source of intellectual vitality. When teachers collaborate with one another, hearts and minds open for rich conversations and intellectual challenges. Collaborative relationships are the power, the vigor, and the energy of teaching—a source of passion in the art of teaching.

Intellectual vitality, achieved through dialogue, reflection, and revisiting ideas, is one thread that emerges as we seek to recast Reggio to inform practice in the United States. Our educational culture isolates teachers in classrooms, and this contributes to the staggering number of young teachers who leave the profession in their first five years (NASBE, 1998). American visitors to the schools in Reggio Emilia are astounded by the low turnover rate of Italian teachers. Similarities in pay and benefits seem to rule out the obvious reasons for the vast discrepancy between the Italian and American child-care teachers' commitment to the field of early childhood education when measured by turnover rate. Rather, it may be the *collaborative approach* to teaching, one that invites reflection and critical thinking, one that is renewing and revitalizing, that accounts for the difference.

Teachers' engagement in the process of teaching and learning is sustained and fed by intellectual vitality and by the questions that emerge in the midst of a collaborative dialogue. In our studies, teachers repeatedly asked for a theory to explain their observations of children (Elliott & Tegano, 2000; Tegano, 2000). In one study group, the process of collaborative dialogue brought teachers to a place where they began to know what they did not know—to know that they needed to know more.

Why Calendar?

Three months into the bi-weekly meetings of an REA study group, the discussion turned to calendar. In this school system, the kindergarten and first grade teachers had adopted a prescribed technique for "doing calendar" each morning. The study group facilitators challenged the teachers to revisit the objectives of the calendar technique. What were the children learning and was it relevant and valuable? Were the teachers hoping that the children would construct an understanding of measured time (days, months, years) or were the objectives more about broadening math skills (number sense, sequencing, place value)? What kinds of knowledge were the children really constructing? Was this the best way for the children to learn?

The discussion extended over two meetings. The facilitators' reflections leaned toward an awareness of a void in the teachers' theoretical knowledge about how children learn math: "We were talking from opinion and not putting theory tested ideas out on the table." The facilitators' reflection goes on: "Perhaps what we needed to do was to go back and look at the theories. One teacher said that she couldn't remember when she actually studied theory last. Another said that she loved the summer course where we actually studied theory, especially Dewey, and it changed her thinking. So maybe this is what we should be doing, reading Vygotsky and Piaget and others and debating them" (Tegano, 2000).

The facilitators brought their reflections to the research group, where another level of dialogue and reflection occurred among the teacher-educators, university professional staff, and graduate students. The discussion went like this:

Most of these study group participants have been teaching for over 15 years. Their educational background is generally from a curriculum and instruction teacher training model, rather than child development. One interpretation is that the professional development to which the teachers have been exposed since college has been predominately subject/content driven workshops. None of these veteran teachers are familiar with Vygotsky, and few of them can recall much about Piaget. In fact, Vygotsky's ideas only reached the United States after these teachers were out of college and Piaget's ideas were taught in only the most progressive teacher education programs before the mid-1970s. Thus, in the study group, the discussion on calendar moved to a session on "convincing," perhaps because the teachers were arguing on opinion and experience but not on theory. Because the teach-

Lucy Way listens intently to a collaborative discourse about "calendar" and reflects on her approach to "calendar" in her kindergarten classroom.

ers were not familiar with Vygotsky or Piaget, they were unable to hear [the facilitator's] reasoning behind the calendar discussion. The teachers connected the issues surrounding calendar to the content area of math or language arts and to the goals and objectives of their grade level curriculum, but not to an examination of how children may be constructing knowledge of "calendar" (Tegano, 2000).

These teachers continued to revisit "calendar" in their study group throughout the year. This conversation was not entirely different from one shared by teachers in an elementary school in a suburb of Cleveland, where another group of teachers' search for the meaning of the calendar ritual—the recurring "Why calendar?" question—served as an on-going classroom project across several months (Roman & Essex, 1998).

The idea of revisiting is an important element of intellectual vitality for teachers who *choose* to engage in a deeper examination of calender, or of any topic that piques interest and yields relevant questions. It is the extended nature of collaboration, the second or third or fourth discussion about a topic, the deliberate and focused effort, the research, and the rumination that contribute to intellectual vitality. The experience of revisiting is collaboration without judgment, where the search is for the better, or the best, ideas without the notion of right or wrong. Our research team has observed that this is a process that is learned over time and that comes with the establishment of trusting relationships (Tegano, 2000). The research team observed veteran teachers who were new to this experience as they struggled to present an incomplete idea or hypothesis to the group for the first time. The process of revisiting happens when other teachers contribute challenges and alternatives that, in turn, create a deeper discussion. This may be viewed as an extension of the process of creative problem solving made popular in teacher education during the 1960s and 1970s (Osborn, 1963; Parnes, Noller, & Biondi, 1977). Intellectual vitality is embedded in the process where opinion is separated from theory and where new knowledge or new questions are generated each time an idea is revisited. Judgment and "right/wrong" approaches give way to acknowledgment of and respect for new perspectives. New perspectives create the recursive magic of intellectual vitality that sustains itself.

Collaboration as a Humanizing Enterprise

Collaboration brings adult learners together to co-construct theory, to represent their learning, and to engage the process of metacognition. The intense look on Amy's face in the following photograph portrays a sense of concentrated intrigue during this Reggio-inspired study group experience. One can almost see the questions forming in her mind, the theories being tested internally. Her small group of colleagues became the natural forum for discussion as she shared her theories of how a pepper grinder works—a clear, acrylic pepper grinder, deliberately selected to invite investigation. Teachers in Amy's group used sketch pads to sort out and represent their ideas about how the pepper grinder worked and then they presented their process of theory construction to the larger group. This activity[5] allowed teachers to recognize their potential and capacity for constructing theory.

Collaboration, from the perspective of Reggio-inspired teaching, is rooted in social constructivism and humanistic psychology. Humanistic perspectives emphasize human potential, capacity, and creativity (Maslow, 1968). In *The Social Construction of Reality,* Berger and Luckman suggest that face-to-face conversations are "the prototypical case of social interaction. All other cases are derivatives" (Berger & Luckman, 1966, p. 28). The spirit of collaborative dialogue combines the ideas of humanistic perspectives with a belief in a socially constructed world where a child's or a teacher's potential, capacity, and creativity are realized through a continually evolving system of social interactions. This was the case when Amy brought the efforts of her concentrated examination of the pepper grinder to her group for dialogue. The group recognized their potential when they began sharing and comparing theories.

....
[5]This activity, "Learning to See Learning," was developed by Tom Drummond and may be found on the Reggio listserv.

The question, "How does a pepper grinder work?" provides intense concentration and study by interning teacher Amy McGaha Cox.

The key ingredient of true collaborative dialogue may be the flexibility of the participants and the mutual recognition of their intersubjective roles. True collaboration is predicated on one's openness toward change—we are recreated by, and through, each social interchange. Berger and Luckman expound on this idea:

> . . . relations with others in the face-to-face situation are highly flexible. Put negatively, it is comparatively difficult to impose rigid patterns upon face-to-face interaction. Whatever patterns are introduced will be continuously modified through the exceedingly variegated and subtle interchange of subjective meanings that goes on (p. 30).

Collaboration is a humanizing experience that aligns elements of humanistic psychology and social constructivism. It opens doors to extraordinary experiences that are difficult to describe in words, though they hold significant meaning for the teachers who experience them. These experiences are embodied by a sense of awe, of an "aha" moment—the moment when a teacher *gets* it, *feels* it. It may be described as "times when spaces open . . . to interact in a synchronistic and dynamic rhythm" (Garrison, 1997, p. 122), or a place where we "overreach our instincts" and capacities (Botstein, 1998, p. 70.) In the next picture, Katie is describing such an experience. She is a participant in a graduate class where her collaborative group has met several times to have "clay parties" and extend their understanding of this media (clay was one of the themes that ran throughout the course). In the photograph, Katie is presenting the documentation of her own collaborative experience of using clay to represent her study of flowers. Here is one of the reflections that Katie shared in her presentation:

> Once finished, I found it very difficult to destroy my flowers. This was an interesting feeling in that it was not that my flowers were so amazing—it was that I had taken such careful time exploring, collaborating, and sharing. My flowers were a representation of my entire experience with clay and it was a meaningful experience.

Katie went on to explain that the work with her collaborative group had been a kind of transcendent experience where she, like the preservice teachers described earlier, "*got* it" or "*felt* it." The members of her group echoed her feelings of enthusiasm mixed with confusion and laced with awe. Another teacher in the group reflected on the group's work with clay, commenting that "revisiting the clay over numerous oc-

First grade teacher Katie Moody expresses her sense of being immersed in, and transformed by, an exploration of clay.

casions was powerful" because each time we felt more "confident" and we "took more risks."

Throughout the teaching of this graduate course, I engaged in lengthy, collaborative, reflective sessions with my co-teacher and colleague, Kathy Fitzgerald. As instructors, we were also caught up in the intellectual vitality and the power of relationship. We were intrinsically motivated to push ourselves toward what we intuitively knew were the limitless capabilities and potential of the class. To quote our own reflections on this experience: "This class was exhausting and renewing." Collaboration is a source of renewal even in the midst of overreaching ourselves.

PASSION AND THE ART OF TEACHING MEANS OVERREACHING OURSELVES

Perhaps this is what each of the examples in this chapter brings to us—the overreaching of our own understanding of the teaching and learning process. We have said that passion and the art of teaching requires discipline, concentration, invention, action, and overreaching one's own instincts. Reggio brings us to teaching as an art. "What the arts do is create something that does not already exist, that is not predictable or entirely rational, which forces us to talk to ourselves and to other people in new ways" (Bostein, 1998, p. 67). By extending ourselves, being mindful of pedagogy, and being supported by colleagues, we take risks toward teaching as a creative and humanistic experience.

Teachers who study the Reggio Emilia approach experience intellectual vitality, and this is seen in their disciplined and concentrated conversations about the teaching and learning process. These conversations force teachers to reach down to reformulate and revisit questions about how to help children make meaning in their lives. The process of continuous co-construction is both exhausting and exhilerating and this tension is the source of passion. It refuels the process anew.

Invention and action in teaching take on perceptible form as teaching becomes an art. This artful form of teaching may be seen in one teacher's awareness of the variety of ways to continue her "dance with children" or another teacher's realization that teaching is an unpredictable and constantly changing "journey." While artful teaching is creative and full of possibilities, these possibilities are embodied in action, and invention and action are guided by the theory and principals of the Reggio Emilia approach.

Malaguzzi (1998) said that "school is an inexhaustible and dynamic organism" (p. 63). It is the teachers' investment in the challenge of this constantly changing entity, their willingness to experience the tensions and see the possibilities in these challenges, and their innate responsiveness to the pedagogy of relationships that impassions teachers who study the teaching approaches of the schools of Reggio Emilia. As we explore Reggio-inspired practices, the teachers and teacher/educators we have met have found their voice and intellectual vitality in passionate, collaborative dialogue about the teaching and learning process. We are growing toward the art of teaching.

REFERENCES

Berger, P. L., & Luckman, T. (1966). *The social construction of reality: A treatise in the sociology of knowledge*. New York: Anchor Books.

Bostein, L. (1998). What role for the arts? In W. C. Ayres & J. L. Miller (Eds.), *A Light in dark times: Maxine Greene and the unfinished conversation* (pp. 62–70). NY: Teachers College Press.

Darling-Hammond, L., & Sclan, E. M. (1996). Who teaches and why: Dilemmas of building a profession for twenty-first century schools. In J. Sikula (Ed.), *Handbook of research on teacher education*. (2nd ed., pp. 67–101). New York: Macmillan Library Reference.

Dewey, J. (1987). Art as experience. In J. A. Boydston (Ed.), *The collected works of John Dewey, The latter works* (vol. 10). Carbondale, IL: Southern Illinois University Press. (Original work published in 1934.)

Dewey, J. (1998). My pedagogic creed. In L. A. Hickman & A. M. Thomas (Eds.), *The essential Dewey, Volume 1: Pragmatism, education, democracy*. Bloomington, IN: Indiana University Press.

Edwards, C. (1998). Partner, nurturer, and guide: The role of the teacher. In C. Edwards, L. Gandini, & G. Forman (Eds.), *The hundred languages of children: The Reggio Emilia approach–advanced reflections*. (2nd ed.) Greenwich, CT: Ablex.

Edwards, C., Gandini, L., & Forman, G. (1998). *The hundred languages of children: The Reggio Emilia approach–advanced reflections*. (2nd ed.). Greenwich, CT: Ablex.

Eisner, E. W. (1994). *The educational imagination: On the design and evaluation of school programs*. (3rd ed.). Upper Saddle River, NJ: Merrill Prentice Hall.

Elliott, E., & Tegano, D. W. (2000). *Interns and mentoring teachers: A qualitative study of collaborative, reflective dialogue*. Manuscript in preparation. The University of Tennessee, Knoxville, TN.

Fitzgerald, M. K., & Tegano, D. W. (2000). *At least they came to the table: Reflections on a writing and drawing activity*. Manuscript in preparation. The University of Tennessee, Knoxville, TN.

Garrison, J. (1997). *Dewey and Eros: Wisdom and desire in the art of teaching*. New York: Teachers College Press.

Greene, M. (1988). *The dialectic of freedom*. New York: Teachers College Press.

Groves, M. M., Tegano, D. W., & Eddleman, G. (2000). *Pedagological investigation as an agent of change*. Paper presented at the American Educational Research Association meeting, New Orleans, LA.

Malaguzzi, L. (1998). History, ideas, and basic philosophy: An interview with Lella Gandini. In C. Edwards, L. Gandini, & G. Forman (Eds.), *The hundred languages of children: The Reggio Emilia approach–advanced reflections*. (2nd ed.). Greenwich, CT: Ablex.

Maslow, A. (1968). *Toward a psychology of being*. Princeton, NJ: Van Nostrand Reinhold.

National Association of State Boards of Education (NASBE). (1998). *The numbers game: Ensuring quantity and quality in the teaching workforce.* (The report of the NASBE study group on teacher development, supply, and demand). Alexandria, VA: National Association of State School Boards of Education.

Neufeldt, V., & Guralnik, D. B. (Eds.). (1997). *Webster's new world dictionary* (3rd ed.). New York: MacMillan.

New, R. S. (1998). Theory and praxis in Reggio Emila: They know what they are doing and why. In C. Edwards, L. Gandini, & G. Forman (Eds.), *The hundred languages of children: The Reggio Emilia approach—advanced reflections.* (2nd ed.). Greenwich, CT: Ablex.

Osborn, A. (1963). *Applied imagination; Principles and procedures of creative problem-solving.* (3rd ed.). New York: Scribner.

Parnes, S., Noller, R., & Biondi, A. (1977). *Guide to creative action.* New York: Scribner.

Roman, S., & Essex, G. (October, 1998). *Professional development for teachers: Reggio and the Ohio experience.* Invited presentation at Applying Reggio in Tennessee Schools Conference, Knoxville, TN.

Spaggiari, S. (1998). The community–teacher partnership in the governance of the schools. In C. Edwards, L. Gandini, & G. Forman (Eds.), *The hundred languages of children: The Reggio Emilia approach–advanced reflections.* (2nd ed.). Greenwich, CT: Ablex.

Tegano, D. W. (2000). *A community of learners: Partnerships in early childhood education.* (Goals 2000 Report, The University of Tennessee, Knoxville). The Nashville Department of Education.

Tegano, D. W., & Stott, A. M. (1999). *Re-thinking teacher education at The University of Tennessee: Negotiated relationships.* Paper presented at the meeting of the National Association for the Education of Young Children, New Orleans, LA.

Tegano, D. W. (1998). *Collaboration among a university, state department of education and teachers: Ingredients for change.* Paper presented at the National Association for the Education of Young Children meeting, Toronto.

Tegano, D. W., Distler, G., & Fox, C. (1999). *Public school adaptations of the Reggio Emilia approach.* Paper presented at An Aesthetic Encounter: Recasting the Reggio Emilia Approach to Inform Teaching in the United States, Blacksburg, VA.

Vecchi, V. (1998). The role of the atelierista: An interview with Lella Gandini. In C. Edwards, L. Gandini, & G. Forman (Eds.), *The hundred languages of children: The Reggio Emilia approach–advanced reflections.* (2nd ed.) Greenwich, CT: Ablex.

Wells, G. (1986). *The meaning makers: Children learning language and using language to learn.* Portsmouth, NH: Heinemann.

Part IV

Progettazione and Documentation: Learning Moments among Protagonists

We must listen "with an active mind and an active heart," Carlina Rinaldi informed the Lugano-Reggio Collaborative at the 1998 Winter Institute in Reggio Emilia, Italy. Alise Shafer has taken this tactic to heart and implores us to appreciate the ordinary moments with children. Finding the complexity of an idea that results in a seemingly simple comment or happening makes the ordinary extraordinary. Only listening well can ensure us of the magical transformation. Pam Oken-Wright and Marty Gravett agree and speak of a deeper kind of listening that is in search of the child's intent. How respectful is the resulting responsive, fluid, inclusive curriculum that they share so eloquently in this section of the book?

Chapter
12

Ordinary Moments, Extraordinary Possibilities

Alise Shafer

Evergreen Community School is a small, non-profit preschool and parent–toddler program in Santa Monica, CA. Our interest in the Reggio approach began in 1989 when we first saw the video, "To Make A Portrait of a Lion" (1987). We were captivated by the images of children breathing life into the firmly rooted, stone figure guarding the local piazza. Seduced by the beautiful imagery, we set out to find the map to Reggio. For years, we were searching for the "right" path—in retrospect I think we were really looking for a short-cut. Eight years later, we abandoned the need to know *how to get there* for the need to understand *why we should make the journey*. From this more reflective place we could see that the road to Reggio was a familiar road, one that we were, with small, tentative steps, already traveling. There were no sudden left turns or radical departures. Our roots in social constructivism had already defined our course. These images from across an ocean gave us the vision to move forward, to see beyond the juncture at which we stood.

Still, we proceeded carefully, questioning whether imitation *is* truly the greatest form of flattery or a productive goal for a school. Picasso as a young painter studied the work of VanGogh and Gauguin. Their *influence* on Picasso's work is clear—the vibrant colors, expressive lines, and strong indication of mood. Yet who today would call a Picasso a Van Gogh? After all, imitation was never the goal.

Just as Picasso was drawn to Van Gogh's vivid palette, we are drawn to the rich palette we see in Reggio. It is a palette of possibilities. It opens our minds; it allows us to think in ways we had not considered; it requires us to question long-held paradigms about what it means to learn and what it means to teach. Color by color we explore the many layers of the thick and complex canvas of Reggio Emilia. Initially, we are captivated by its ever-prominent aesthetic qualities: the lovely environments, the artfully designed panels, and the attention to light. But as we look deeper, beneath the surface layers of enticing colors and striking impressions, we reveal the underpainting that supports this masterpiece. The fundamental dictum, *listen,* is present in every color and embedded in every stroke of the brush. It's a message that is so simple that it's easy to overlook. After all, we know how to listen, or do we?

OUR BEGINNINGS

During our early years of exploring the Reggio approach, the parents and teachers from our school met often to view the video and discuss the long-term project from La Villetta School, The Amusement Park for Birds (Forman, G. & Gandini, L., 1994). The project took several months and was so complex that the city water company installed a water line for the fountains and waterways that the children had designed! Still new to the Reggio approach, but convinced of the merits of long-term explorations, we set out to find the "big project." We looked and we looked. Nothing seemed big enough, meaty enough, or profound enough. Through our telescopes we peered out to the distant horizon while children dropped seeds at our feet that were left unnoticed. We were looking, but we were not listening. Months passed, and we still had not found what we considered an appropriate long-term project. Then one day it happened. The children had just completed making a cardboard box skyscraper when one child announced, "I don't like it. I wanted to build a real building!" The moment had finally arrived—a big project was knocking at the door. We opened it without a moment's hesitation. Building a real building was certainly a BIG PROJECT. We were so eager to begin that we didn't stop to clarify what was meant by a "real building." It was weeks before we realized, much to our surprise and disappointment, that the child had envisioned building a TV room in which three children could watch TV!

Over the course of the next several months, we examined windows and doors throughout our campus. A local architect talked to the children about form and function and helped us design a blueprint. By June of that year, we had built quite an impressive building—a small play house of sorts, 6′×5′ with a tin roof, wooden walls, three windows, and a door!

It was somewhere in-between the study of doors and the exploration of windows that we started having an uneasy feeling that the project had taken over rather than the children. In an effort to construct the building, we were hardly listening at all. Many of the most valuable moments during our design and construction phases were, in fact, detours. But we didn't allow ourselves or the children to linger too long on these diversions. We were conscious to stay on track to complete the building before June.

Then, as an afterthought, we made 12 small panels that recounted what we could remember of the building project. The beauty and curse of documentation is that your errors hang there on the walls as a constant reminder of your shortcomings. Such was the case with our building project. The 12 beautifully designed panels hung in the hallway for the next two years, casting a glaring light on our faux pas. I suppose this is good—it certainly kept us from making the same mistake twice. As a result, we called a moratorium on long-term projects, realizing that we first must learn to listen. We spent the next couple of years learning how to document the everyday interactions and discoveries happening at Evergreen. Deborah Meier's (1995) words echoed through our school, "Teaching is mostly listening—learning is mostly telling." When three-year-old Justin, who had been designing a carwash, bolted across the playground to a teacher shouting, "Get your clipboard. I have an idea!" we knew, and more importantly, we knew our children knew, that we were beginning to really listen.

As we continued to gain proficiency in listening and documenting, we made two profound discoveries. First, we found our own Lucias and Simones (Forman, G. & Gandini, L., 1994). We found Nicole and Jesse and Adnan who taught us to trust their ideas and to believe in their strengths and their competencies. Second, as our image of the child was slowly transformed through our commitment to document, we began to appreciate the complexity and brilliance of ordinary moments—moments we wouldn't have even noticed in years prior. Connecting with these seemingly mundane moments has led us to extraordinary explorations.

AN ORDINARY MOMENT

It was a cool morning in February when four-year-old Avery attached a bucket to the back of his tricycle, filled it with rolled-up papers, and made his rounds along the bike path calling, "Newspapers! Newspapers! Who wants a newspaper?"

"Want a newspaper, Alise?" Avery asked as I passed by with a visitor.

"I sure do, but I'll have to read it later when I'm finished giving Nancy a tour of the school," I answered, as I tucked the newspaper under my arm.

Our days are filled with moments like these—moments with great potential that slip in just as we're about to read a story or prepare for lunch. We used to let these moments go by, in part because we didn't recognize their potential, and in part because the timing wasn't right because there were other tasks to do. As we've shifted our focus from looking for the big project to recognizing the potential of ordinary moments, we've come to appreciate the complexity of an idea that results in a seemingly simple comment like, "Newspapers! Who wants a newspaper?" When these moments appear at inopportune times, we return later to recapture the moment.

"So what's the news today?" I asked an hour later, after my visitor had gone.

Avery unraveled a story about a chocolate dinosaur complete with an interior structure made of bones, batteries, and cement.

"That's hard to imagine. Would you like to draw it? A drawing might help me to understand."

Using a drawing as a platform for dialogue (Forman, 1998), Avery's ideas were illuminated beyond what his words could convey. The conversation that followed was a result of having the additional information that Avery's drawings provided.

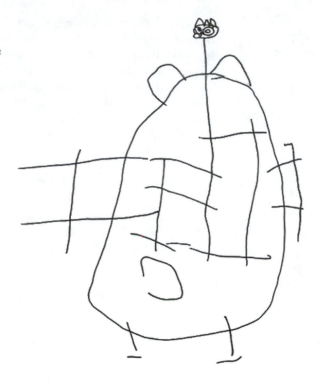

FIGURE 12.1 Avery's interest in conveying his ideas through drawing could have been thwarted by his frustration with the eraser. Helping Avery move beyond the impasse by providing technical assistance enabled us to continue discussions and move to deeper explorations.

Avery made three drawings. The first included the internal workings of the dinosaur, which he carefully eradicated with scribbles saying, "And this is the skin 'cause you can't see the bones." I asked Avery if he would make a second drawing without the skin so we could more easily examine the bones together. Avery's second drawing included only the skeletal structure, which Avery described as " The same shape bones as we have 'cause dinosaurs are animals and we're animals." As he talked and drew simultaneously, Avery changed his mind, "They have the same bones as we have, but actually no ribs." Avery quickly began to erase the lines he described as ribs but found the results unsatisfactory. To avoid the technical difficulty that was frustrating Avery, it was suggested that he take the picture to the light table where he could trace his drawing while omitting the ribs.

Avery   They have the same bones as we have, but no ribs. They have bending bones, long bones. Bones are everywhere. It has very long arms. It has two arms and they are attached together. It has a tail but I can't do a tail because it's behind—you can't see it.

Avery and I looked carefully at his drawing noticing each bone. We observed together that the leg bones were shorter and less intricate than the arms or spinal bones.

"Do you think it bends its legs when it walks?" I inquired, wondering if Avery understood that a single bone cannot bend without a joint. Asking children to explain their drawings encourages them to work with deliberation and forethought. Though I couldn't be certain that Avery had considered the function of the dinosaur legs while drawing them, I proceeded with the assumption that his lines were purposeful. If indeed Avery's lines were intentional, my question and his response would help me to more clearly understand his thinking. If Avery's marks were haphazard or arbitrary, my question would help him to develop the capacity to self edit and work with greater deliberation. Either way, my questions conveyed my interest in his drawing and in his thinking. I cared enough to notice the shortness of the legs; I cared enough to ask why and to ponder with him how his dinosaur walks. The questions caused Avery to try walking with straight legs. "If I don't bend my knees then I just stand still. Dinosaurs bend their legs." Avery demonstrated a dinosaur walk down the long hallway: BOOM, BOOM, BOOM!

Our discussion lasted nearly forty-five minutes and ran the gamut from dinosaurs eating yellow jackets with their sticky tongues to a whimsical carousel made of dinosaur bones that go up and down. Our meeting was tape-recorded and captured on a digital camera. In rapid succession Avery brought many ideas to the table, any one of which could have been explored further, but first we needed to look at the array of topics. Given Avery's rich descriptions and varied subtopics, I opted to begin a small, temporary panel, including excerpts from the transcript, drawings, and photos. Documentation panels are a powerful vehicle for extending one child's ordinary moment to a larger group. It seemed likely that Avery's panel would provide fertile ground for his peers to enter the discussion. I prepared the panel not knowing where it might lead or which avenue might pique the interest of his classmates. It was hung the following morning under a window sill in the main hallway.

The panel attracted much attention from Avery's classmates. His enthusiasm about the display of drawings and photos spread quickly and resulted in many children stomping down the hallway in dinosaur fashion. Each step began with a knee pulled high, followed by a resounding thud as the foot hit the ground. With great dramatization and gleeful laughter, the children made their way down the long corridor: BOOM, BOOM, BOOM!

Noticing that every child had adopted a similar walk, I wondered whether this stereotypic gait was based on a theory the children held about dinosaurs, perhaps relating to their size or weight, or whether they had been influenced by media representations. We often look for the child's unspoken theory and bring it to the surface where it can be exposed, articulated, and explored. Why did all the children adopt a walk that reverberated through the hall? What is the origin of the notion that dinosaurs walk with a thud and a boom?

In rethinking the role of the teacher, it's been useful for us to consider the metaphor of child as professor, teacher as student. The professor has a theory. It is the job of the student to seek clarification, to ask questions, to uncover the meaning. When we assume this role with children we can better understand and respond to their ideas. I assumed that Avery and his classmates had a theory about dinosaurs that resulted in the children's heavy stomping and loud sound effects as they made their way down the corridor. As teacher, now student, it was my role to understand the theory:

Teacher	Why do you suppose dinosaurs walk that way?
Cassie	So everyone will know they're a dinosaur. Then they can bend down and eat the people with their claws. First they take your eyeball out.
Jesse	If people lived with the dinosaurs that would happen, but they don't. There's an imaginary book in the library that says people live with dinosaurs.
Cassie	Do the dinosaurs creep behind the people and then eat them?
Jesse	No!
Cassie	Do they just eat them? What if they're hungry in the nighttime, do they eat the aliens?
Avery	Aliens live in outer space!
Cassie	What if the dinosaurs live in outer space?
Jesse	They never live in outer space because they don't like to float around.
Avery	'Cause there's no gravity in outer space. There are only aliens and flying *saucers* that are not *sausages*.

This hallway discussion among children inspired by the small panel of Avery's work had moved from dinosaurs to gravity. Following the children through an array of topics, I listened for motivation, interest, cognitive knots, and inconsistencies in thinking. There have been times when we've made the mistake of following for too long, as the children moved from one idea to the next, never landing long in one place. Often it is the teacher who helps the children to zero in on one of the many ideas they uncover. A well-constructed question, or a clarifying remark, will shift the focus back to an earlier point or more salient idea to allow for further investigation.

"So things in outer space float around? I wonder why?" I pondered aloud.

This marked the beginning of a series of discussions over a two-month period that the children called "the gravity meetings."

Teacher	Jesse said that dinosaurs don't live in outer space because they don't like to float around. What do you mean?
Avery	In outer space astronauts float around. Do you see us floating around? NO! Do you see the cars floating around? NO! Gravity makes us stay on earth.
Teacher	What is gravity?
Jesse	Gravity is the thing that makes you stay down on earth.
Avery	Gravity is clear—you can't see it. It's clear stuff that makes you stay on earth.

Jesse	If there's no gravity. . .
Avery	. . . we would be floating. Do you see anything floating? NO!
Jesse	Tables aren't floating. These [pointing to a container of pencils] aren't floating.
Avery	Here there's gravity, but in outer space there's no gravity.
Jesse	Everywhere except space there's gravity.

For the next eight weeks, a small group of children regularly came to my office to talk about gravity. The meetings were usually initiated by the children, who would bound into my office at 9:00 A.M., to announce the need for "another gravity meeting." Mostly I listened, trying to understand their theories and assumptions. Often I asked a question to clarify my own understanding or to prod them to look harder and think deeper. I looked for what Eleanor Duckworth (1996) calls "soft spots" in their thinking—loosely formed ideas that need further exploration:

Teacher	Where does the gravity come from?
Cassie	Maybe the gravity is in your body so you stay down. So if there's no gravity in your body you stay up.
Teacher	So the gravity is in your body? Do all people have gravity?
Cassie	Yea, real people, but the aliens in outer space don't have gravity in them.
Avery	I think Cassie is really right. Gravity is in your body.
Jesse	Maybe how you stay down is friction from your feet.
Teacher	How does that work?
Jesse	Maybe some friction stays in your body and it comes down to your feet.
Teacher	How does friction work?
Jesse	How it works is that it really sort of sticks to the ground.
Teacher	So friction works by making you stick?
Jesse	But you walk from friction—it's only a little bit sticky.
Avery	Friction can mean also another thing. Friction is when you walk and you get a watery bump on you. One time I got a friction.

Later I asked for more clarification on Cassie's theory:

Teacher	So Cassie had the idea that gravity is inside our bodies. I'm wondering how gravity gets inside our bodies.
Cassie	There's these little holes inside the sky that you can't see. And it sends gravity down through your mouth.
Avery	And also it comes through your nose.
Teacher	So if we talk too much what happens?
Avery	You'll float around in outer space!

FIGURE 12.2 *Cassie made a drawing to explain how gravity enters the body.*

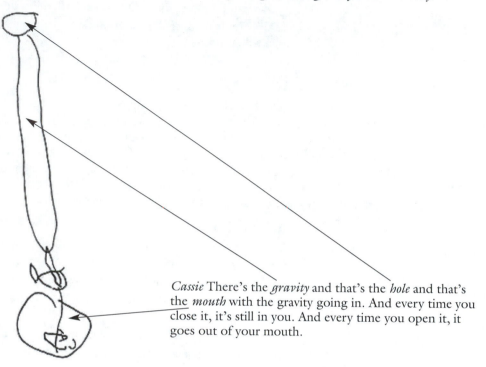

Cassie There's the *gravity* and that's the *hole* and that's the *mouth* with the gravity going in. And every time you close it, it's still in you. And every time you open it, it goes out of your mouth.

Cassie   If the gravity goes out, you could float up into the sky, into outer space. Then you can't get out of outer space because there's no gravity in you.

Cassie's theory was only partially developed. She had not accounted for the possibility of escaped gravity caused by an open mouth. The question, "So if we talk too much, what happens?" was meant to challenge her theory. The teacher's role as provocateur can stimulate children to more fully formulate their ideas and to consider new evidence or alternative theories.

Three-year-old Jesse, the youngest member of the gravity committee, often acquiesced to the four-year-olds, even when his ideas were more credible. This time, however, Jesse could not accept Cassie's theory. He knew from experience that an open mouth does not send one hurling into space. Still, he maintained a certain reverence for the wisdom of his older classmates, making it difficult for him to disagree entirely. Instead, he mediated the situation by making a slight adjustment in Cassie's theory. He hypothesized that an internal control restricts the flow of gravity.

Jesse   Well, my idea about how you get gravity is there's a little lung and it has a control in it and the control makes the lungs open and close.

Cassie	There's no control in bodies. There's only controls in toys and stuff.
Jesse	But the control is invisible—in the body it is invisible. Each time you breath out and in, the control stays in your body. That's my idea.
Cassie	Every time you eat, the control goes out.
Jesse	And every time you breath in, the control comes back.

APPROPRIATENESS OF TOPIC

Years ago I would have argued that gravity is not an appropriate topic for preschoolers to discuss at length. I would have advocated for more concrete topics more easily understood by young children. Today I make no such arbitrary assumptions. After all, the children initiated this discussion and it was their passion that sustained it. Had it been beyond their zone of proximal development (Vygotsky, 1978), the discussion would have dwindled on the first day. The gravity discussions continued for eight weeks because the children had enough information from which they could extrapolate. Their investigation provided the opportunity to think hard, argue, gather data, reconsider, graphically represent their ideas, and co-construct meaning from a natural occurrence that is part of their everyday experience (Katz & Chard, 1989). The accuracy of the children's understanding is less important than the fact that existing schemes led to more complex schemes, and eventually to a well-defined theory that could be articulated and defended. Their discussions provided a context in which their natural disposition to make sense of the world was supported and strengthened (Katz, 1996).

LEARNING THE FACTS

One day, Jesse's mother Alison raised a concern. At home, Jesse was eager to talk about the gravity meetings. He shared with his family the many ideas and theories he and his friends had constructed. It was difficult for Alison to know how to respond to the inaccuracies of Jesse's thinking. "I feel like I'm withholding information, yet I know if I just give him the facts, the group will hit the wall and their theory building will be over." Her concern was important and warranted a parent meeting. Alison's question caused us to thoughtfully consider our objectives. Is it more important to know the facts, or is it more important to develop a style of thinking and discourse that is analytical and inquisitive? We agreed our goal was to engage children in high-level thinking where *possibilities* could be explored. Our children are given permission to explore their world, create their own theories, and test them accordingly. Ultimately our goal is to nurture the disposition to wonder, to explore, and to construct meaning (Katz, 1993). Resisting the temptation to correct a child's misconception, to not "teach," may be one of the most difficult tendencies we struggle to overcome and one of the most valuable gifts we give children.

THINKING METAPHORICALLY

As the children formulated their ideas, learned to articulate their points of view, and considered the theories of their classmates, I, too, was learning. I was learning about their remarkable perceptions and their skillful use of visual imagery as they communicated their thoughts and made connections between new and familiar experiences. Like poets, their words painted pictures that captured the essence of their thinking. Their words became windows into the prior experiences that illuminated their understanding.

Cassie	You can't see the hole [referring to the one in the sky from which gravity comes]. It's invisible.
Jesse	Yea, but there isn't a hole in the sky.
Cassie	Yes there is. You can't see it.
Avery	It's just a little tiny hole, right?
Cassie	Yea, like a blood test.
Avery	A little tiny, tiny, tiny hole.
Cassie	Like when you put a needle in you. Well the gravity is really small. You can see the gravity in my picture. I need an eraser.

Dr. George Forman visited Evergreen during the gravity discussions and was able to join one of our meetings.

Dr. Forman	Why do you need gravity?
Jesse	I need gravity 'cause that's how you stay down.
Dr. Forman	What does it do once it goes into your body to keep you down?
Jesse	It just makes you stay down forever and friction and gravity are only a little bit sticky so you are still able to walk.
Dr. Forman	I see. So if you were stuck too much on the ground, you couldn't move at all.
Avery	No, you would just stand there on the sidewalk.
Dr. Forman	And you just couldn't move at all—'cause you'd be so sticky or so heavy.
Avery	And you would be like the Statue of Liberty.

THE GRAVITY DISCUSSIONS COME TO A CLOSE

With the support of parents keeping us abreast of what was being said at home on the gravity front, the children were able to move forward in their thinking. Cassie maintained the main premise of her theory with a few minor concessions about the controls once we tested her hypothesis about people who talk too much. Jesse changed

Figure 12.3 *Jesse explains his new understanding of gravity.*

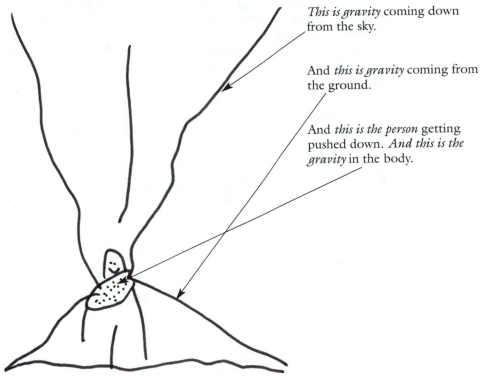

This is gravity coming down from the sky.

And *this is gravity* coming from the ground.

And *this is the person* getting pushed down. *And this is the gravity* in the body.

his position weeks later after noticing that walking down a hill is much easier than walking up a hill.

Jesse	That's cause gravity is pulling us down.
Teacher	Where does it pull from?
Jesse	It comes from the sky and the ground.

Eventually the children stopped asking to meet, so there is no climactic ending to this story. It was not a project, a unit study, or a thematic investigation. It was simply a moment in time, a moment that began with the playful call, "Newspapers, get your newspapers here." Imagine if I had only said, "Thank you, Avery," as I tucked the paper under my arm.

WHY IN THE WORLD?

Early one morning, while Dr. George Forman was consulting at Evergreen Community School, Robbie arrived to find steam rising from the water table. The cool morning air, coupled with the warmth of the water had produced a phenomenon that Robbie had not expected. As I was passing by, three-year-old Robbie asked, "Why does the water smoke?" His words hung in the air like the vapor he had noticed as I grappled for a response. It was a good question—the kind we hope children will ask. Robbie stared up at me as I considered my options. Alas, I couldn't find the right words or an appropriate explanation or meaningful question with which I could respond. "I don't know," I finally retorted then hurried away to avoid further questioning.

Robbie's question and my paralysis lingered in my thoughts for most of the day. A lesson on evaporation is not what Robbie needed—of that I was sure. And I was glad I had resisted the temptation to respond with the standard "why do you think the water smokes?" Being a person who asks many questions, I know how flat and unsatisfying that response is. Discussing Robbie's question at a staff meeting later that day, Dr. Forman explained:

> If a child asks you a why question and you just turn it back to the child, you have a good chance of reducing the number of why questions that the child will ask in the future. Afterall, he did ask a question and wants some level of help. A child might enter a wondering phase with you, but he does not want to do it all by himself.

Robbie's question was born from a theory he held that was violated (Forman, personal correspondence, 1998). To him it was incongruent for water to smoke. Fire smokes. Water is used to put out fire. His knowledge of water did not include smoking. Had I helped Robbie to articulate the incongruity that provoked the question, we could have moved forward. Perhaps I could have said, "Smoking water, that's pretty unusual." That simple response would have acknowledged the paradox between water that doesn't burn and smoke that comes from fire. Again, Dr. Forman explained:

> It does not matter if your theory of the child's theory is wrong. It only matters that you have a theory conversation with the child, and a good start for such a conversation is for you to venture a guess. We have faith that the child will enter this frame of discourse and will agree or disagree but will continue with the negotiation, the co-construction of what this simple observation means to Robbie.

When we venture a guess about a child's question or comment, we are prompting further inquiry, reflection, or the correction of our own misconception. Even when we guess incorrectly, chances are good that we may gain a clearer insight into the child's line of thinking as the exchange proceeds.

CONCLUSION

Watching and listening to everyday occurrences has proven to be a fruitful way of working and being with our children. The supply of ordinary moments is limitless. Uncovering the extraordinary within the ordinary is, to a large extent, a matter of listening. Considering with colleagues and parents the implicit assumptions or questions that lie just beneath the surface has been the key to finding meaningful, self-sustaining material for exploration. The ideas of children continue to inspire, inform, and transform our practice.

Willy, a graduate of Evergreen, is now in public elementary school. He told his father after the first week of kindergarten, "No one at my new school cares about my good ideas." With certainty, the greatest lesson we have learned from Reggio is the one that is free and requires no props and no fancy tools. We need just two ears, the passion to listen, and a willingness to value the ordinary moments we have with children.

REFERENCES

Duckworth, E. (1996). *"The having of wonderful ideas" & other essays on teaching & learning.* New York: Teachers College Press.

Edwards, C., Gandini, L. & Forman, G. (Eds.). (1998). *The hundred languages of children: The Reggio Emilia approach—advanced reflections.* (2nd Ed.) Norwood, NJ: Ablex.

Forman, G. (1998). Negotiated learning through design, documentation, and discourse. In Edwards, C., Gandini, L. & Forman, G. (Eds.). (1998). *The hundred languages of children: The Reggio Emilia approach—advanced reflections.* (2nd Ed.) Norwood, NJ: Ablex.

Forman, G. & Gandini, L. (1994). *The amusement park for birds.* Amherst, MA: Performantics Press.

Katz, L. & Chard, S. (1989). *Engaging children's minds: The project approach.* Norwood, NJ: Ablex.

Katz, L. (1993). Disposition: *Definitions and implications for early childhood practice.* Urbana, IL: ERIC/EECE.

Meier, D. (1995). *The power of their ideas.* Boston: Beacon Press.

Vygotsky, L. (1978). *Mind in society: the development of higher psychological processes.* Cambridge, MA: Harvard University Press.

Chapter
13

Big Ideas and the Essence of Intent

Pam Oken-Wright ◆ Marty Gravett

What is it that makes the particular curriculum of the preprimary schools in Reggio Emilia so very responsive, fluid, and inclusive? Perhaps in Reggio Emilia they would say, "It is progettazione." In *One Hundred Languages of Children*, Carlina Rinaldi writes, ". . . at the initiation of a project, the teachers get together and proceed in terms of progettazione, that is, fully discuss all the possible ways that the project could be anticipated to evolve, considering the likely ideas, hypotheses, and choices of children and the direction they may take" (Rinaldi, 1998, p. 118). In an effort to define the sizable and elusive concept, progettazione, some have embraced Elizabeth Jones' term "emergent curriculum." Jones and John Nimmo caution in *Emergent Curriculum,* "People who hear the words 'emergent curriculum' may wrongly assume that everything simply emerges from the children." The search for progettazione leads us to realize that our work with children can be far more collaborative and that it can require far more of us as teachers than "following children's lead." We have come to believe that the teachers' reading of children's *intent* is central to our effort to engage in the kind of responsive, fluid, and inclusive curriculum which could be one of Reggio's greatest legacies. (For more information on the concept of progettazione, see Chapter 3.)

We hear about teachers in Reggio Emilia catching the ball of a child's idea and then choosing to keep that ball in play, keeping the idea alive, helping the child grow toward a deeper and deeper understanding of the idea through investigation. Children may toss the ball, but we must recognize the toss. We must also recognize, or at least be inclined to try to find out about, what exactly has been tossed our way in order to know when to intervene and how to offer support to keep the ball in play. We want to learn to read children's *intent*. What is the child saying with her words, play, representation, or even with body language? We may hear and understand the words she is using, but what thinking is behind it? What is the child's image of the idea at hand? What does she know, what ignites her passion, what confuses her, what throws her into disequilibrium about the topic she is considering? Rinaldi urges us to listen with an active mind and an active heart (address at 1998 Winter Institute in Reggio Emilia). We believe that a key to this deeper kind of listening is the search for children's *intent*.

> *One evening when my daughter was three, she came upstairs from playing with her older cousins, dressed in an ancient and tattered fur coat. "Mommy, I can't think of that word. What is that word? Rope rope?" I had no idea, so I began with the question, "What is it like?" She couldn't answer. "Where did you see it?" I tried again.*
>
> *"A BOOK! You know," she told me.*
>
> *"Which book?"*
>
> *"The book with the goat man. YOU KNOW!"*
>
> *I still didn't know.*
>
> *"What happened with this thing you're thinking of?"*
>
> *"They went in and it snowed, YOU KNOW! . . . and the LAMP!"*
>
> *Only then did it occur to me that she was talking about* The Lion, The Witch, and the Wardrobe *(Lewis, 1950) and that "rope rope" was the wardrobe.*
>
> *In this simple example Sarah was asking, demanding, for me to read her intent. I was willing to work for it. Once I thought I understood and responded, she was able to continue in her attempts to engage her cousins in play about a trip through a wardrobe into a magic land. With that little bit of support she was able to expand the play and go deeper into her idea.*

In the classroom it is often a more elusive intent we are trying to read. We might ask ourselves, "Why is this child or this group of children so fascinated with a particular idea that they return to it over and over? Could there be more than meets the eye when a child represents the same idea over and over, or when one child's idea sets afire the intellect of others to the point that the idea becomes part of the culture of the class?" It may well be a mystery to both the child and us. Still, the exercise of trying to read and give voice to the child's intent draws us in as collaborators as she expands her thinking and representation.

One Christmas Eve, we experienced a rather violent ice storm. Trees were down, sometimes through roofs and cars, and families lost electricity for five or six bitterly cold days. Many had to evacuate on Christmas Day. Those who did not were still affected, as they were certain to be housing family and friends who sought refuge from the cold and dark. The children returned to school from Winter Break full of excitement, fear, and passion about the storm and its aftermath. Day after day, the children engaged in impassioned conversation; it was a topic that hung on for many days. With an eye toward discovering what was behind the tremendous emotional energy with which the children talked about ice, we observed children's experimentation with large hunks of ice and studied the transcripts of our conversations. We were not looking *for* something, exactly; rather we were trying to look *through*. Patterns emerged. The following is the author's reflection, quoted from a documentation panel, "The Children and The Ice."

The children are impressed with the strength of ice and the damage it did during the storm. Their interest seemed to fall into two categories: the power of ice (or Ice vs. the World) and breaking ice (Child vs. Ice).

Ice vs. the World

Charlotte	When I was at my house the bad thing was that a tree fell in my backyard, and it almost squished my play area.
Kristen	I know one of my friends had lots of trees, and they couldn't even count them. . . falling on the ground, and they couldn't even count them. Because of the ice.
Kelsey	Different reason! The trees were just frozen, and if you touch them, my Daddy said they would fall down.
Kristen	I touched my tree and it didn't fall down.

Child vs. Ice

Claire	I had to smash my chair with that hammer. My Dad had to give me one. All that white stuff was plunking out. I smashed it, and I just did a big hammer, it was so heavy.
Mrs. O-W	You smashed the chair with the hammer?
Claire	See, I was getting the ice off of it.
Hannah	When Charlotte was over, there was a big thing of ice over there, and we tried to break it, but we breaked a little, and when she left I broke more of it.
Kelsey	I knocked icicles off my house.
Caroline	I found lots of icicles on my car. I ate them.

Excerpts from children's conversation while experimenting with a large hunk of ice:

Claire	Put some water on here so it will skate. We're making it slipperier.
Kristen	My hand is starting to freeze!
Claire	(with fingers in her mouth) It tastes like icing!
Kristen	You want to damage it a little?

Later, after many conversations, much experimentation and representation, and after a riverfront encounter with ice formations, the children's interest shifted to a more cognitive question: What makes ice stick to things? The children posed and co-constructed theories, tested them out, and represented their theories spontaneously in a rich investigation of the properties of ice. We wondered: Could our entering into the

Children investigate how ice sticks to things.

I'm gonna make it stay a really long time.

I think I might know one idea. Air! I need a fan!

I know! I'll put a stack of ice cubes together until it sticks!

Child represents ice sticking to branches of a tree.

journey with children as they delved into their initial feelings about ice and our helping them clarify the crux of their interest and passion have freed them to pursue more cognitive intent?

INVITING CLUES TO INTENT

We'd like to make a distinction between two levels of intent at this point. The first level (Explicit) is the intent of which children may be, and certainly can be, aware. As children learn to declare intent: "I want to paint," or "I'm going to make a treasure map," and as they begin to make decisions less intuitively and more consciously, they take a step toward greater purpose in their work and play. As useful as awareness of one's own intent can be, however, we hope to go beyond thinking about children's growing *intentionality* and to examine a second level of intent (Imbedded). Behind a child's intense interest in a topic may lie a deeper meaning for the child. She may not be aware of that meaning in the beginning. However, she may revisit the initial idea over and over and over, not necessarily expressing dissatisfaction with what her investigation or representation produces, but not satisfied enough to let it be either. Behind the intent of which the child is aware could be a bigger idea. If, with respect for the fluid nature of such ideas, we help her to uncover that idea, we also help her find greater meaning in her endeavors.

EXPLICIT INTENT

The more adept children are at declaring intent, the more they can help us understand what they are thinking. The more we understand, the better we can support the children's work and learning.

Children may grow through several levels of complexity in declaring intent.

❀ Declaring intent with the body, either by taking the teacher to the place in which he or she wants to work, or by (perhaps unconsciously) representing some aspect of the activity with his or her body. Toddlers, in particular, may do this. For example, as the very young child thinks about rocking on a rocking horse, his body may rock back and forth.

❀ Declaring intent verbally to go to an area of the classroom or to wherever a particular friend is playing. "I'm going to blocks." "I'm going to do what Mary does."

❀ Declaring intent to engage in a particular activity. "I'm going to make a book about mummies."

❀ Increasing sophistication and greater awareness of one's own agenda, process, and thinking.

Teachers can ask questions in order to help children become more conscious of, and specific about, their intent, such as:

"What's your plan with the blocks?"
"I remember you were building a castle in blocks last time. What's your plan now?"
"What's happening here?" (An invitation for children to tell what they mean in a specific drawing, for example, rather than have us assume we know based on appearances).

We can invite children to reflect on their process by asking of them, for example:

"How did you know that?" or "How did you figure that out?"
"_____ wants to make one like yours. Will you please tell him how you figured it out?"
"I noticed _____. What were you thinking when you drew (built/made, etc.) this?"
"What gave you the idea to _____?"

Such questions, carefully worded, may also serve to inspire children to revisit their work in order to move toward a deeper understanding.

Eventually, children begin to declare increasingly specific intent: "I'm going to go see if I can get a friend to collaborate with me on my block castle. We're working on getting the flags on top." Parents report that children who have become accustomed to declaring intent and seeing it through will often make plans ahead of time for what they will do the next time they are at school. Teachers notice that those children seem to hit the school door in the morning with specific agendas and great purpose.

The ability to plan extends beyond making a choice of activity, to adding clarity, purpose, and detail to declared intent.

> *A small group of children wants to construct a house for the cat they anticipate the class will adopt. As they discuss this house it becomes clear to the teacher that each child has a different image of a house for cats. One child seems to be thinking about a bed-like structure. Another about a house like the one she lives in. Another imagines a house that looks like a large hunk of cheese with holes for ingress and egress. The teacher asks the children to draw what they have in mind.*
>
> *With the drawings in front of them, the children can see the discrepancies in their images—where those differences were not clear in conversation. The drawings served as referents, as embodiment of the children's ideas, and they were able to continue the discussion, choose one drawing to work from, and proceed with the construction of the cat's house.*

Plans for the cat's house.

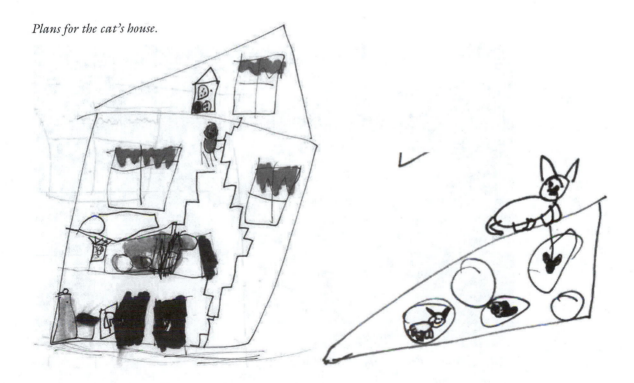

The plan the children chose as the design for the cat's house.

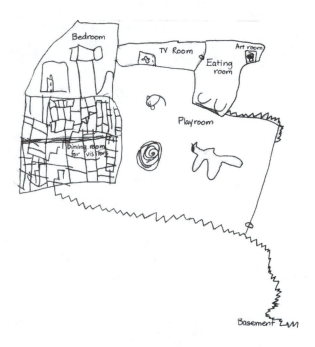

Children negotiating revision of cat's house plan.

Cat's house.

TRUST AS A FACTOR IN HELPING CHILDREN GIVE VOICE TO THEIR INTENT

Collaboration between child and teacher weaves a narrow path, one which early childhood educators have long negotiated. Inspired by the support for learning teachers in Reggio Emilia offer children, we are reaching farther down that path. Children have wonderful ideas, often large, often intricate. What if, we ask, children were to hold on to those ideas, to believe that no matter how great or reaching the ideas, they could be made visible? What if, in addition to the disposition to hold on to the ideas, the children had the help needed to remember pieces of their process and trusted that the adults (and other children) around them *would* help them make their ideas visible? And what if teachers, doing their best to read children's intent and asking, "What is the child really trying to do here?" were to offer tools, techniques, and strategies responsive to the child's agenda? People look at the work that children do in the schools of Reggio Emilia and marvel—unaccustomed to seeing such remarkable representation from the hands, minds, and hearts of young children. I propose that some of the reasons this is possible *are* the disposition, collective memory in the form of documentation (see Chapter 10), trust in adult collaboration, and responsive provision of tools available to children in Reggio Emilia.

In my setting, where children enter at age five after one to three years of preschool experience, many come to school without the expectation that they can make their ideas visible. Those who have not given up trying or set their sights only on the familiar are often easily frustrated in their attempts to represent their ideas. The trust

Clay cat (front) sculpted by three children, age five-and-a-half.

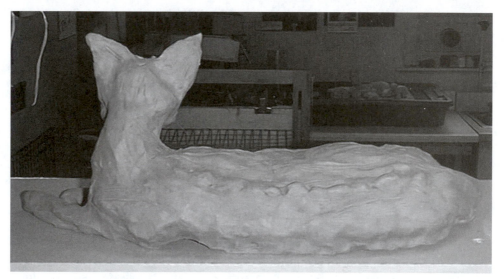

Back of clay cat sculpture.

Images of Ellen's bird and referent.

that the adults in their lives will help them make their ideas visible frees children to set their sights as high as their imagination goes.

> *It was September, and Ellen wanted to draw a duck. She made a few attempts and was clearly unhappy with the results. "It's not right!" she complained, and dropped her arms to her sides in helplessness. I asked Ellen to tell me what wasn't right, so that I could get some idea of her intent. She had a mental image of "duck," I could see, but I couldn't tell if the image was clear enough to inform Ellen's representation. So I acted as coach in a way, asking her what a duck "had." Sometimes it is enough to think one's image through aloud. In this case, however, my attempts did not help Ellen come any closer to realizing her intent. I asked her if she would like to look at a picture of a duck as she drew. We hunted together for a duck that fit Ellen's image. Still she was unable to make a duck that pleased her. I invited her then to trace the duck, to feel its shapes under her pen. She was happy with her traced duck.*
>
> *One month later, Ellen wanted to draw a bird as a toy for our class cat. By then she was learning that her teachers would help her represent her ideas, so she asked for help before becoming overwhelmed by the helplessness that had beset her earlier. Once again I tried to talk Ellen through the drawing, to help her become more conscious of her mental image of "bird." Once again, this was not strategy enough. But Ellen remembered how she had accomplished her duck drawing, and she asked for a picture to use as a referent. She found a photograph of a bird that fit her image, and from there Ellen was able to draw a bird that satisfied her.*

IMBEDDED INTENT
Finding the Clues to Intent

We can set up provocations in the environment that will inspire the kind of representation and expression that offer us clues to children's intent. Then we can listen. We can listen for children's understanding, for their confusion, for cognitive conflict. We can listen not only with our ears, but also with our minds tuned to two vital mantras, one an assumption and the other a question. The assumption: Children are powerful thinkers. The question: What is the child's intent? We want to listen not only with the goal of hearing what the child is saying but also mindful of the possibility that she is seeking meaning beyond her words. If we decide too soon that we understand what children mean, we may not be as inclined to search for intent beyond that.

Reading Group Intent

Some of the examples in this chapter represent adults' reading of intent of individual children, and others reveal group intent. In a sense the intent of a small group with a common purpose is co-constructed by the group. An investigation may begin with intent declared by one child, or it may be inspired by several children's individual takes on a single environment—or teacher-initiated provocation. From many images of a topic, children must construct a single purpose before the task becomes a group endeavor. The teacher can play a key role in supporting that co-construction.

Conversation, creation of shared referents (like the drawings to plan the cat's house), and the teacher's roles as memory proxy and provocateur all contribute to the honing of an idea to one shared by all members of a group. That consensus may not always be permanent. Often, part way into a group investigation, a provocation will arise that could take the intent in a different direction. Whether the intent shifts or not may be a matter for negotiation within the group. Here is one example:

> *About mid-way through the clay cat project, a small group of children began to urge the clay cat group to make the sculpture hollow so that they could show the insides of the cat. The sculptors considered the arguments of the children campaigning for transparency. After some discussion, they decided it would not be practical for them to make the insides of a clay cat visible, and they declined the suggestion of the second group. However, shortly afterward, they did decide to include the vertebrae of the cat, as this was a part of the inside of the cat that they could feel when they pet our class kitten and one that they apparently felt would not compromise their initial. . . and maintained. . . intent.*

Sometimes, the direction of an investigation may shift to what looks like a novel topic, but it actually represents a move deeper into the idea children started with. The transition from "mice" to "mousetrap" to "invisibility" seemed to me to be a *continuum* of the same idea, rather than representing a *change* in topic per se.

My hypothesis is that the mice appealed *because of* their elusive nature. It may have taken a little time for the adults involved to figure out that invisibility/making visible was the Big Idea which helped the children give voice to it, but that does not mean that the mice themselves were ever really what interested the children.

In order for the teacher to determine her role in any aspect of any one investigation, she must remain responsive, flexible, blowing with the wind in a way, ready for the text of children's intent to shift, at times rather radically, midstream. It is in this way that the children lead us to greater understanding of their intent.

Having Good Conversations

If we want to set the stage for the exchange of powerful ideas in class or small group conversations, whether they emerge serendipitously or out of our provocation, we must negotiate our role as teachers the same way we would a tight rope. We don't want to exert our control or guide toward our agenda; nor do we want to simply sit in and "moderate." Rather, we want to learn how to ask the questions that keep conversations going or that invite a response that tells us more.

Our first task, I believe, is to listen with that same active mind and heart, and to always avoid assuming we understand what children mean too quickly. In the search to read intent we want to ask questions or offer provocations that will inform the child as well as us, such as:

Clarifying questions: "So, you are saying that. . . . ?"
Challenging questions: "Well, if _____, does that mean _____?"
Memory proxy prompts: "Earlier you said _____."

One role of teachers in conversation with children is to hold the group memory. Each of us tends to remember the parts of a conversation that we own in one way or another; we may have made the point ourselves, we may have agreed with it, or at the very least, we have understood the point. When the teacher holds "memory proxy," she makes the rest of the conversation accessible, so that children can work with each other's ideas. Or she may remind a child of his own statements in order to challenge him to consider an idea more deeply. Here is one example:

Claire's grandfather had died. We anticipated that she might want to talk about the event at school, but it was several days until death surfaced as a topic on our morning circle. Claire brought pictures of her grandfather to share. The children were curious about how he had died; Claire was not entirely clear about how he had died and her friends, intensely interested in this subject, had numerous suggestions on how they thought he had died or how it is that people can die. Their theories, of course, related to their own experience of older people dying (i.e., His heart must have stopped. He was old.) or media messages (A cobra squeezed him to death). I was reasonably comfortable with the conversation, and since Claire seemed comfortable, we continued. Matthieu said, "Maybe he died of poison ivy." I knew that Matthieu had just recovered from an irritating case of poison ivy and suddenly I realized that Matthieu could be talking from his own place of fear. I became anxious to convey to him that poison ivy is very uncomfortable but that people don't die of poison ivy. I did. In retrospect I realize that I stopped the conver-

sation, and that in giving the children information, I'd ended what might have become even more invested theorizing about death and dying.

One must only observe infants with an open heart and mind to recognize that they have readable intent from birth. Here is one example:

Lukin, at three weeks, makes eye contact when I come close. I smile and talk to him: "What a clever boy!" I say. "What big, big eyes you are using!" When I approached Lukin, he was at rest. Now he is waving his arms, squirming a bit, his focus not wavering from my face at all. I break eye contact to talk to his mom for a moment. Lukin calls me back by waving his arms and doing that same squirm until I reengage and he once again latches on with his eyes. We assume that Lukin is not aware of his own intent. Yet, it is clear to me that he has intent: to engage me in conversation, to interact, to relate. When I respond according to my hypothesis as to his intent, he answers with engagement and possibly even takes a small step toward eventual awareness of his own intent.

All parents of toddlers have struggled alongside their children with their early verbal communication. We *know* they have meaningful intent, but the words are hard to decipher. We guess at their meaning. We hope we won't frustrate them to the point of their giving up before our clumsy attempts at reading their intent pay off. When we are successful, we may learn something new about the meaning of this one utterance. By helping our child give voice to his intent, we help him learn not only about language, but also a bit about our trustworthiness.

Body language becomes a useful clue for the reading of children's intent. We rely on it heavily with infants and toddlers whose communication may be primarily physical. However, even older children will often rely on physical communication, *showing* us what they are thinking when the idea at hand is more complex and bigger than they can express with the words they have. I have no doubt that children readily grapple with ideas far bigger than those they can express verbally. Two examples follow. One includes a situation with Melina and Gabrielle, and the other includes a situation with Jacob and his friends.

Gabrielle and Melina were fast friends. Often one or the other of them came to school dressed in "fancy" clothes. One day they both arrived at about the same time. I watched as they came together and talked excitedly. As I came closer to greet them, they both looked at me with beaming expectancy. Their clues were all nonverbal but I had seen this look before on children's faces, and knew I was expected to notice something about them. Then I saw that both were dressed in special clothes, one in a pink fringed dress and the other with a colorful "twirly" skirt. It appeared that not only was each enjoying her own personal transformation, but also they were delighting in their shared transformation. I invited them to come enjoy themselves in a large mirror. They accepted with alacrity and passion and immediately began to frolic and dance in front of the mirror. Later, noticing their continued engagement, I invited the girls to use animator's clay (they had used the medium before) to make relief portraits of themselves. They spent the

Gabrielle's work

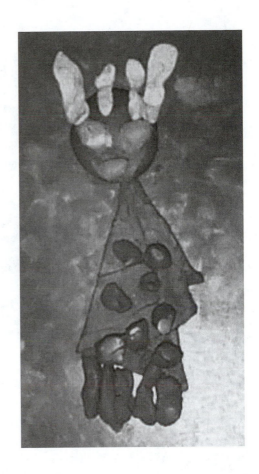

morning refining the detail of strand after strand of fringe and the nuances of a skirt that floated about the body of a little girl. They could not name their intent but they could expect others to notice it, they could delight in it, and they could represent the outward manifestation of it.

Four-year-old Jacob often runs up to other children, growls, and then "shoots" them with his finger and shouts "Pow!" The teachers' initial interpretation of Jacob's approach to other children could have been that he was anti-social or driven by aggression. However, when they asked themselves what Jacob could be trying to do, they wondered if perhaps his intent was to engage the other children in play but that he did not know how to ask. The teachers decided to try to help Jacob become aware of his intent by asking, "Are you trying to tell Justin and Alex that you want to play with them?" They believed that showing Jacob a strategy for realizing his intent would result in greater satisfaction for him and less stress for his friends.

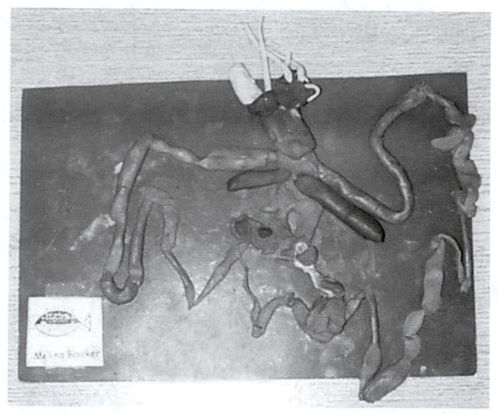

Melina's work

The Role of Documentation in Reading Children's Intent

It is one thing to live a moment with a child and to make a guess about the child's intent. It is another to live that moment and document it and then to make a guess about the child's intent after studying the documentation. No matter how attentive we feel we have been during a conversation, for example, when listening to a recording of the conversation we invariably discover that we have missed exciting moments. In many ways, revisiting an experience with children through its documentation makes us more keenly *present* in that experience. The photographs, transcripts of conversations, children's work, and teacher's notes around a particular encounter are the vocabulary with which we may read children's intent in that encounter. It may take documenting many encounters with the same idea for us to see a pattern of intent (see a description of the search for specific "threads" through documentation, Chapter 10).

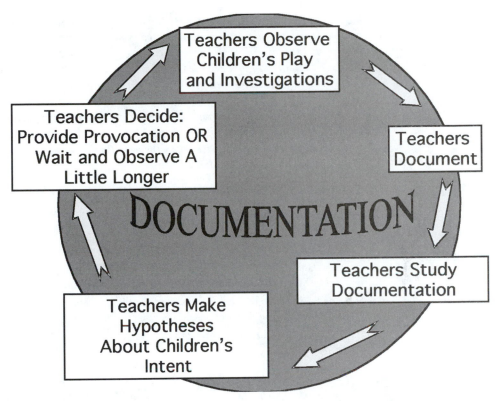

Documentation model

Provocations and Hypotheses about Intent

Studying our documentation of children's work, play, and representation will eventually lead us to making hypotheses as to children's intent. We may offer provocations not only as invitations to children to engage in (further) investigation of a topic, but also to test our hypotheses about children's intent. Here is one example:

> Over the course of the first six months of school, we noticed that the children often walked around peering at the world through the prisms we keep in the classroom. We also noticed that they spent much time with the mirrors, not only gazing into them, but also investigating the way reflection could transform images. The children made "telescopes," tubes with ends covered with colored cellophane, to look at the world in different colors, and checked new visual experiences with transforming tools such as magnifying glasses and holographic goggles. They gravitated toward the Tana Hoban book, Look, Look, Look, a perennial presence in our classroom, but never loved as much as by this group. As we reviewed documentation

long term, looking for trends and patterns, we wondered if this remarkable and persistent interest was a sign of some deeper intent, if it were a portent of possibilities yet untapped. We offered provocations to test our hypothesis that somewhere in all these encounters lay a big idea, and boldly guessed that the children were interested in transforming visual reality. We offered more tools for looking at the world in a new way—mirrors in different configurations, and more books like Look, Look, Look. *The children responded with continued energy, and we documented and offered more provocations. Eventually we engaged in a study of reflection, which became particularly rich when the provocation of a mirror taped to the floor inspired the invention of "Mirror Land."*

Children's Thinking about Mirror Land

❀ "Children are supposed to be upside down [in the mirror on the floor], because it's the mirror's job."

❀ "You get into Mirror Land by falling asleep for a long time on a mirror."

❀ "You have to have the magic to suck into a mirror."

❀ "Everything in Mirror Land is made of mirror, including the people."

❀ "The floor will be the ceiling to us and the ceiling will be the floor to us. We wouldn't be able to see the calendar because it would be on the roof to us!"

❀ "Everybody could float because there's no gravity in Mirror Land."

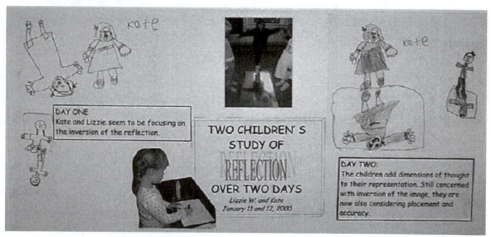

Documentation: study of reflection over two days.

Reading of Intent and the Big Idea

Several years ago, I was witness to an intense period of contagion in my classroom of five-year-old girls. Emma had been to Disney World with her family, a trip the family had anticipated and for which they had prepared for a year. Emma's mother had taken photographs all week without, she discovered later, any film in the camera. So Emma decided to document the trip by making a merry-go-round out of clay. As I supported her efforts to make this merry-go-round, other children began to join her, until nearly every child in the class had made one, and many had made two. The children worked with an intensity we only see when the idea they are representing is calling with a loud voice. What was the Big Idea? Was it merry-go-rounds or was it something bigger?

The next year, before we visited the State Fair, I asked the children to draw what they thought they might see at the fair. Ferris wheels appeared in many of the drawings—many, little more than circles on sticks with spokes radiating from the middle of the circles. I took the children's drawings back to them and we began to talk about those ferris wheels. How do people get on such a high ride? How does it work? They proposed hypotheses and constructed theory together, and so began an intense study for some children of ferris wheels. They drew ferris wheels, constructing theory about how they work, and then made them in clay. Some children would finish a clay ferris wheel after days or weeks of work and would appear to be quite pleased with the result, but they immediately chose to revisit it by beginning another clay ferris wheel. Some question, it seemed, or some idea was not yet resolved for them. Whatever the Big Idea was for them, their intent had not yet been satisfied. Then I became aware that in other cities, in other countries, at other times children had expressed a similar fascination with ferris wheels. I wondered if the paddle wheel experience in the Amusement Park for Birds came out of a similar call to those children at La Villetta School in Reggio Emilia?

The next year, the children in my class remained engaged in a more abstract manifestation of what I have come to consider the same Big Idea—circularity. It began with our observation of the children's spontaneous exploration of line in their drawing: intersecting lines, radiating lines, and lines in symmetrical designs. In hopes of encouraging the children to continue with the study and to give us clues to their intent, we offered them the provocation of sheets of paper, each with a line drawing of a shape in the middle: square, circle, triangle, or arc. The children explored and extended all the shapes but then focused intensely on only the circles. Hoping to extend their interest and the depth of their exploration, we presented an extension of the provocation, a line drawing of a circle in the middle of a circular piece of paper. The children responded to the provocation by spending enormous amounts of time, care, and attention developing an understanding of circularity through drawing. They explored rotational symmetry, concentricity, and apparent movement in a circular path. They explored arcs and semi-circles and quarter circles. They took the concept off the page and into three dimensions and with languages other than drawing. They explored the symbolic nature of circularity. By this time we were so keenly attuned to the possibility of circularity as a Big Idea that when children manifested a particular interest in circular concepts we made certain to document it. We became more awake to any clues to their intent that the children offered in their play, conversation, and representation.

We see this same circularity in human symbolic thought and representation throughout history, across cultures, and across religions. The circle has symbolized continuity, wholeness, unity, and "containing." Children all over the world play circle games and spin until they fall with dizziness. If you look for the circle as a symbol, you will find it everywhere. I propose that circularity, in its physical, emotional, cognitive, and symbolic forms, is indeed a "Big Idea."

WHY THINK IN TERMS OF BIG IDEAS?

If we listen deeply enough, if we assume that children are powerful thinkers and that there may be some bigger idea behind what they are doing, we enter a place where possibilities abound. The search for the Big Idea encourages us to look deeper when we first think we see a good project topic emerging in children's interests. If we jump on what initially appears to be of interest to the children we risk never discovering the essence of the children's intent: What *about* the idea so fascinates this group of children? The question, "What's the Big Idea?" can keep us looking for children's intent. It can be the guardrail that keeps us from assuming too quickly that we understand what children are interested in. We might say, "They are interested in dinosaurs? Let's teach them about dinosaurs." But is the children's fascination really about the characteristics of specific dinosaurs, or is it the even bigger idea, "Power/Danger/Safety" played out with those most dangerous, yet safely extinct, characters? If we slow down to listen, if we ask ourselves, "What's the Big Idea?" we may gain insight into children's intent, with which we may offer more salient provocations and support.

Big Ideas set children's intellects on fire. When children stay engaged in a topic long enough to afford a deeper understanding of a set of ideas, they stay awake to the topic. Any information that comes their way about that topic is instantly theirs.

A small group of five-year-olds was engaged in constructing a large cat, a see-through cat whose insides were visible. They had made the wire structure and were working on the skeleton when they encountered a problem. One of the children brought a picture of a cat's skeleton to school. The children noticed that the picture showed no ear bones. This puzzled them because they had felt our kitten's ears, and the children were sure they had felt ear bones. In addition, they reasoned that if the cat did not have ear bones, the ears would flop over, as do some dogs' ears. But our kitten's ears stood up, and so there must be bones. Perhaps the cat in the picture was angry, one child suggested. Her cat at home laid its ears back when it was angry. That could explain the inconsistency between her observation and the picture. Perhaps the picture of the skeleton was merely in profile, one child suggested. She knew that part of a figure is invisible when it stands in profile to the observer; perhaps the ears could disappear in a similar way if the cat were in profile. Perhaps that picture was simply wrong. We needed to look for other pictures. We went to the Internet and found drawings and photographs of skeletons and even CAT scans. No ear bones. One child suggested everyone look on her computer at home. She knew her Internet was different from the one at school, because her computer was purple. The children lived with this question for many days. I would think that they had resolved the issue only to observe it arise again another day. Much later, one of the group was home sick. She emailed us that she had come across a bit of information about cat's ears that she thought we'd want to have.

I am convinced, that though this group of five-year-olds never did resolve the question, "Do cats' ears have bones?" their minds will remain primed for any information about the topic that comes their way because of the theory they constructed. In essence, they made a mental web that can catch all related information if it comes anywhere near.

BIG IDEAS TRANSCEND TIME, GEOGRAPHY, AND, IN SOME CASES, CULTURE

It is of some help in our attempts to discern children's intent to be aware of Big Ideas that seem to capture children's imaginations and intellects across time and geography and, in some cases, culture. In fact, it was my observation of the ubiquity of certain investigations in classrooms where negotiated learning happens that first piqued my curiosity. How was it that the children in my class were making ferris wheel after ferris wheel with intensity and unspoken purpose, and the children in Reggio Emilia had done a similar investigation with the water wheel for The Amusement Park for Birds? Or that the year after the children in my class had engaged in a yearlong investigation of trees, I read about the children at Louise Cadwell's school in St. Louis investigating trees? (Cadwell, 1997). These studies are not initiated by teachers following some list of "good topics." The tips of these topics most often emerged out of children's play. How is it, I wondered, that when we go after the essence of children's intent with them, we discover that they are drawn to the same topics as are children in vastly different circumstances? I began to identify other Big Ideas, using the criteria: The topic must be rich enough to sustain in-depth investigation; it must be powerful enough to call children to it over and over; it is the essence of what interests a child about a particular topic or idea. Other possible Big Ideas: Embryology (what it's like for babies before they are born), trees, water, bridges, and human body and form. (Tangentially, I have observed children's interest in representing houses for years. Houses did not feel like a Big Idea to me, yet here was this recurring topic. Until I learned that in human symbolic life houses symbolize the human body, it made little sense. However, as I had identified human body/face and form as a Big Idea, houses as symbolic of this Big Idea made sense.) Light, or some aspect of it (rainbows, reflection, shadow, transparency, color), seems to compel children's intellects—is it part of "Invisibility" as Big Idea? Power/Danger/Safety and death/redemption may be Big Ideas, as may precipitation (snow, rain), flight, and circularity. I have wondered if there may be a Big Idea around children's exploration of what I call "the malleable self," the boundaries of self through transformation of outward appearance. "If I wear your shirt, am I more you than I was? If I become a little bit of what I seem, do I lose some of myself?"

I have proposed other Big Ideas, but it is not the list that is important. Awareness of ideas that are considered Big is of use *only* so that we might recognize where children's intent may lie. It is of use only to broaden the question and never to narrow the field. It is for the sake of complexity, not simplicity.

If we are able to read and give voice to children's intent, perhaps children will learn that others are interested in what they think. Perhaps they will not learn to hunt for what adults want them to say, but will use that energy to give voice to their own theories. Perhaps they will learn to set problems for themselves and come to teachers less for approval than for support in their investigation. And perhaps they will be more inclined to develop a disposition toward co-constructing theory, a disposition toward investigation, and an inclination to represent in order to learn.

We have heard of projects in the pre-primary schools of Reggio Emilia lasting months. When we are able to give voice to children's intent, they may well engage in a year-long project, or one that is just hours long. The length of time matters less than the ability to engage fully until, for whatever reason, it is not desirable to keep the ball in play any longer. In the process, children's understanding of the topic goes deeper, and when children remain engaged long enough to go deep into an idea, they are likely to progress from magical thinking to more logical thinking.

The five-year-olds in my class responded to the presence of an incubator with six goose eggs in the classroom with the following theories, co-constructed in the course of two class conversations:

- ❋ *There is nothing in the egg. The gosling magically appears, fully formed, after 28 days.*
- ❋ *There is a fully formed gosling in the egg when it is laid, and the gosling works for 28 days to peck out.*
- ❋ *The yolk "becomes" the gosling.*
- ❋ *There is a seed inside the egg, and that becomes the gosling.*

The first two theories seemed most plausible to the children at that time.

Over the course of the 28 days of incubation, the children talked more about their theories and drew them. They fed their construction of theory with observations (e.g. candling the eggs) and information from books and older siblings. Note that they sought the information out themselves, with two exceptions. I invited the children to participate in candling the eggs, which must be done within a certain time frame in incubation, and I offered provocations periodically. In "How does the gosling get in the egg? Five-year-olds and the co-construction of theory" (1998), I wrote about the children considering the growth of the embryos in the eggs. ". . . I showed the children three drawings from a book: a chick embryo, a fish embryo, and a human embryo at stages of development when they looked nearly identical. Until that moment, the classroom had been alive with outpouring of ideas and theories and sophistry. The tenor of the class changed with the introduction of those three drawings. The children seemed more reflective, almost ruminating. . .and behaved as if pondering a profound issue, asking questions or raising the subject out of the clear blue throughout the day."

By the end of the incubation period, the children were considering contradictions and problems with the very theories they had constructed. They hypothesized that the gosling grows out of the yolk. However, earlier in the investigation they had agreed that the gosling must eat the yolk in the egg. This presented a problem, as the children argued that if the gosling ate the yolk it couldn't possibly grow FROM the yolk. It would, in essence, be eating itself. They also thought that if the gosling ate the yolk it would necessarily be yellow. They projected that if, when the gosling hatched, it were not yellow, it would prove their second theory false. When our lone Toulouse goose hatched yellow and brown, the children agreed that it could have eaten SOME yolk. By that time, the children's theories had evolved: There is a seed in the egg, which becomes a gosling and the gosling in the egg eats the yolk through the blood vessels (which they saw in photographs of chick embryos in books when we candled the eggs).

"How interesting that, without having been told how the gosling gets in the egg in the first place, these five-year-olds actually have constructed an ultimate theory that is not only plausible but remarkably accurate!" (Oken-Wright, 1998).

LABYRINTH

I sometimes think about this journey into negotiated learning with children as a walking labyrinth. A labyrinth differs from a maze in that the maze is designed to fool the walker. If you follow the path of a labyrinth, starting on the outer edge, you will always be led to the center. We may not be able to see the center when we begin, but

Labyrinth from Chartres Cathedral.

we know it is there, and so we are patient as we follow the winding path, negotiating the turns and twists, not always being able to predict where we'll be next. Walking a contemplative labyrinth is meditative, and as with any meditation, there is potential for new revelations along the way. All this comes with negotiated learning. . .the winding path, revelations along the way, and a Big Idea, or perhaps just a bigger idea waiting in the center.

REFERENCES

Cadwell, L. (1997). *Bringing Reggio Emilia home*. New York: Teachers College Press.

Edwards, C., Gandini, L., & Forman, G. (Eds.) (1998). *The hundred languages of children: The Reggio Emilia approach—advanced reflections*.

Hoban, T. (1991). *Look, Look, Look*. New York: William Morrow & Co.

Jones, E., & Nimmo, J. (1994). *Emergent curriculum*. Washington, D.C.: NAEYC.

Lewis, C. S. (1950). *The lion, the witch, and the wardrobe*. New York: MacMillan Publishing Company.

Oken-Wright, P. (1998). How does the gosling get in the egg? Five-year-olds and the co-construction of theory. *Innovations in early education: The international Reggio exchange. 5* (4).

Rinaldi, C. (1998). Talk to the 1998 Winter Institute, Reggio Emilia, Italy.

VIDEO

Forman, G., & Gandini, L. (1994). *The amusement park for birds*. Amherst, MA: Performanetics Press.

Reflections

Lessons Learned and Possibilities for the Next Steps

It is the intention of the authors—Vickie, Andy, and Lynn—in crafting this chapter to capture the thoughts, feelings, and voices of all the authors who have contributed to this volume. Our collaborative reflection in this chapter is grounded in the context of where we began our journey, articles that are presented in this volume, our own personal journals, and our own constructions and meaning-making. Where do we begin this reflective process? How can we capture each other's voices? What questions should we ponder in order to give the readers a sense of time and place, of where we've traveled, where we are now, and where we want to go from here? Furthermore, we want to provide some images and thoughts, if not answers, to the questions often asked by those who have never been to Reggio Emilia: "What makes Reggio a unique experience?" "Why do you and/or others keep going back?" Thus, to facilitate the writing of this chapter we decided to post our thoughts and have a reflective conversation on our listserv guided by the following questions:

1. What were your impressions, expectations, and learnings during your first visit to Reggio Emilia? Why do you go back to Reggio Emilia again and again? What are your changing images, learnings, and expectations?
2. What has been your experience with our Lugano-Reggio Teaching Research Collaborative? How is this experience tied to the chapter you wrote for this book? Where do you plan to go next with this topic of exploration? What are your recommendations for the next steps to be taken for teachers and teacher educators?

The rest of this chapter will be loosely organized based on the above questions. While we share many similar thoughts and feelings about the schools in Reggio Emilia, there are also many differences. As you read this chapter, you will detect individual differences in intentions, ways of seeing, listening, and meaning-making (i.e., many different minds). These differences challenge us to build intersubjectivity and to find shared meanings and understandings through dialogic conversations while scaffolding each other on our journey to recast the Reggio Emilia approach to inform teaching and learning in our diverse contexts.

CHANGING IMAGES OF THE TOWN AND THE SCHOOLS OF REGGIO EMILIA

First Impressions of Reggio Emilia

At the time when we first got together as a group, some of us had been to Reggio Emilia a number of times, while for others it was the first visit. Regardless of the times each of us had visited Reggio, we tried to recall and reflect on the images and feelings we experienced during our first visits.

Jeanne: My "first visit" reactions to Reggio Emilia were a mix of joy and wonder by the "beauty" (in terms of the school environments, the teachers' and children's competence, the engagement of the larger community, etc.) of what the educators of Reggio Emilia had managed to accomplish, and discouragement and deep fatigue in response to what felt like the gulf between the vision they inspired and the reality of our context.

Carol: There are similarities between my memories of the first trip to Reggio and those from my recollections of childhood Christmas mornings. Excitement to actually be there experiencing the awe of finding the lions of Piazza San Prospero only an hour after arriving; Visiting the schools and meeting those who could describe in such vivid ways the evolution of the schools. In particular, I remember Anna who described in such wonderful detail the history of the school *XXVAprile*. The sadness of leaving after only one week in this wonderful town was like Christmas morning. It was over too soon. On my first day back at work in the states, I visited a community school in which, much to my dismay, the major activity of the day was coloring teacher-made Indian headbands that were to be worn the next day when they made butter! When I left I was literally in tears. The Reggio visit had provided me with wonderful images of what is possible when we really listen to young children. It helped give so much more focus to my work, helped sharpen my beliefs, and created a new excitement for my work as a teacher-educator.

Diane: I went to Reggio for the first time in May 2000. Although I had many reactions and thoughts during and after the trip, the 1,000 lire bill made the biggest impression on me! One side of the bill features a portrait of Maria Montessori and the other side consists of a beautiful drawing of children (a young boy and girl) reading and writing. In addition to being much more colorful than our bills, the images on the 1,000 lire note make quite a statement about the place of young children and the people who teach them in Italy. This message was especially clear to me when I contrasted the images of Montessori and the children with the images on U.S. currency— former presidents and other national symbols. This highlights to me the importance of advocacy in all of our work—advocacy to increase the visibility and importance of children and their education and care at a national level in our country.

Dee: I had very little understanding of the Reggio programs as I embarked on my first visit back in 1991 . . . I expected to see some beautiful environments and a community which valued their youngest members. I was not prepared mentally for the experience that first visit offered. I was totally overwhelmed by the environment, amazed at the vast array of materials, and confused about everything I had previously known about quality programs. I came away with the environment imprinted firmly on my brain, a vague idea about the value of projects, and an interest in, but little understanding of, documentation. My immediate connection with the Reggio Emilia programs, however, was that their basic philosophical beliefs in the competent child, their value on social constructivist principles, and close observation meshed very well with our own program. It seemed like we had the same foundations, but in Reggio Emilia they had developed these in more depth (this is an understatement!) and with much more attention to a larger community of learners. Upon returning I immediately began making changes in our environment . . .

Marty: For me, the initial pull to see Reggio was precipitated by seeing slide images of the extraordinary environments and images of children's artwork. While I had long been attracted to the use of art materials in my work with young children, I did not understand, until I saw in Reggio, how children could use various media to represent their thinking. In that first visit that understanding did not go very far.

The most lasting reaction to my first visit to Reggio has been my decision to leave an academic administrative role in early childhood and to return to the classroom. The opportunity and decision followed immediately upon my return from my week in Reggio Emilia.

Lynn: My first visit to Reggio Emilia in the company of Marty was in 1995. Although I had read, studied, and attended lectures in preparation for this first visit, I, like others, was not prepared for the enormous emotional response that I would have to the experience. I remember walking around in the Arcabolena school and crying as I viewed the visually stunning environments that reflected a strong respect for the child . . . and then crying again as I was forced to admit that our children back home had so little in comparison. I struggled with the question of how to bring this way of thinking home and I immediately joined with my friends and colleagues at Rainbow Riders and Virginia Tech in beginning to make some shifts in our systems of educating children.

Andy: I have been to Reggio Emilia twice in the last three years. Like most people who experience Reggio for the first time, I was captivated on my first visit by the breathtaking beauty and splendor of the environments of the Reggio schools. In particular, the remarkable and beautiful representations of the children convinced me of the mystery and sacredness of artistic self-expression, wonder, and discovery that are at the heart of teaching and learning, and indeed all of life. I was especially interested in the "image of the child," the notion that children are strong, competent, intellectual, and born ready to learn and to be the protagonists in their own learning and development, not mere consumers of information and ideas. This interest influenced my thinking and research as presented in my chapter in this book.

Vickie: On my first visit to Reggio Emilia with Lynn, the beauty and aesthetics found in the schools captivated me. I paid special attention to the effect the environment had on learning and teaching, and especially, the notion of the art of teaching. Being a student of social constructivism and inquiry-based education, I realized that the Reggio Emilia approach offers the possibility of connecting theory to practice—teachers as researchers observing and listening to the children to support their interests and extend their learning. I was keenly aware of the culture of the town and its reciprocal relationship with the schools and the families. On returning to the United States, I joined my colleagues, Andy and Lynn, in their effort to make a paradigm change at the lab school—a change in the learning teaching environment, where the three protagonists are active contributors to learning.

Reflection

Many other people share these sentiments on their first visits to Reggio Emilia. There is a feeling of being caught up in the beauty and aesthetics of the learning environment and the art of teaching, and observers are often overtaken by the complexity and multiple learning opportunities. The resulting feeling is a desire to return to study and learn more about its philosophy and practice. The contrast between what we observed there and the reality of many schools in the United States challenged us to want to reflect and learn more about the possibilities afforded by the approach. And, above all, to begin to make changes in our own schools, our ways of teaching, and our understanding of learning.

Changing Images, Changing Intentions

On subsequent trips back to Reggio Emilia, each of us went with different perspectives and expectations. After having reflected on, and made, changes in our lives and in our schools, we were more intentional in deciding on the foci of each of the later visits.

Jeanne: Since then (the first visit), I've come to appreciate the less-visible beauty of the schools of Reggio Emilia. For example, I became interested in the role of organization and the development systems that make everything they do possible (from documentation to planning parent meetings) and their ongoing involvement in their community's political agenda. In fact, my reasons for returning to Reggio Emilia reflect my changing lens and agenda. In the beginning, I went to see if all I'd heard and read was "true" (like many, my cynicism quickly turned to awe), later I wanted to learn more about their documentation process, and later still I wanted to share my experience with the teachers of our center. Now, my agenda is largely a political one—I want to engage my Vermont community in creating similarly "beautiful" contexts for all our young children. I have brought, and hope to continue to bring, representatives from our state government, business sector, public education, etc., to Reggio Emilia . . . I feel hopeful, and I am determined to make Vermont a better place for young children and their families—I thank Reggio Emilia for that.

Carol: My last visit, in May 2000, was another onion-peeling experience—discovering new layers while shedding some tears! I wondered, "Are they telling us MORE about the organization of the school, the ways in which they work together each day, the resources they have available, the challenges they face?" or "Am I listening differently as a result of who I am now?" I think it may be a bit of both! Their total commitment to inquiry within teaching means that they are continually growing as well. The word passion that Deb uses in her chapter pretty well sums up what this whole experience has meant to me . . . thanks, everyone!

Deb: On my first visit to Reggio I was most taken by the cultural attitude toward time and the slower pace of the Italians . . . (as opposed) to the hectic pace of our culture that is seen in our schools, our universities, our classrooms (from preschools to graduate classes). We never seem to have enough time. Time was a concept that our group repeatedly discussed with the Italian educators on our first visit to Reggio Emilia. We learned to reframe time in terms of looping and emergent curriculum. When we returned to the United States, and as we began to understand the Reggio principles, we MADE time. We changed some parts of our program so there might be just a little more time to dialogue, document, and reflect. Every one of us has discussed this as a structural change that emerged from our philosophical understandings as we have grown into this approach to education.

Dee: After two years of floundering and reading more about the approach, we returned to Reggio Emilia. This visit felt slightly more comfortable. We made the decision that when we returned to the United States we would begin actively documenting, not only with our staff but with our students. . . . We learned about video printing as a means of gathering photos for documenting. This seemed like the logical next step in our process of having students observe and record behavior. It added a visual component. . . . Over the next few years, we honed our writing skills, learned about photography and graphics, video print machines, computers, aesthetics, and above all, how to use our time. During this time of concentration on documenting, other changes were taking place that reflected the lessons learned from Reggio Emilia. We changed our teacher rotations so that the youngest children stayed with their primary teachers for three years, and we changed our students' courses so that they stayed with children for a full year. Our environments were more carefully planned with careful thinking about aesthetics, and we began to see the value of documenting to further children's thinking, advocate for children's competencies, and communicate with parents and students. Going back to Reggio Emilia in 1996 found us looking more closely at the documentation. We looked at methods of data collection, organization techniques, and ways to use documentation for curriculum development. Fifteen of us went on this trip. This trip was most valuable to our documenting efforts. As a classroom teacher I began to understand more about the many things we had discussed before, and so I think we looked at the programs in more detail. We heard many of the same words from the Italians, but they had new meaning. Two years later all the teachers, as well as some students and our secretary, made the journey to Reggio Emilia. This trip was such a validating experience for our teachers. They realized how far they had come, and of course, they were able to go even deeper when they returned with investigations and use of the environment as a third teacher.

The last nine years have truly been a journey in exploring the Reggio Emilia approach. Actually, in writing these words I realize the real journey has been in the discovery and development of our own center, as a mirror to my own, and other staff and faculty's developing understanding of this approach.

Marty: Personally, by returning, I came to a larger understanding of the dynamic nature of the Reggio schools: their environments and their systems evidenced change in the two years since I had visited. There were new teachers and the process of their growth and mentoring was more evident. Nothing had stopped, nothing was static, and their willingness, as a collective, to take risks was jarringly evident when I returned to find big, new ideas (for example: citywide intentions) being implemented.

Deb: Before going to Reggio Emilia, Jeanne asked me, "So, what are you hoping to get this time?" I told her that I was going back to see the schools and to hear the teachers, administrators, and scholars *without* the sense of awe that, in some way, interfered with my lens on my first visit. I wanted to see how the day-to-day operations of the school really transpired, and I think that I did just that. I realized on my second visit that these seemingly amazing schools deal with the same issues that we deal with, and I saw that the Municipal

Preschools of Reggio Emilia are not perfect. How could I have missed that the first time?

On my return visit I was impressed by the integration of professional development of teachers into the day-to-day happenings of the schools. I think that this is one of the things that sets them apart from us. Their image of "teacher-researcher" provides a professional expectation that is supported by the broader systemic structure. And this, of course, is directly related to my chapter on "Passion and the Art of Teaching." Passionate teachers have a sense of intellectual vitality (akin to a teacher-researcher image) that is sustaining for them.

When I returned to Reggio, I didn't notice "time." I had questions about teacher education after my first trip, and these questions evolved into a series of changes in our approach to teacher education at the University of Tennessee and into qualitative research studies designed to investigate these questions. For me, intellectual vitality is the most pervasive and exciting finding of our research on teachers who are learning social constructivist approaches to education and who are engaging in meaningful collaborative dialogue. It is part and parcel of passion in a profession that is plagued by burnout. On my return visit to Reggio I looked for intellectual vitality and passion. We talked with Tizziana at lunch about her perceptions of professional development. (Tizziana Filippini is a pedagogista of the coordinating team for the infant-toddler centers and preschools in Reggio Emilia.) We talked about the image of the teacher. We listened. We came back with ideas about how to create the systemic structure that will support this level of professional development.

Lynn:　Subsequent visits for me, like others, have been with more focus. I found that I tended to be so overwhelmed by the experience itself, that I had to put blinders on and force myself to consider one or two aspects of the approach in order to make the most of the visit. My first return visit, then, was focused on environments. Our lab school space was in need of revamping and this seemed to be a piece that our small community could take on together and learn something about philosophy and each other in the process. Subsequent visits have helped me to refine my notions about the role of the atelierista, to begin thinking about recasting the approach for a middle school, and to consider in great depth the ways that our teacher-education program might better reflect what we have learned from our friends in Reggio Emilia. Co-leading (with Vickie) a group of future teachers last summer as they participated in the study tour was a recent highlight as we entered into the extraordinary relationship of teacher/student co-researchers. Living this important lesson from Reggio has drastically changed the way that I will now teach and think about teaching.

Andy: When I returned this past summer, I went with the intention to focus on the interactions between children and adults. My observations confirmed the importance of the teacher–child relationship and collaborative and meaningful engagement in the learning process. From visiting Reggio and having numerous occasions to dialogue and reflect on what I have seen and what it all means, I continue to reflect time and again on our own program at the Virginia Tech Child Development Lab School.

Vickie: On my second visit, I paid special attention to the role of the pedagogista, since I had taken on the role of a pedagogical consultant at the lab school. I listened carefully and tried to make sense of the role of the pedagogista in the schools. I also tried to find deeper understanding of the breadth and depth of documentation and its multiple possibilities. Being with my Lugano-Reggio colleagues, I gained understanding and appreciation of the art of documentation through shared dialogue and reflecting together. Most importantly, because of our shared goal to reconstruct and recast the Reggio Emilia approach in the context of the United States, my reflections on the experience took on a social, cultural, and political turn which led me to ponder on the meaning of "education in a democracy" in our country.

During my last visit in May 2000, I was able to go even deeper into understanding the Reggio philosophy and the reasons the schools are considered to be some of the best in world. The reason, I think, lies in that the approach is grounded in theories and philosophies of teaching and learning in social context. The teachers are knowledgeable of this framework and put theory into practice. Reflecting on practice with others makes a difference in learning how to teach. As I listened to Carlina Rinaldi, Sergio Spaggiari, other teachers, atelieristi, and pedagogisti, I realized that since my first visit to Reggio Emilia three years ago their new, shared insights gleaned from revisiting and reconstructing theories and practice. The approach is being revised and reconstructed in the face of new knowledge and needs. This idea affirmed my conviction that in order to effect educational change in the United States we need to advocate for an inquiry-based education that fosters change through reflection with others in diverse contexts.

Reflection

These reflections remind us that the main reason for revisiting Reggio Emilia is to use these opportunities to find meanings and understanding of various areas of the philosophy. The foci might differ among the authors driven by their individual agenda and needs. As Jeanne said so well, once we're over the initial sense of awe and wanting to know everything about the approach, we become more purposeful in the search for meanings that may inform our agenda for change in our diverse contexts. It is also interesting to note that every one of us, upon visiting Reggio Emilia, came home to effect change in ourselves, our teaching, and our schools. It is as if there is an urgency to reconstruct our practice, document, reflect, and reconstruct our practice again with our colleagues, friends, the children and college students we teach, and the families we serve. We—Lynn, Andy, and Vickie—are continuously reconstructing our teaching and our curriculum inspired by the Reggio experience in the context of our University and our Child Development Laboratory School. We have also taken our colleagues to Reggio with us to share in the experience, to reflect, and to effect change. The importance of bringing those who work with us to Reggio is common among all of us. We believe that true social constructivism and inquiry, learning, and teaching take place in relationships, an education based on relationships, where different perspectives and ways of knowing are valued as means for building intersubjectivity and multiple ways of knowing.

Another reason for revisiting is that the Reggio Emilia philosophy and practice is ever changing, renewed, and revised. In revisiting Reggio Emilia we know that we will gain new insights and challenges. This willingness to change is a lesson for all educators and policy makers in the United States not to be satisfied with the status quo but, rather, be willing to effect change in our educational system with thoughtfulness grounded in theory and research in the classrooms. Change involves a willingness to take risk. Lynn and Vickie reflected in an article about our collaborative group experience at the 1998 Reggio Emilia Winter Institute, "In our minds, one of the important reasons that the philosophy and the practices in the schools of Reggio Emilia work is because they are willing to risk. We promised to support one another in our attempts to risk . . . to try something different and unknown . . . to think beyond the usual . . . to challenge each other to stretch for new ideas and ways of being (maybe most importantly) to risk being wrong . . . to value the process, we hope to become more reflective practitioners," and to advocate for change (Fu & Hill, Summer 1998). All of the authors have taken risks to change after our visits to Reggio Emilia because in the schools of Reggio Emilia, as it is in our minds, change is an expected way of life.

Maybe another reason to revisit is to use these opportunities to gauge our own development. It has become venue for us to realize that we are in the process of change, to recast the approach, and to make it our own. Our changing agendas may very well be a reflection of this process.

THE LUGANO-REGGIO TEACHING RESEARCH COLLABORATIVE: A COMMUNITY IN THE MAKING

As we write this chapter, it is almost three years since the collaborative came into being. During this time, because of shared interests among a group of educators, there have been many moments of transcendence, and as in any community, there have also been times of challenge. Even with the best intentions, do we know how to collaborate? What keeps the group thriving? How can we be supportive of each other in our efforts to learn and to meet our ever-changing, reconstructed individual and group goals? How can we, together, recast the Reggio Emilia approach to make it our own? Here are the reflections:

Pam: In Riva, I found the minds for which my mind was searching—a community of folks struggling with similar issues around adapting Reggio principles in our various contexts. Many of us do not have local learning communities and must look abroad for support or provocation. I, for one, have had to do most of my thinking alone or, at best, through internet discourse. In Riva San Vitale, Switzerland, two of us slept little, sitting up into the wee hours talking about ideas. That enduring collegiality and friendship is a gift. In Riva, our small group, self-formed to investigate issues around progettazione, struggled to construct shared meanings. The need to become articulate with one another, to consider multiple perspectives yet find a common lexicon, was a gift of another kind.

Over time we have "touched in" more than abided in each other's lives and work. Whether it is a day-to-day collaboration or a "checking in" kind of alliance, I think that the more complex and difficult the topic at hand, the more vital the community becomes. In taking risks and departing the beaten path, I have needed members of the group to tell me that I am not also jumping off the earth entirely—to co-construct with me as I represent emergent ideas in order to make them grow and to encourage me to continue on when I think "no one really wants to hear/read about this!" Even if no project were to ever again come out of the Lugano group, the experience, the group, and the individuals will be a piece of me forever. Could anyone have come home from that experience unchanged?

The next steps? For us as a group, I've no idea. At our first meeting in Riva, it became clear that the path of this group would be negotiated, emergent, and sometimes unclear. I'd like to see us all delve more deeply into the layers and possibilities of documentation. Once we have made the shift to a more active form of listening, we can think more deeply about children's thinking. For in-service and pre-service teachers alike, can we find ways to help them look deeper? to find the big ideas behind children's play, conversation, and representation? to move from the superficial to the profound in our interpretation?

Dee: Going to Lugano was surely one of the highlights of my professional career. Sharing so many ideas, challenging our thinking, forming new friendships, and joining a community of learners with a shared history are but a few of my memories. My participation in the Lugano experience is directly reflected in the chapter Jeanne and I did on teacher preparation. Because of the discussions we had on pre-service training, I came back with a heightened interest in teacher training. I also vowed to look more closely at how students come to shed the inevitable image they have of teachers as dispensers of information and how teachers become active researchers of their classrooms and partners in learning. Realizing that everything is a process and not an end product keeps teaching alive and meaningful. Each year is different and raises new potential for the children, the students, and the staff. The cycle spirals and there is no lid.

Marty: Other pieces of the Reggio puzzle came into focus for me because of the collaboration that continued after my visits. It has been my impression that because the Reggio approach is so complex, each individual comes away with learnings that are dramatically their own. In fact, in the beginning, comparing notes with colleagues, I sometimes wondered if we had seen the same system of schools. Later, perhaps addicted to the process, I began to seek out the differences in my colleagues' perspectives in order to allow myself to experience the disequilibrium that I had come to recognize as a precursor to greater understanding.

Lynn: When I think back to the first gathering of the Lugano-Reggio Research Collaborative, the memories that come to the forefront are the ones of the shared time together as we ate, drank, and studied. It was in the villa in Riva San Vitale where the Blacksburg Middle School project was launched. At that point, it was only a dream and a far-fetched one. But now, almost three years later, it is a reality. So, my most profound memories are ones of exciting beginnings.

However, if I coax myself to think beyond the positive experiences, I have to admit that those first few days together as a "collaborative" were not so collaborative. We had come together because we shared a passion for children, their programs, and the possibilities for better systems that we had each embraced from Reggio. That was a strong common thread among us, but we quickly found that it was not enough to justify having spent lots of money and given up lots of time to come together in Switzerland. The early talk among the group indicated that there might have been a lack of respect for our varying places in the journey to understand Reggio and for our varying ways of transgressing that path. We had all been members of collaborative communities before and we all knew the heady exhilaration, the sense of pride and camaraderie, and the welcoming feeling of being provoked to think and act beyond our current levels of being. What we were finding out in those early days in Riva was what it felt like when a collaborative didn't work: it was personally painful, it was threatening, it inspired defensive reactions in many of us, but thankfully, it was provoking.

We have a saying in our lab school at Virginia Tech—"Make the problem the project." Well, we certainly had a problem and it seemed that the only way that we all might survive the experience was to shape this problem into a force that could be reckoned with. As I reread my journal from those days, this question leaps out at me now: How can we turn this powerful dissonance into an equally powerful provocation?

Marty: A year and a half after my first visit, I was invited to join the Lugano-Reggio Teaching Research Collaborative. I resolved to bring my teaching team with me. The difference in viewing these schools as an independent agent and then as a member of a teaching team within a larger national collaborative was extraordinary. Four of us journeyed to Riva San Vitale by Lake Lugano and then on to Reggio Emilia. Having my colleagues as a sounding board to discuss our environment, our approaches, our children, our visions, and our challenges against the Reggio foreground moved our work forward enormously. Fitting that dynamic within the rich diversity and discussions of the Lugano Collaborative challenged our work even further.

Carol: My second trip included the week in Riva. I think the key to the success of this trip for me was in the relationships that were established and the dialogue that occurred day after day as we ate, worked, traveled, and stayed up until the wee hours of the morning. I had the feeling early on that this was a group that truly valued discourse, deep and complex ideas, ambiguity, different points of view, and joyful work. I needed to be a part of such a group in order to continue the transforming journey I had begun in my study of the Reggio approach. The visits to the Reggio schools, in particular Pablo Neruda, helped to extend this notion of the value of being part of a community of learners. It would take many more pages than you desire to explain the understanding about community and collaboration that I took back to my school and my work. I was inspired by the work of fellow members of the group and knew that I could go to them for support when the work seemed too daunting. When our undergraduate students are afforded this same opportunity to construct a community of inquirers, we are continually amazed at the depth and richness of their thinking about teaching and learning. We have seen that this community provides the support for us to become passionate change agents in their internship schools. There are many wonderful stories, particularly in the area of parent participation.

Andy: Reading the reflections of my colleagues and fellow sojourners, I am struck by the transformations that have occurred in each of them—changes in perspective, agenda, and approach—that have deepened their understandings of teaching and learning and their commitment to making learning communities better for students, children, and families. The one thing we all seem to have in common, perhaps as the result of our collaboration, is the desire to create continued opportunities for stimulating and engaging dialogue about our work in order to move us forward. I was particularly moved by a statement Marty made that "those individuals who have come together by virtue of their attraction to the Reggio Emilia approach see some inequities erased because the Reggio Emilia approach, by its very nature, emphasizes the need for all players (starting with children) to foster at least one characteristic disposition—the disposition to research." I love this statement because I am convinced that research, like theory, should derive from and apply to the common stuff of our lives, the children and students with whom we work, our realities, and our lived experiences.

WHERE DO WE GO FROM HERE?

Pam: After visiting with Jeanne and the University of Vermont Lab School again this summer, I have come to believe that the issues for teachers and the issues for teacher-educators are not as different as they may seem. Students' documentation there reached toward the deeper meaning; clearly it was not all about the visual impact of a panel. Rather, the process seemed in itself to be both the education and the framework around which further construction of meaning could occur. I have sometimes felt as though the Lugano group is divided into teacher-educators and others. I am suggesting that reunification might be beneficial for all (though I am aware of issues of majority and of greater access to funds of those at universities, and that, in itself, creates somewhat of a divide). Of course, I could be entirely alone in this impression . . . in which case, ignore me, please!

Jeanne: Next steps? We need to come back together . . . if not in Lugano, then someplace else. We have so much to learn from each other and yet when we finally do come together, we usually have 10,000 other commitments to attend to as well. At the very least, let's keep talking—whether it's about teacher education, the use of images to communicate, writing books—I don't really care, I just want to stay connected.

One final word: Pam, I learn so much from teachers like you. There simply aren't a whole lot of folks out there who are actually "doing it" AND are able to talk about it. Our collaborative has to overcome what is a largely logistical challenge—maybe that should be the next conversation?

Marty: Thoughts on teachers and teacher-educators. Because teacher-educators are teachers, too, this is an ideal bridge between the early childhood teaching community and the academic community. The inequities in pay and status, even where education and experience are on level, create an unnatural divide in what can and should be a natural alliance between the early childhood teaching community and early childhood academics. Those individuals who come together by virtue of their attraction to the Reggio Emilia approach see some inequities erased because the Reggio Emilia Approach (REA), by its very nature, emphasizes the need for all players (starting with children) to foster at least one characteristic disposition—the disposition to research. The REA does not appear to give greater credence or distinction to the player's age, experience, education, or social status in this domain.

Within the Lugano group there are strong pockets of commitment to address the barriers between early childhood educators and academics. From the beginning of this collaboration, both groups were sought out and included. Certainly there is mutual valuing of the opinions and contributions of both groups. Outside resources have even been directed toward the early childhood educators. While inequities in the time and resources available for collaboration are likely to exist for a long time, the group has opened the conversation. I cannot help but feel that marriages such as this between teachers and teacher-educators hold enormous hope and promise for the future of the field.

Vickie: In reading my colleagues' reflections, I am sorely aware that I share their sentiments and wishes. There is a need for more dialogue in different venues and in a variety of ways. We need to create opportunities to talk, share ideas, work on joint projects, challenge each other, and continue to find ways to get together. We need to share our learnings with the larger education community of teachers and other stakeholders who are committed to the best education for all our children across the span—preschool, elementary, middle, high school, and college.

Reflection

It is quite obvious that we all value our collaborative community and hope that it will continue to thrive in spite of the many obstacles we have to negotiate. One of the most rewarding ties of this community of learners is bridging the "divide" between teachers and teacher-educators. There is a need to find more opportunities to be together to eat, drink, talk, share our stories, and learn from each other. Teaching is relationship, yet often we do our work alone, reflect alone, and reconstruct our knowledge and practice alone. This Collaborative of a community of learners, in some ways, has created a space in time that meets our need for professional relationships across teaching contexts. This community, as any, is not perfect. The diversity of needs and perspectives among us challenge us to face each other as we best know how and with a willingness to find ways to keep this community alive. Maybe, this is how a strong community ought to be—it is always in the making, as is life.

LAST BUT NOT FINAL THOUGHTS

Andy: Four things stand out to me as I consider the way we conduct teacher education and how it resonates with principles of Reggio Emilia. First, if teaching is a relationship and we see the child as strong and competent, then we need to find better ways to welcome and receive our children and parents into our community of learners. So I have pondered the questions: "In what ways have we tried to receive our children and their families, to listen to their needs, and to honor their voices?" "In what ways have we treated our children and families like friends who honor our house and leave it having made their own contribution?" Second, as teacher-researchers, we seek to uncover the wonders and mysteries of the child's world, and through practical inquiry, we seek to construct new understanding of our practice as teachers. Third, teaching starts with faith and ends with transformation of self. I have come to value the fact that teaching is an act of faith in the belief that children and the students we work with are capable, even though they don't always show their gifts. It is our role as teacher-educators to challenge them to listen to, reflect on, and be open to who they are and what they bring to the classroom and learning community. Fourth, for me at least, the whole Reggio experience and the community developed from this experience has helped me understand that theory and research need not be generated exclusively by those who reside in the hallowed halls of academia. Rather, it is in the presence of those who live in the daily realm of the classroom, where children, students, parents, and teachers bump into each other, where we tell our stories and develop our most meaningful questions, that we can discover far more exciting truths.

Vickie: In crafting this final chapter with Lynn and Andy, I was brought back, in my mind, to the beginning of our group's journey to Reggio Emilia in January 1998, to learn about teaching and about ourselves as teachers. It is rewarding to find that the questions we posed then are still relevant today and will continue to challenge us as we recast the Reggio approach to make it our own. These questions challenge us, teacher-researchers, to define our "way of life," as we continue to revisit and research: What is life? What is teaching? What does teaching mean? After all, teaching is a transformation of self that happens in a community that embraces and lives the notion of an education based on relationships. As Bruner (1996) said, "We do not learn a way of life and ways of deploying mind unassisted, unscaffolded, naked before the world. Rather it is through the give and take of talk, the active discourse with other minds, that we come to know about the world and about ourselves." I am fortunate to have a group of collaborators to challenge and support me in my continuous journey to research and find answers to the questions about life and teaching.

Lynn: How can we find ways of celebrating our multiplicity, of embracing our pluralist thinking, of finding comfort in our cognitive dissonance, of realizing that there are multiple truths, and of uncovering the power in our community? I believe that this book is our attempt to embrace our conjunctive relationship and to share the intersubjectivity that has become our way of thinking and working together. The reader won't necessarily find complete theoretical or practical agreement between and among chapters. And that's just fine, because there is no universal logic to the work that we do. This book is a celebration of our realization and transformation into a true community of learners that is inclusive and powerful because of the relationships that we share. In my mind, this experience echoes one of the most important teachings from Reggio Emilia, which is captured in this description by Gatto:

A community is a place in which people face each other over time in all their human variety—good parts, bad parts, and all the rest. Such places promote the highest quality of life possible, lives of engagement and participation. (Gatto, 1992, p. 56)

REFERENCES

Bruner, J. (1996). *The culture of education*. Cambridge, MA: Harvard University Press.

Fu, V. R., & Hill, L. T. (Summer 1998). Learning within and between communities: reflections on the 1998 Reggio Children Winter Institute. *Innovations in Early Education: The International Reggio Exchange, 6,* (2).

Gatto, J. T. (1992). *Dumbing us down: The hidden curriculum of compulsory schooling*. Philadelphia: New Society Publishers.

Index